DESIGNING AND TUNING High-Performance FUEL INJECTION SYSTEMS

Greg Banish

CarTech®

CarTech®

CarTech®, Inc.
6118 Main Street
North Branch, MN 55056
Phone: 651-277-1200 or 800-551-4754
Fax: 651-277-1203
www.cartechbooks.com

© 2009 by Greg Banish

All rights reserved. No part of this publication may be reproduced or utilized in any form or by any means, electronic or mechanical, including photocopying, recording, or by any information storage and retrieval system, without prior permission from the Publisher. All text, photographs, and artwork are the property of the Author unless otherwise noted or credited.

No portion of this book may be reproduced, transferred, stored, or otherwise used in any manner for purposes of training any artificial intelligence technology or system to generate text, illustrations, diagrams, charts, designs or other works or materials.

The information in this work is true and complete to the best of our knowledge. However, all information is presented without any guarantee on the part of the Author or Publisher, who also disclaim any liability incurred in connection with the use of the information and any implied warranties of merchantability or fitness for a particular purpose. Readers are responsible for taking suitable and appropriate safety measures when performing any of the operations or activities described in this work.

All trademarks, trade names, model names and numbers, and other product designations referred to herein are the property of their respective owners and are used solely for identification purposes. This work is a publication of CarTech, Inc. and has not been licensed, approved, sponsored, or endorsed by any other person or entity. The Publisher is not associated with any product, service, or vendor mentioned in this book and does not endorse the products or services of any vendor mentioned in this book.

Edit by Josh Brown
Layout by Tom Heffron
ISBN 978-1-61325-900-9
Item No. SA161C

Library of Congress Cataloging-in-Publication Data

Banish, Greg.
 Designing & tuning high-performance fuel injection systems /
by Greg Banish.
  p. cm.
ISBN 978-1-932494-90-7
 1. Automobiles—Motors—Fuel injection systems. 2. Automobiles—Performance. I. Title. II. Title: Designing and tuning high-performance fuel injection systems.
TL214.F78.B359 2009
629.25'3—dc22

                          2009000046

Written, edited, and designed in the U.S.A.
Printed in the U.S.A.

CONTENTS

Introduction: Welcome to Electronic Fuel Injection 4

Chapter 1: Common Tuning Mistakes 8
- Unwillingness to Learn 8
- Improper Injector Characterization 9
- Failure to Perform Steady State Measurements ... 9
- Mechanical Problems 11
- Tuning for Dyno Numbers 12
- Tuning Only on the Street 12
- Tuning Only on the Dyno 13
- Trusting Marginal Measurement Equipment ... 14
- Getting Good Advice 16

Chapter 2: Components of a Standalone 18
- Why Use a Standalone? 19
- So What's In It for Me? 20
- Drawbacks of SA Controllers 21

Chapter 3: Combustion Basics 23
- The Great Equalizer 24
- AFR and Torque 25
- Fuel Economy and Emissions 26

Chapter 4: VE Equation and Airflow Estimation 28
- Engine Load 34
- VE and Torque 35

Chapter 5: Fuel Injector Behavior 37
- Batch vs. Sequential Injection 38
- Saturation vs. Peak and Hold 40
- Flow Rate vs. Time 42
- Choosing an Injector 44
- Fuel Pressure 44
- Multiple Injector Arrays 47

Chapter 6: Ignition Angle and Cylinder Pressure 48
- Spark Hook Test 49
- Knock 51
- Torque Control 52

Chapter 7: VE Table Zones 53

Chapter 8: Introduction to Setups and Calibration 58
- Laptop 58
- Wideband Oxygen Sensor 59

- Dynamometers 62
- Additional Equipment 67

Chapter 9: Initial Setup 69

Chapter 10: Creating a VE Table from Scratch 73
- Getting Moving on the Dyno 76
- Working Downward 81
- Higher Loads 82
- Boosted Operation 84

Chapter 11: Acceleration Enrichment 87
- Calibration of the Transient Fueling Correction . 89

Chapter 12: Timing Maps from Scratch 91
- Rule #1: Don't Knock! 91
- Rule #2: Advance Timing with Increasing Engine Speed 92
- Rule #3: Reduce Timing with Increasing Cylinder Load 93
- Rule #4: Don't Run MBT at Idle 94
- Finding MBT on the Dyno 95
- WOT Spark Advance 96
- Boosted Spark Advance 97

Chapter 13: Startup Maps 99
- Fuel Delivery 100

Chapter 14: Auxiliary Outputs 102
- Cooling Fans 102
- Camshaft Actuation 103
- Boost Control 105
- Traction Control 107
- Nitrous Oxide 108
- Two-Step Control 111
- Transmission Control 112

Chapter 15: Alcohol and Ethanol 113
- Oxygen Sensors and Alcohol 114
- Calibration Setup for Alcohol 115
- Ethanol 116
- Pump Gas 118

Appendix 119
- Tuning Example 119
- Conversion Charts 125

Glossary 126

INTRODUCTION

WELCOME TO ELECTRONIC FUEL INJECTION

So you've decided that fuel injection is for you, but you still want to know more. Undoubtedly, there are a lot of questions surrounding what appears to many as more of a black art than science. Engine tuning used to be the hallowed ground of vehicle engineers, and the most elite of cutting-edge hot rodders. For years, the carburetor filled the needs of enthusiasts and provided simple adjustments at the end of a flat-bladed screwdriver. As long as you were willing to spill a little gas, changes to the engine's fuel delivery were as close as the toolbox.

Today, electronic controls for engines are the norm. Every car coming off an assembly line in Detroit and around the world uses electronic engine controls. Enthusiasts who have relied upon the trusty carburetor for years are now turning to affordable electronics in search of consistency, convenience, and perhaps those extra few foot-pounds of torque. The consistency is the primary reason that has driven the OEMs from carburetors to electronic controls, since they are required by law to meet some very stringent emissions standards today. The level of precision necessary to achieve these targets just cannot be found with a set of jets, power valve, and accelerator pump.

But the OEM engineers are not the only ones who stand to benefit from more precise controls. Weekend racers have become progressively more competitive through the years.

Here's an excellent application of modern technology to improve the enjoyment of a classic. The owner of this 1956 Crown Victoria has installed a 2001 Mustang Cobra driveline, complete with the fuel injection system. All he has to do is get in and hit the key to start it on any given Sunday afternoon.

The classic big-block Chevrolet with a carburetor has long been a staple of the performance world with its simple layout and clean installation. Don't worry, it's still possible to maintain this clean and simple look with fuel injection.

The difference between advancing to the next round of eliminations on a Saturday night is often a matter of a few thousandths of a second. If the weather changes between mid-day testing and late-night racing, the precision of a properly tuned electronic fuel injection (EFI) system may be the deciding difference when it counts. Racers are quickly discovering that it's easier to spend a couple hours ahead of time calibrating an electronic controller than it is to scramble for the right jet change between rounds.

Even the casual enthusiast who actually drives his favorite hot rod on the streets can easily see the benefit of increased precision when he fires the car up for the first time each spring. A properly tuned EFI system rarely needs anything more than the turn of the key to come to life. Likewise, that same finely tuned EFI system requires no changes as the summer heat of July and August comes with its change in air density. The car simply runs right even into the cool autumn evenings of the late season. All the while, we find that not only is the car running smoothly, but it's also getting respectable fuel economy. That's right, high-power engines are usually efficient ones. All that high-compression, low-pumping losses, and plentiful natural EGR from the lumpy camshaft is actually good for fuel economy. As long as the tuner takes the time to properly map the engine, it should be able to cruise down the road at the optimum air/fuel ratio with proper spark timing. These are the conditions that make for good fuel economy and a more enjoyable overall experience with the vehicle.

Historically, many professional tuners have regarded their practices as a bit of a secret. Lessons were often learned the hard and slow way, so many were reluctant to share their findings with others in an attempt to maintain their control of a captive market or position as "the tuning expert." This cloak of secrecy still exists today in many shops across the country, but these are luckily a dying breed. Knowledge of electronic fuel injection is rapidly becoming more common among enthusiasts as the market becomes more savvy with how each high-performance dollar is spent.

The best tuners in the industry today are the ones with nothing to hide. Having trained many of them and worked side by side with some of the brightest people in the horsepower industry, I found long ago that collaboration goes a lot further than concealment. There will always be those who do nothing more than copy others' work and cleverly conceal it as their own. The best in the industry are the ones who can apply the laws of physics and thermody-

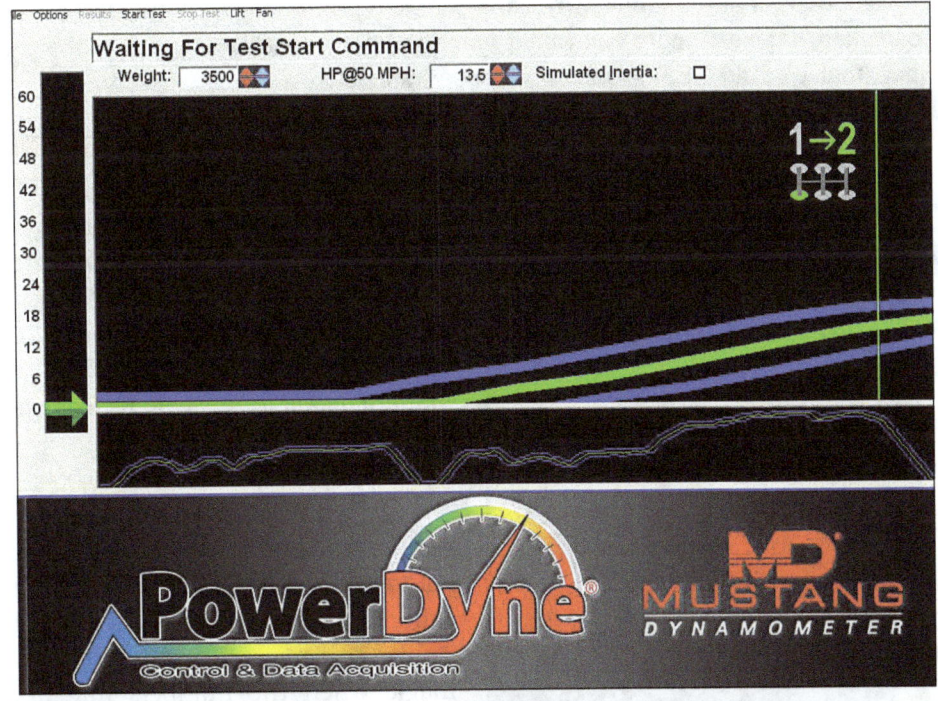

Vehicles are often tested for emissions compliance on specific drive cycles. These cycles can be "driven" on a load-bearing chassis dynamometer where resistance changes in relation to wheel speed just as it does in the real world. The IM240 is commonly run at individual testing stations in states where actual testing is required for vehicle registration.

INTRODUCTION

Case Study

I once had a customer bring me a classic car for tuning. He came in, much like many others, looking for more horsepower on the dyno. His combination was the typical small-block V-8 with a healthy induction and exhaust package and a standalone controller. The EFI system was running a "baseline" calibration that was given to him by the system's manufacturer as a starting point for that family of engines. The car ran "okay" by his own account, but could certainly use some improvement. Initial inspection found that the vehicle would cruise at an air/fuel ratio of 12.0:1 with roughly 28 degrees of timing. Fuel economy had been in the 15 mpg range for his random city driving, although the owner never really complained.

After the tuning session, an additional 15 hp were found up top with the proper fuel delivery and ignition timing at wide-open throttle (WOT). While this is usually worth noting on many cars, it wasn't what gave me the most satisfaction. Before I ever got to the WOT tuning, I spent time on a load-bearing dyno mapping the bulk of the volumetric efficiency (VE) table. It was found that his particular combination of heads, camshaft, intake, exhaust, and compression yielded a map that was as much as 20% different than the "baseline" file in some areas, including the region used for cruise on this car. By changing the values in the VE map to better match this particular vehicle's hardware, the EFI system could more accurately predict actual airflow on the fly. Additionally, timing was tested to find that maximum brake torque (MBT) was actually closer to 34 degrees at these loads. The net result was that during cruise, the new (lower) airflow was used to properly predict the fueling needs of the engine. This relieved the engine of its excessively rich and under-sparked running condition and brought the fuel economy to more than 20 mpg!

A week later, I followed up with the customer to ask how his first day at the drag strip went with the newly tuned vehicle. After relaying to me the predictable increase in trap speed (based on dyno gains), he commented that he no longer needed to stop for gas on the long trip to and from the drag strip. His wife even noticed that the car didn't smell as bad when idling in the driveway. Now here is a guy who will be able to get more enjoyment from the hobby as a direct result of the EFI system's increased precision.

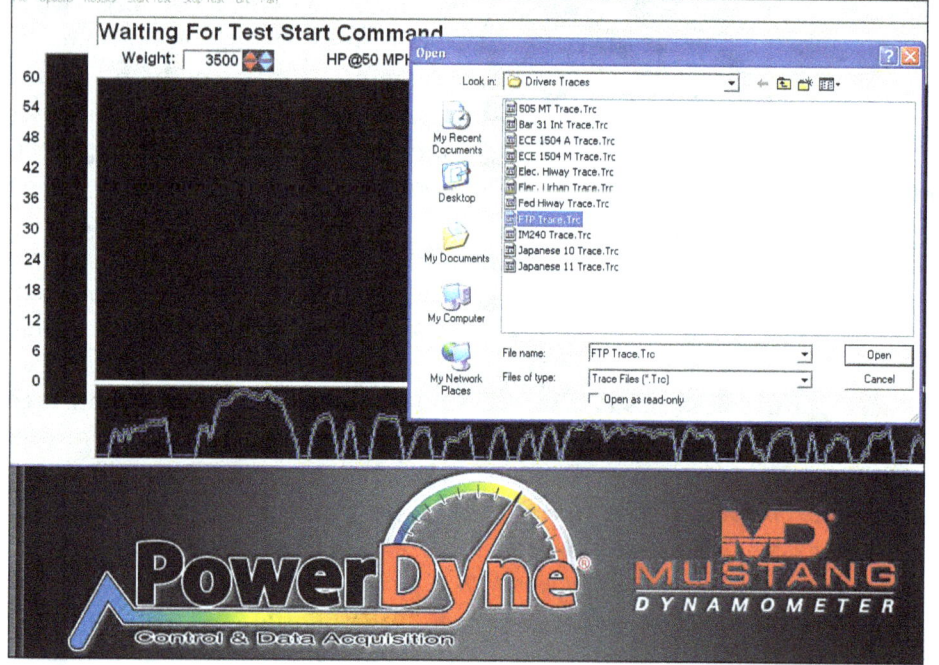

New production vehicles must pass stringent federal emissions standards before they are legal for sale. The most common test cycle is the FTP72 seen here with its 18 unique "hills" that are meant to replicate typical city driving conditions.

namics to almost any engine put before them and develop a working calibration based on sound testing results and math. There is no black magic when the numbers line up. Understanding where the numbers come from is the first step, followed closely by practicing the application of this knowledge in a controlled environment.

WELCOME TO ELECTRONIC FUEL INJECTION

The import performance crowd is driven almost exclusively by fuel injected engines, but domestic drag racers can take a lesson or two from this very clean install in an import drag car. Notice the individual EGT wires on each exhaust tube, firewall mounted vacuum manifold, and liberal use of AN fittings to avoid loose connections.

I encourage my students and readers to observe a properly tuned factory system at work before attempting to blindly leap into tuning their own unique combination. Engineers at the OEM level have been paid to develop these calibrations over a series of years using the best of testing equipment. Taking a few moments to view their tables at work can go a long way toward knowing the "why" behind the "how." Once the fundamental operating principles are understood, it is a lot easier to begin developing a revised calibration for your own unique combination of hardware. The objective is to develop practices that arrive at the right calibration values for the right reasons.

That is the fundamental goal of this book. Once you're able to do it once, it's time to do it again and again. Practice makes perfect. I leave you with a quote:

"He who loves practice without theory is like the sailor who boards ship without a rudder and compass and never knows where he may cast."
—Leonardo da Vinci

The Gen III fuel injected small-block installed in this 1964 Corvette has this owner spending more time enjoying his car and less time working on it. All he has to do is get in, turn the key, and drive without worrying about the weather, choke, or bad mileage.

Another example of old sheetmetal meets new powertrain and fuel injection can be seen here. This classic Ford was spotted at the legendary Woodward Dream Cruise where it had been fitted with the 5.4 L supercharged and intercooled engine from a 2000 Ford Lightning pickup.

CHAPTER 1

COMMON TUNING MISTAKES

Just like many readers of this book, I've spent plenty of time observing the progress of others. The advent of the Internet has made it that much easier to follow along with projects put forth across the country by various speed shops and enthusiasts. Each project has its own motivation and merits as people tend to want to build something unique each time. Even as these individual projects come into shape and they inevitably hit the testing stages, some go noticeably smoother than others.

Along the way, I have observed many of the same mistakes being repeated by both novices and experienced professionals. These mistakes are surprisingly easy to make and just as easy to fix, in most cases. Unfortunately, it seems that all too often pride, ego, or just plain bullheadedness gets in the way of progress. The performance industry seems to be fueled by confidence and a relentless need to be better than others. It's not until one can swallow his pride and take an honest look at what he's doing (or has been doing for quite some time) that he realizes how silly it is. In the end, scientific method

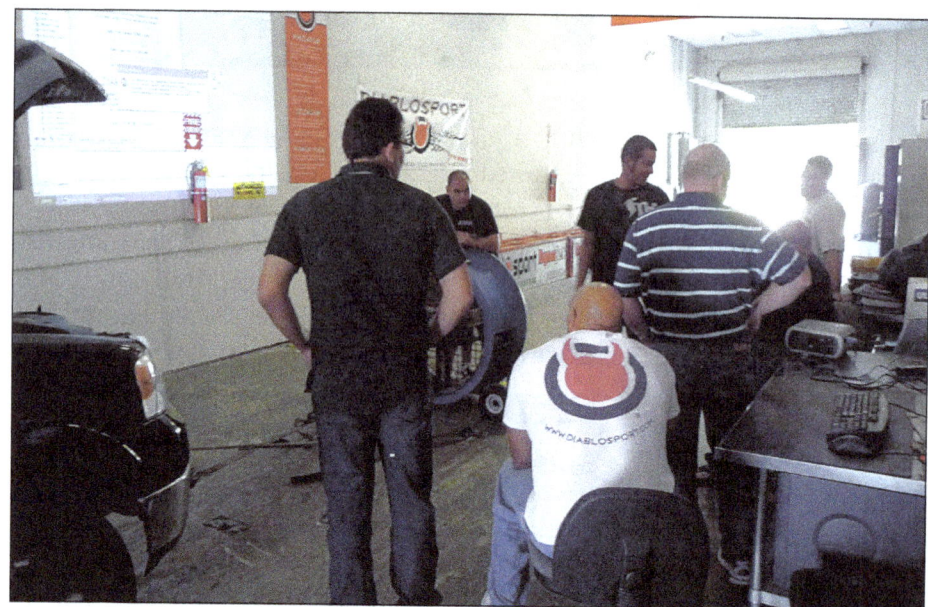

Nothing beats some good-old-fashioned hands-on training. Here, a group of professional tuners have gathered at Diablosport's headquarters in Florida for one of my EFI training classes that includes several live tuning demonstrations.

and the laws of physics prevail. Any attempt to outsmart these laws leads to a very difficult tuning experience, at the least. Sure, there is more than one way to get any engine running, but working against common sense and nature's laws isn't the easiest.

Avoiding frustration during the calibration process is often just a matter of learning from others' mistakes.

The following are some common mistakes that I see repeated all too often in dyno shops, racetracks, and discussion forums around the world.

Unwillingness to Learn

The best engine and powertrain calibrators I've met have been the ones who are both their own honest critic and the ones most eager to learn a method to improve their craft. Even as an experienced OEM calibration engineer, I find myself constantly learning and updating my techniques in the vehicle and dynamometer cell. If you haven't ever asked yourself "Is there a better way to do this?" when struggling, you are either already perfect or have your head in the sand. Too many performance industry "experts" refuse to take a step back and look at what they're doing when a problem arises because they let their ego get in the way.

Solving a problem in a newer, faster way is one of my supreme joys as a calibrator. Just as good, is finding out why I've been making some error all along and seeing an instant correction when the proper method is discovered. Often, this boils down to identifying the physical condition at hand and tuning the software to optimize the systems within these conditions. With the added layers of control in many modern ECUs, it's easy to get lost between them and adjust the wrong table to get the desired result. Avoiding this in the first place goes a long way toward making you into a more efficient calibrator. It never fails to amaze me how stupid I once was. If you're not learning something new with each engine tuned, watch out. Even the most experienced calibrators learn every time they're at the controls.

Improper Injector Characterization

When it comes to proper calibration methodology, this is probably the single most common mistake that gets repeated over and over. Fuel injectors do not behave as lin-

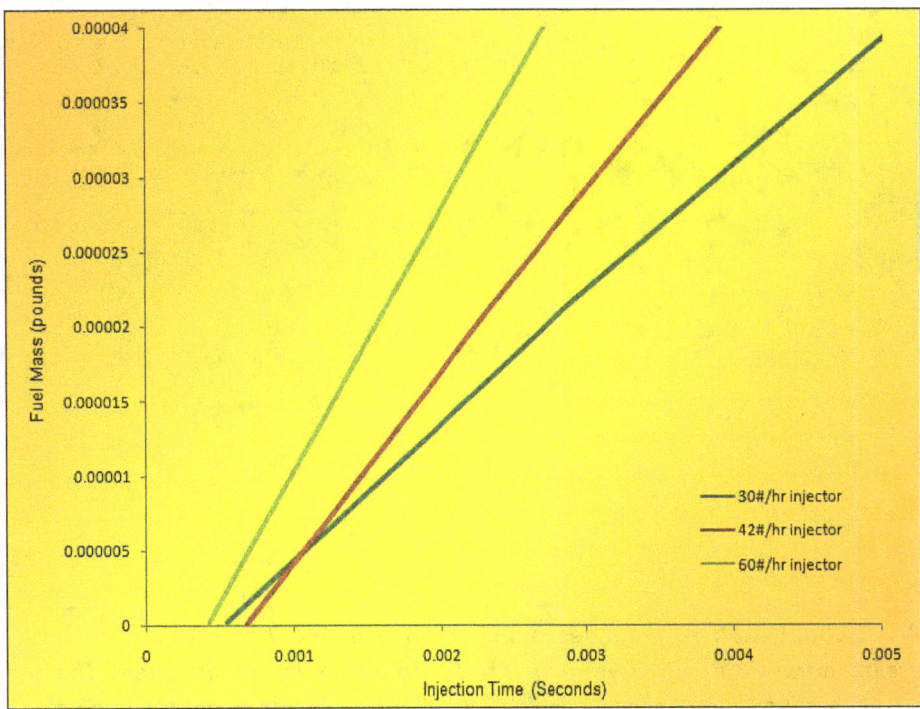

Here we see the difference between three common fuel injectors at short pulses. Notice how the on-time (X-axis) required to deliver a specific amount of fuel (Y-axis) varies greatly between all three injectors, especially during short injection events.

ear devices. Each design has slightly different characteristics, particularly in their low-flow region. The details of how an injector behaves during short pulses are covered later, but I can't emphasize enough right now the importance of being as precise as possible with the characterization. If it sounds like I'm repeating myself later on about this, it's for good reason. I don't think I can emphasize this enough.

So much of our tuning logic revolves around the delivered fuel mass that any error here will be echoed in multiple tables later on. Differences in delivered fuel mass versus calculated fuel mass almost always lead to improper volumetric efficiency (VE) or airmass calculations. These bad airmass calculations can in turn lead to poor idle airflow control, dashpot behavior, and more. Bad airflow esti-

mations can exaggerate a rolling or hunting idle, poor shift quality, and stalling. All of this stemming from a seemingly simple and minor error in fuel injector characterization, who would have thought?

Failure to Perform Steady State Measurements

The underlying code in the ECU is clearly divided into two regions, static and dynamic airflows. Like it or not, the base fuel maps are all based upon static airflow and fuel flow rates. Your target air/fuel ratio, VE, mass airflow (MAF) transfer function, and spark advance tables are all modeled to represent static conditions even though you may pass dynamically through many of their cells per second. Each cell's value represents an equilibrium point at steady state

CHAPTER 1

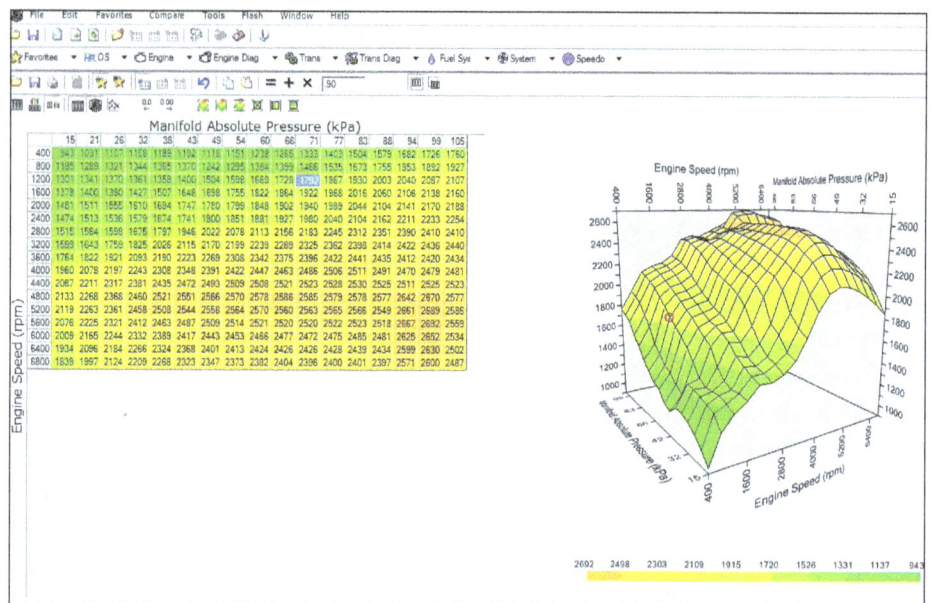

This VE table was modified based on poor measurement practices that included transient data from randomly driving the vehicle on the street. The result is a lumpy, inconsistent table that doesn't really represent the engine's real pumping efficiency and will cause more problems as the calibrator moves further along the tuning process.

that provides an accurate representation of what is happening within the physical engine. As such, the calibration work performed on these tables should be done in as close to steady state conditions as possible.

If and when the steady state models do not give the desired engine behavior, there are other transient tables available to fine tune the engine's performance. Most commonly, this means that steady state fueling is a function of the VE table's airflow estimation multiplied by the base fuel table's target air/fuel ratio. During an acceleration event, you may see a momentarily lean ratio on the wideband and the proper solution is to address this in the transient fueling tables only after you have confirmed that the steady state models are correct.

The mistake commonly made during tuning is to recognize a legitimately lean condition during a transient, and apply the correction to the base table such as VE or MAF transfer function in the area of the lean spot. While this may address the symptom of leanness during that particular transient event, it may also result in an over-fueled condition when holding the engine steady at the same point, perhaps while driving up a grade under load. I have seen this on many professional tunes that were done either solely on the road/track or on unloaded dynamometers. Don't fall into the trap of confusing tip-in or converter flash with steady state conditions.

The proper solution here is to map the engine's base performance in steady state so that the delivered air/fuel ratio closely matches the steady state target first. Accomplishing steady state testing across such a wide range of points on the typical speed-load-based VE table requires some form of vehicle loading to be done right. Usually, this means employing the services of a load-bearing dynamometer or a test track where the vehicle can be driven indefinitely at any given speed without the need to stop for road hazards, pedestrians, or other emergencies.

Steady state mapping can be very time consuming up front, but the rewards are worth it. Chances are

Any mechanical problems with the engine must be diagnosed and fixed prior to starting the calibration process. Here a mechanic is using a can of brake cleaner to listen for the telltale engine surge of a vacuum leak if the combustible fluid is drawn in through a leak.

that if this step is done correctly for the majority of points on the base map, there will be even less work to do when the time comes to address transient fueling differences later.

Mechanical Problems

Any engine with mechanical problems isn't ready for calibration. Time spent tuning an engine with known mechanical issues is almost always time (and money) wasted. These issues can be as simple as incorrectly set fuel rail pressure (which effectively changes the injector flow rate) or as serious as bottom-end clearance problems. At best, a tune is developed based on a series of bad assumptions such as airflow numbers derived from a wrongly assumed fuel flow rate and accurate wideband measurements. At worst, catastrophic engine failure results from the high-stress testing environment of full-load mapping. Proper testing should expose the engine to almost all the stress it will ever see in its daily exercises, so if there are borderline mechanical parts the act of calibration will usually root them out.

Let's take a look for a moment at a seemingly simple problem, a poorly torqued intake manifold. Without the proper sealing that results from the normal torquing sequence, small gaps are left to act as either boost or vacuum leaks, depending upon the immediate conditions. These gaps are often just small enough to be an annoyance when calibrating the base VE map, but sometimes not large enough to sound alarm bells for most tuners. Vacuum leaks mean that the pumping efficiency of the engine is no longer tied 100% to the throttle position, but also to some unmetered hole that can play games

Load-bearing dynamometers like this Mustang MD-250 allow the calibrator to hold the vehicle under very steady conditions almost indefinitely. Testing on a chassis dyno is far safer than street tuning and doesn't need to stop for traffic or pedestrians, or become compromised for turns and changing road grades.

with idle airflow control and airflow distribution within the intake manifold. Even worse, the difference is usually local to only one or two cylinders. With one cylinder running slightly leaner than the rest on the same bank, it becomes difficult to acquire an accurate lambda reading with the wideband sensor. The lean cylinders' gases are mixed with those of the normally functioning cylinders adjacent to it, making the entire bank appear leaner. When and if this is detected by the operator, fuel is typically added until the whole bank delivers an average lambda reading close to the target ratio. The result is one slightly lean cylinder flanked by several over-fueled cylinders and poor overall operation. Left unchecked, this can lead to premature liner wear on the over-fueled cylinders or spark knock at high load on the leaner and hotter cylinder near the leak.

In the case of the vacuum leak, it is most easily detected on V-engines by differences in measured air/fuel ratio between banks for the same injector pulsewidth. In a closed loop system where the ECU is constantly trying to draw bank averages toward lambda=1.00, a vacuum leak can manifest as a difference in learned

CHAPTER 1

Taking a look around the dyno cell at a shop will give you an idea of what level of work is being done there. Steady state calibration work generates a lot of heat, so good shops are equipped to deal with this. Don't forget to have a fire extinguisher handy either!

fuel trims and average pulsewidths between the two banks. For literally pennies, the diagnosis can be made with a can of brake or carburetor cleaner. Spraying the mating surfaces with this flammable mixture will yield a surge in engine speed if any of the mixture is drawn into the intake through gasket leaks. Tuning around this or any other mechanical failure condition just opens the door for more headaches in the future.

Tuning for Dyno Numbers

The first thing that comes to mind when comparing two similar engines is power or torque output. Since these are measured on a dynamometer, the ultimate goal when building or tuning an engine is commonly expressed by vehicle owners as some specific desired power level. It's very easy to get lulled into this thought process as an engine calibrator as well, especially if you have worked on similar engines before. I can't count how many times I've heard "This should make XXX horsepower" during bench racing sessions.

The careful distinction comes, however, when it's time to calibrate and measure. When all is said and done, the engine flows some fixed amount of air at maximum effort. Once the throttle is fully opened or the wastegate is working, there is no magical ECU table that forces more air into the cylinders. All the calibrator can do at this point is quantify how much airmass is trapped on each cylinder stroke and attempt to deliver the corresponding fuel mass and ignition angle for the present conditions. Sure, the calibrator can choose a less-than-optimal fuel mass or spark angle, but once the optimum is found there's not really much else he can do. If the final result is an engine that only delivers 495 rwhp on a chassis dyno safely, that's it. Any attempt to show a bigger dyno number is usually the result of an eroded safety margin, unethical manipulation of the numbers, or some other error. Correction factors are imperfect at best, so don't get wrapped up in the need to deliver beyond some magical threshold for power.

The only exception here is that if power is way off from the expected, it may be time to look for mechanical issues. It may be belt slip on a blower pulley failing to deliver full boost, or it may be three cylinders down on compression. Either way, it would be prudent to step back for a minute and take a sanity check. Pull one or all of the spark plugs and investigate. If everything checks out mechanically, chasing a dyno sheet in the name of impressing everyone is seldom a rewarding venture in the long run.

Tuning Only on the Street

There are a lot of skeptics out there who don't feel that a dynamometer accurately reflects the way we drive a vehicle. They claim that an actual vehicle on an actual road gives them the exact conditions they need to tune to. They're right. However, loaded dynamometers do accurately reflect how the fundamentals of the ECU's control system works. The real objective is to calibrate a control system to a mechanical device. Doing this means playing by the rules set forth in the controller. If the controller uses a series of steady state reference tables to determine engine conditions, it's best to populate these tables in steady state. The load-bearing dynamometer allows the calibrator to dial in the exact conditions he is looking for and tune these steady

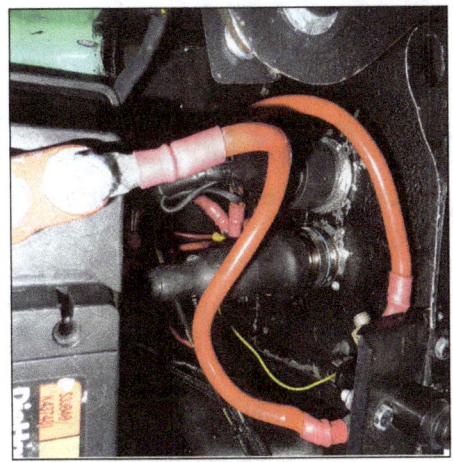

Robust electrical connections can prevent loads of frustration, both during the tuning process and later on as the vehicle is subjected to vibration and a harsh environment. This military spec bulkhead connection is about as good as it gets for connection security.

state tables in fairly short order.

At the OEM level, all ECU calibrations start out on the dynamometer before ever seeing a vehicle. The engine's efforts on a load bearing dynamometer can be both above and below those seen when driving down the road. What's important is that each breakpoint of the reference tables be individually optimized so that any time the engine is between two of them, an accurate interpolation can be made. Driving on the road can make it very difficult to hold the engine precisely at each cell in the table if the available load breakpoints don't line up with easily achievable loads seen in the various gears. Even more importantly, it's just about impossible for anyone in an urban area to find a road long enough with zero traffic to safely perform the necessary steady state measurements. Skipping the steady state measurements only opens the door for more confusion from transient fuel delivery as previously mentioned.

The simple fact here is that a skilled calibrator can get more work done on a proper load bearing dyno than most "tuners" can do in weeks on the road. Getting the fundamental steady state tables correctly calibrated on a dynamometer can save endless hours and gallons of fuel during road testing. When done correctly, dynamometer calibration makes the overall tuning process faster, more accurate, and more enjoyable. It's just as important to recognize that tuning usually doesn't end with the last dyno pull.

Tuning Only on the Dyno

Just as there are those who swear by "real world" tuning only on road surfaces, there are those who insist that their dynamometer is the only method by which calibration can and should be done. Certainly, dyno tuning is an excellent start to any complete calibration procedure. The trick is to recognize that the engine does not live in a steady state world. Even steps on the dynamometer do not precisely replicate the transients seen as a vehicle shifts through the gears on the street or track.

Worse yet, many paid tuning professionals swear by testing on an unloaded dynamometer as the only necessary approach. At WOT, the sweep rate of an unloaded or inertial dynamometer can be much faster than the vehicle sees in the outside world. This allows less time for combustion temperatures to stabilize, perhaps giving a false sense of security when adding that last cou-

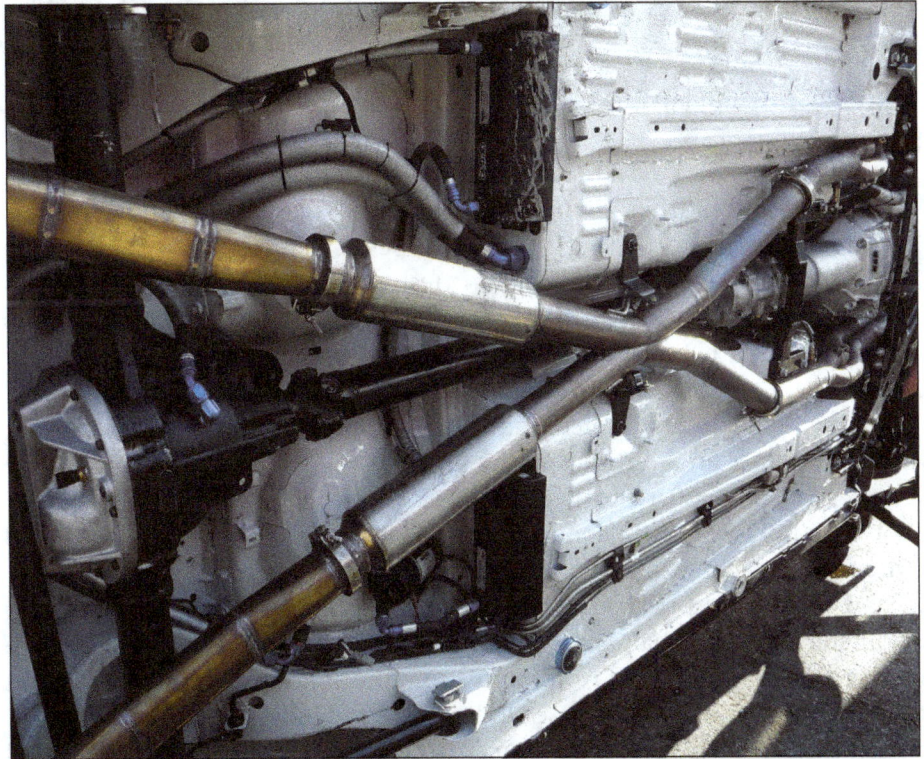

Before beginning any tuning session, it's a good idea to look the vehicle over for fluid leaks or other mechanical issues. All fluid lines should be routed away from hot exhaust components, as a failure on the dyno can be very dangerous in a confined space.

CHAPTER 1

This is not the place to be performing testing for calibration work. The controlled environment of a dyno cell is a much safer and more consistent setting. Testing on the street should be limited to final drivability critiquing.

ple degrees of spark advance during the power pulls. Even though the engine may pull clean and strong on the dynamometer with lower load, it's not uncommon to see the same engine self destruct at the 1,000-foot mark of the drag strip where aerodynamic and thermal forces have aligned against an overly aggressive tune. That extra 20 rwhp from the hot tune-up are of little condolence when staring at an expensive rebuild.

At lower loads, an inertial dynamometer is still a handicap. Since the inertial dynamometer works fundamentally upon Newton's second law ($F=ma$), any increase in the force provided by the engine results in some acceleration of the dynamometer. This makes it impossible to hold a constant load at anything other than light loads equal to the friction of the dynamometer and driveline. At best, the result is a series of sweep tests dynamically through the speed range that still does not yield valuable steady state calibration data for the base maps. In short, an inertial dynamometer is the wrong tool for tuning speed density systems where it is critical to get a wide range of stable readings at specific speed-load points.

While a loaded dynamometer certainly makes for a more flexible and precise tuning experience, it still doesn't define the entire range of tests necessary for truly optimized engine calibration. The load-bearing dyno should be used as a tool to develop the steady state maps and controlled sweep rate tests at WOT in a safe environment. After these objectives have been met, it's preferable to actually drive the vehicle in a free environment to experience as many possible operational conditions as possible. A quick test drive after an initial dynamometer tune may help the calibrator zero in on a specific speed-load point in a particular gear where something does not feel right. This allows the calibrator to return to the dynamometer with the more specific task of fixing either fuel or spark trims in a narrower range of cells that may not have been completely optimized the first time around. Driving on the street also exercises the transmission, driveline, and brakes differently than on a dyno. The addition of new forces may open up the calibrator's eyes to some other area of the software that may need additional attention such as dashpot or coastdown airflow control. It is strongly encouraged to test drive the vehicle after tuning is completed whenever possible.

Trusting Marginal Measurement Equipment

The high-performance aftermarket is rife with affordable tuning aids these days. Test equipment is one of the areas where the old adage, "You get what you pay for," still holds true. Everything from chassis dynamometers to wideband oxygen sensors is available to the public in a surprising amount of variety and cost. Research-grade equipment still tops the market in price and precision, but there is also a glut of bottom feeders that produce and sell garbage to those foolish enough to shop on price alone.

The biggest change over the last decade or so has been the availability of wideband oxygen sensors to the general tuning public. The first wideband oxygen sensors were priced close to $10,000 and only used in research applications where the budget allowed for such accuracy and precision. Since then, prices have plummeted with units now available for little more than the cost of the sensor itself. Many of these wideband sensor kits use the commonly available Bosch LSU or NTK UEGO sensors that have been implemented in mass-production vehicle applications through the years. Either of these sensors is light years ahead of traditional narrowband binary sensors when it comes to calibration work, although it has been my experience that the NTK sensors have the edge in precision and durability, at a slightly higher cost, of course.

But just using a decent wideband sensor does not automatically make one armed for precision engine calibration work. The sensor itself is only as useful as the data that can be extracted from it, which depends largely upon the controller used. Wideband sensor output varies with temperature, pressure, and age. All of these factors require unique controller hardware and logic that is completely different from the older binary sensors. It is the design and functionality of these wideband controllers that makes all the difference when it comes to accurate and precise engine calibration in the field. It's not that difficult to simply

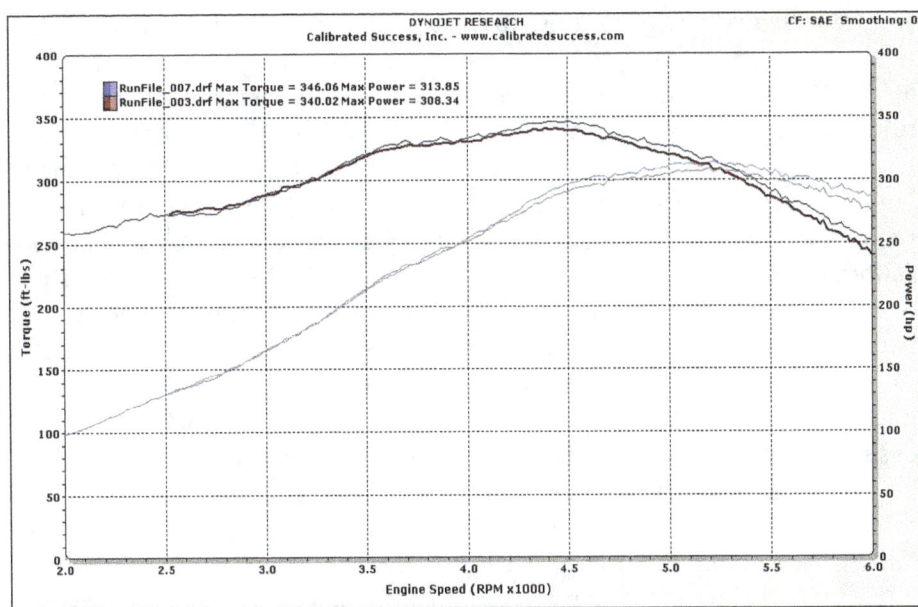

A printout from the chassis dyno often represents the final step in the tuning process for many tuners and can be easily confused with the primary goal of the calibration process. The pumping efficiency that determines maximum power potential is tied to the mechanical parts of the engine. It is up to the calibrator to put a number on things in order to deliver the proper fuel and spark to unlock this potential. Properly quantifying the pumping efficiency everywhere (not just at WOT) should be the goal of the calibrator.

design an electronic box that converts the UEGO pump cell current into either an LCD display or output voltage. Getting the same translation between actual gas chemistry and controller output as temperatures change is what separates the real test equipment from the toys.

During a typical WOT pull in gear, exhaust gas temperatures can rise by several hundred degrees. This temperature-based error becomes

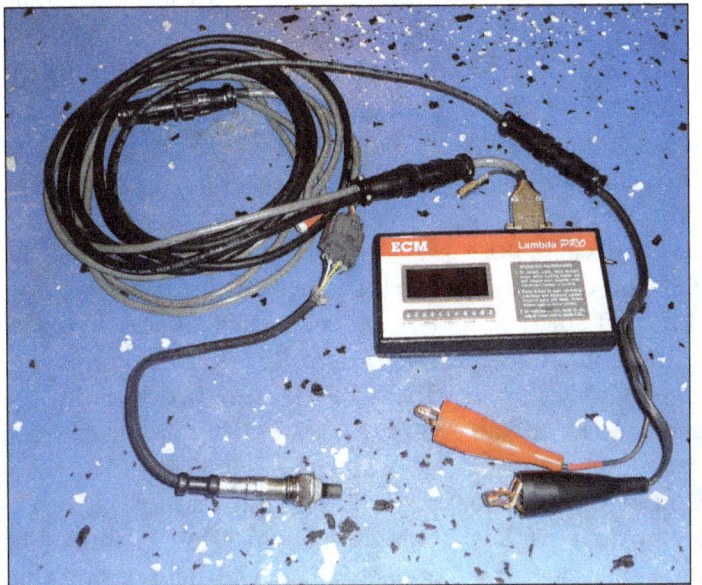

My own personal wideband is an ECM LambdaPro. This unit, while not cheap, is one of the absolute best wideband controllers on the market, especially when working with supercharged or turbocharged applications or alternative fuels.

worse at richer air/fuel ratios, just where the accuracy is needed most at WOT. An improperly temperature-correct wideband controller may read this as a change in delivered lambda, even as actual gas chemistry remains constant. An inexperienced calibrator may see what he believes to be good data from a cheap wideband and make what he believes to be the right corrections until his measured air/fuel ratio matches the desired value. In reality, he may have just introduced an additional error to the airflow model due to the bad data. The best fix for this problem is to avoid it in the first place by purchasing a good-quality wideband controller.

Most skilled calibration professionals who charge good money for their work use professional-grade equipment. It's not impressive to walk into a shop and see the cheapest wideband available sitting on the bench next to the dyno knowing that you'll be paying a premium for the data collected from it. Good shops invest in good equipment all the way around. Chances are that if the calibrator is serious enough about his work to spend over a thousand dollars on a wideband, he also understands why this unit is necessary and will probably be more informed when the time comes to tune a vehicle. Much the same way good mechanics don't use flea market torque wrenches, good calibrators don't buy their wideband controllers based on advertising fluff splattered across every magazine and Internet board.

There's nothing wrong with an individual enthusiast getting a good deal on a wideband monitor. One just needs to recognize it as less reliable and accurate than the professional-grade units. Bargain widebands may be reasonably accurate near stoichiometric mixtures (a balanced ratio of components is known as "stoichiometric"), but their accuracy becomes suspect the further away from stoichiometric the mixture goes. If the objective is to precisely calibrate a supercharged engine (whose target ratio will be about 20% rich of stoichiometry under load), a higher quality wideband controller is strongly advised for the critical high-load and high-temperature work.

Even the best wideband controllers and sensors require periodic maintenance. As the sensor ages, it experiences gain shift that must be corrected in order to maintain accuracy. Cheaper wideband controllers simply rely upon a fixed resistor to calibrate the sensor when new, which is not advised. Many controllers offer the option to check the calibration in free air by holding the sensor outside of the exhaust for a few minutes and adjusting the unit to correlate with Earth's normal atmospheric concentration of 20.9% oxygen. Special care should be taken to do this in a well-ventilated area though, since any residual exhaust gases or fumes will displace oxygen in the environment. Checking and correcting the calibration of the wideband should be a routine activity at the start of every tuning session.

The need for accuracy with test equipment doesn't end at the wideband sensor. Most dynamometers are configured to accommodate some form of weather correction. The sensors used to determine the current weather conditions should be checked periodically for accuracy. If the unit cannot be recalibrated when in error, it should be replaced. This will help ensure that the dynamometer is properly corrected before relying upon the power and torque outputs. It may sound obvious, but also check to make sure that the weather station is not placed in a location that is subject to drastic environmental changes.

Once the weather station's barometric pressure sensor has been validated, it can be used to check the vehicle's MAP sensor at initial key-on before running. The ECU should see the same MAP reading as the barometer with the engine off. Any differences here indicate the need to check either the wiring, MAP sensor configuration in the software, or the sensor itself. Collecting bad data from a vehicle sensor is just as misleading as bad data from any other outside source.

I once visited a shop that had installed the dyno controller "stack" that contained the weather station next to the vehicle, just behind the rear axle. This is directly in line with many vehicles' exhaust discharge. The result was a moving correction factor during the session as the thermometer rose in direct relation to exhaust flow. How embarrassing, but it was a surprisingly simple fix that lead to much more repeatable testing going forward.

Getting Good Advice

In this age of instant gratification, it's tempting to want to find the solution to whatever tuning problem is troubling you at the moment from the first source available. It seems that the preferred source for tuning expertise for many enthusiasts is their favorite Internet forum. The Internet shouldn't feel bad, this happens in the parking lots of drag strips, road courses, and car shows around

COMMON TUNING MISTAKES

The Advanced Engineering Technology Conference is one of the best learning opportunities in the performance industry. I recently had the pleasure of speaking at the nineteenth annual conference that was held in conjunction with the PRI industry trade show in Orlando, Florida, where hundreds gathered to learn more about many aspects of the engine.

the world too. All too often, it seems that tribal wisdom trumps physics in some of the reasoning employed by some of these groups. Advice is often sought in a poll format where each person feels compelled to contribute regardless of their experience or expertise. The "winning" solution is usually declared based on the number of votes in favor of it rather than solid scientific reasoning.

First and foremost, there should be some due diligence before heading to the collective well of knowledge. Too many people give up quickly and just make the request for a starter tune or fix to their hunting idle without spending the time to make sure the fundamentals of tuning have been covered. When all else fails, go back to the basics. Make sure that the injector flow is properly characterized and that steady state airflow mapping has been done before questioning why delivered air/fuel ratio is all over the place. Ensure that any mechanical issues are completely addressed before asking for advice on how to tune around them.

Certainly, there are forums where sound advice is freely given to those who ask politely and intelligently. These tend to be more the exception than the rule. Just remember that free advice from many of the public forums is often worth the price you paid for it. Many claim experience and knowledge based upon how often they dispense advice or practice the same failed methods over and over. Take this with a grain of salt and consider the source of the advice. Experienced experts are usually busy performing real work rather than sitting around waiting for an opportunity to hand out advice on the Internet. When these veterans are willing to share, take a moment to weigh what they have to say more carefully than the typical high-post-count armchair expert.

All of this leads back to the earlier discussion of willingness to learn. There are many sources of knowledge available ranging from one-hour seminars at trade shows, to weekend training seminars, to a college engineering degree. Going all the way to a bachelors or doctoral degree doesn't, on its own, qualify anyone to calibrate engines, but it exposes them to the forces at work within the engine. Many of the college-level courses go far beyond the fundamental knowledge necessary to tune engines. There are some golden nuggets hidden in these college courses that get applied in speed shops and at tracks around the world on a daily basis.

Any time I speak to a group about engine calibration, I try to apply the engineering principles I learned during my own education as directly as possible to the tuning issue at hand. I call my calibration seminars a crash course in mechanical engineering where the important points of a four-credit-hour class can be described in plain English to a group of technicians in twenty minutes or less. A formal engineering education is only one piece of the puzzle and even I learn from many of my fellow calibrators on a regular basis. When seeking tuning advice, I'm careful to make sure that the answer I'm given is scientifically sound and not just another "band-aid" to trick the PCM into attempting to break the rules of nature with the engine.

CHAPTER 2

COMPONENTS OF A STANDALONE

A standalone controller has the ability to perform all of its own engine monitoring and control functions from a single box. It does not require any outside assistance from body or chassis modules. As such, they are particularly well suited to race cars, hot rods, and classics where these outside modules seldom exist. Each standalone controller is designed to work with its own wiring harness with connections to the necessary sensors and outputs. Very little outside engineering is required to get most systems up and running on just about any engine.

The same standalone controller can often be used on a wide variety of engines from inline fours to V-8s or even rotary Wankels. This common architecture keeps production costs reasonable and allows the user to remove the hardware from one vehicle and install it in another by simply changing the programmable configuration and a few sensors in most cases. The general control logic remains the same. Lessons learned tuning a standalone controller on one application can often be applied toward another in the future.

While this 240sx engine may look intimidating at first, to the experienced calibrator, it's just another four-cylinder boosted engine. The standalone engine controller uses a 3 bar MAP sensor that can easily measure up to 30 psi of boost and calculate the large amounts of airflow and power that go with that boost.

If the vehicle was originally equipped with a carburetor, there is often no option for a replacement factory controller. A standalone controller allows the user to add the flexibility of electronic controls by using the system's own sensors and harness. The only wiring connections necessary to the rest of the vehicle are a 12-volt supply and ground. This make installation as simple as following the instructions included with most controllers and adding the proper high-pressure fuel-sup-

COMPONENTS OF A STANDALONE

Standalone systems, like the Edelbrock Pro Flo seen here, come with everything needed to convert an existing carbureted vehicle to electronic fuel injection. Notice how the IAT, ECT, MAP, TPS sensor, and fuel pressure regulator are all neatly integrated into a single package on a Performer RPM intake that makes for a very clean installation.

An example of just how clean an EFI installation can be, this Ford could almost pass for carbureted if it weren't for the aluminum fuel rails. This stealthy install still enjoys the benefits of EFI's reliability with the classic look that suits the rest of the vehicle.

The standalone controller can be cleverly hidden just about anywhere in the vehicle. In this Mustang, the ECU is mounted under the passenger-side dashboard, alongside the MSD ignition module.

ply system. Similarly, racecars that have a few extra pounds of unnecessary equipment are easily equipped with standalone controllers. With the elimination of any unnecessary modules, their wiring harnesses and connections do not disturb the operation of the standalone EFI control system.

Since most standalone controllers are capable of working on inlet pressures of up to 3 bar MAP (more than 30 psi in the intake manifold!), they have no problem working with high-powered engines. Most standalone controllers will also allow for engine speeds well beyond factory limits in production controllers, another key benefit to the racer.

Why Use a Standalone?

The primary reason for choosing a standalone EFI system is to add fuel injection to a vehicle where none previously existed. Updating carbureted engines to electronic control can improve efficiency, flexibility to weather changes, and overall

DESIGNING AND TUNING HIGH-PERFORMANCE FUEL INJECTION SYSTEMS

CHAPTER 2

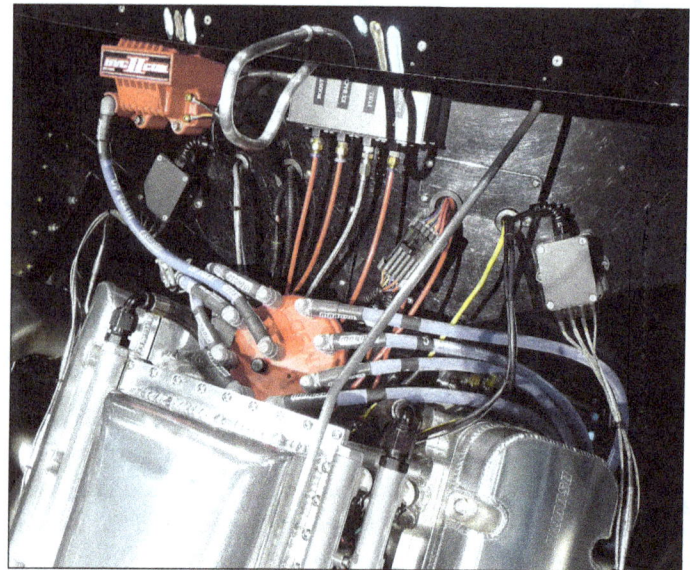

Another key to a clean installation, especially on a race car, is tidy wiring and terminals. Notice how each hole in the firewall is grommeted, wires are cut to length, and weatherpack connectors are used to avoid contamination.

Many late-model vehicles cannot simply have the engine controller removed and replaced with a standalone controller so easily. Modern CAN messaging networks check for the presence and feedback of each module on the communication bus and will not operate properly without all modules communicating as expected.

drivability. The improvement in cold-start quality alone is enough for many to justify the change to electronic fuel injection. Adding fuel economy and better driving manners is often the icing on the cake here.

Another common reason for running a standalone controller is to upgrade from a factory ECU that has limited flexibility. If one does not have proper access to all of the calibration maps in a factory ECU, it can be utterly impossible to get some hardware combinations tuned properly. It can be an extremely frustrating experience attempting to tune around the factory setpoints only to have your final work "leaned out" by automatic correction strategies. There are many layers of control within modern OEM engine controllers. Without access to all of them, it can be a fruitless effort to attempt tuning. With some vehicles, there are no aftermarket tuning solutions whatsoever for the stock ECU. A popular choice here is to install a "piggyback" controller that intercepts and modifies the signals going to and from the factory ECU. This is at best a compromise, and often leads to the same concerns as tuning with only limited ECU access. Bypassing these systems entirely with a standalone engine controller can open the doors to a properly running vehicle, even at significantly elevated power levels.

The key in this case is to ensure that the removal of the factory ECU does not wreak havoc upon other modules within the vehicle. There are often safety checks performed not only by the ECU, but by body controllers that may trigger "limp home" conditions if left unaddressed. When installing a standalone controller in a production vehicle, it is important to do your homework regarding what modules interact with the ECU. In some cases, it is possible to just leave the factory ECU on the harness to make the proper connections, but still have the standalone controller entirely in control of engine functionality.

So What's In It for Me?

Standalone EFI systems have several key benefits over some other alternatives. First and foremost, they're relatively simple in design and operation. While still complex when compared to a carburetor, the intricacy of modern OEM electronic controls makes the average standalone look like child's play in comparison. Standalone EFI controllers usually only have a few layers of control at most. This makes adjustments much simpler for the end user. The simplicity extends to the installation and integration of the controller into the vehicle. Because the standalone ECU does not need any outside communication to run the engine correctly, the setup process is streamlined.

Since most standalone controllers operate on the speed density principle, they are exceptionally forgiving of intake system design. Almost any combination of air filter, tubing, throttle body, and manifold

COMPONENTS OF A STANDALONE

Race cars like this Formula D Mustang are an ideal environment for a standalone EFI controller. The Bosch system used on this 5.0 L cammer engine runs an Alpha-N configuration to work better with the stack intake configuration and individual throttle bodies.

can be employed. There is no need for a MAF sensor, so even multiple intake paths can be used on a single engine. Likewise, the absence of the MAF sensor means that it can never be the limitation in either range or flow capacity for the engine. Many classic car owners prefer to discretely hide the EFI system under what, at a glance, appears to be an original round air cleaner atop a carburetor.

Speed density systems also have the benefit of being pressure-based controls. This means that even if the local barometric pressure changes, the EFI controller has the ability to automatically adjust. Even better, if used in a turbo or supercharged application, the speed density control system can tolerate pretty much any airflow amount imaginable as long as the system's MAP sensor is within the measurable pressure range. Fortunately for the speed freaks of the world, 2 bar and 3 bar MAP sensors are both readily available and affordable. In short, the sky's the limit for horsepower as long as you can measure the pressure.

Drawbacks of SA Controllers

So what am I missing? Why don't all ECUs operate this way? While the simplicity of a standalone controller's layout is beneficial to dedicated racecars, owners of road-going vehicles may not be as quick to embrace them. Many modern cars integrate the ECU's outputs and calculations into other systems. For example, fuel consumption numbers from the ECU are often passed to a body computer that will display instantaneous MPG, average fuel economy, and projected range numbers to the driver. If the

If a vehicle already has a well supported ECU in the aftermarket, it may not make sense to switch to a standalone EFI system. The Ford EEC shown here is surprisingly flexible in its abilty to control a wide variety of engine combinations with the proper reprogramming on the SCT chip (green) seen on the J3 port opposite the wiring harness.

The classic look of the 14-inch K&N filter can still be maintained with a clean EFI installation. Much of the wiring for this GM LSx engine is hidden in the valley beneath the single plane intake manifold.

factory ECU is eliminated, the signal that makes this convenience possible is lost. Not all drivers are willing to make such compromises in the name of increased power or simplified wiring. The same argument can be held for ambient air temperature measurements, trouble codes, and predicted oil change interval calculations. If these amenities are to be retained, then the factory ECU must remain installed and functional. This can seriously limit potential modifications unless a factory ECU remapping tool is available.

Even worse than losing an optional convenience feature, some vehicles have a Controller Area Network (CAN) or similar inter-module connection bus that is required for proper operation. Simply removing a single component on the network or communication bus can send the other remaining modules into a rather disagreeable state to say the least. It is possible that functions such as anti-lock braking systems and stability control may use overlapping signals for wheel speed, throttle angle, engine torque, driver inputs, and ambient temperature that are either shared with the ECU or passed through it. Breaking this connection can have seriously undesirable results up to and including a stranded vehicle.

At first glance, 92.1 degrees isn't "hot" to those used to standard units of measure. Since the thermocouple is completely submerged in the water, it does not register the 100 degrees C (212 degrees F) of the escaping vapors.

The ECU for the aftermarket EFI system can be remotely mounted away from the heat and harsh environment of the engine bay. This racecar has its ECU and all other electronics cleanly mounted to a common carbon-fiber panel in the cockpit, where the passenger seat would be in a street car.

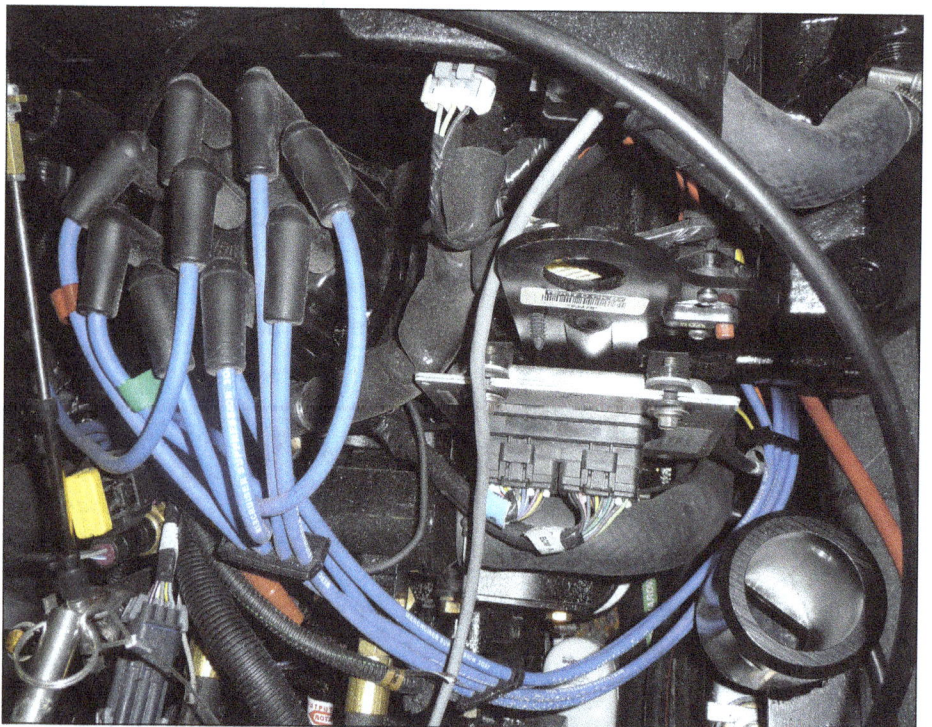

The Delphi MEFI (Marine EFI) controllers are specifically engineered to tolerate a hot and abusive environment. Many ski boats have the ECU mounted directly to the engine, making a short and simple wiring harness for an easy installation.

Units and Examples

A quick note on units and examples.

The majority of the math shown in this book will be done using SI (metric) units. While the scales may be unusual for some at first, a few attempts at tracking the proper Imperial units through the various equations will quickly show the advantages of the metric system. A conversion sheet is included at the end of the book for quick reference, but simply getting used to seeing metric units will definitely make life easier during the calculation and calibration processes.

CHAPTER 3

COMBUSTION BASICS

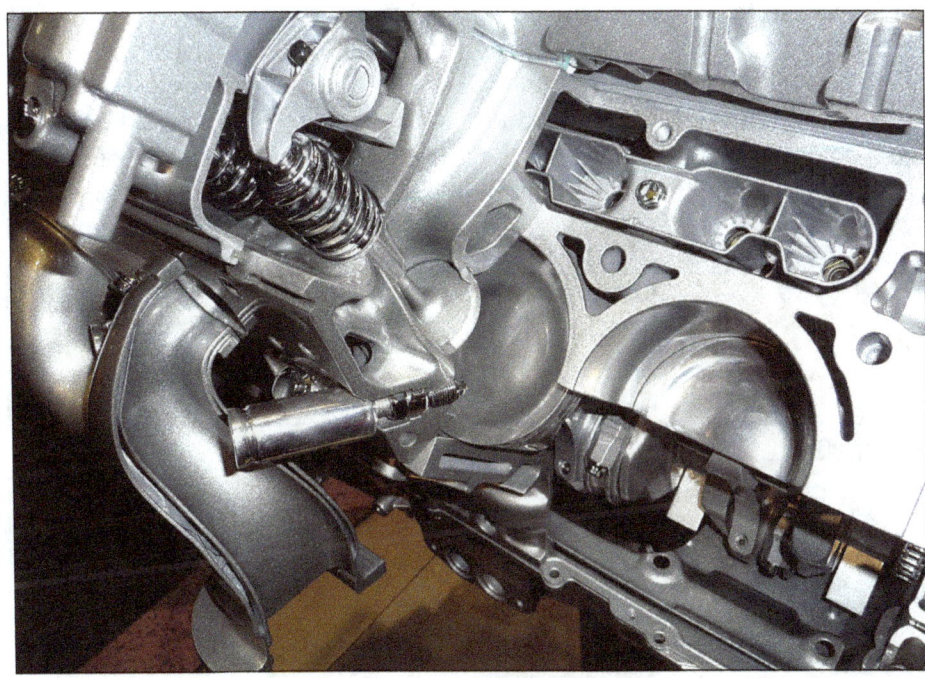

One of the primary functions of any ECU is to determine the exact amount of airmass entering the cylinder on each stroke. The engine's pumping efficiency is largely determined by the port geometry, camshaft profile, and, of course, throttle postion.

Before we dive too far into the controls, it's important to know more about what is actually being controlled. The ECU is not merely in charge of power or torque. These are indirect outcomes of the engine's actual operation state. Conditions such as engine speed, throttle angle, delivered fuel quantity, ambient temperature, and pressure all play a part in how much power the engine is making at any moment. Fundamentally, the torque delivered to the flywheel is a function of how much pressure is present inside the cylinders on each cycle. This cylinder pressure results from a combination of the engine's natural compression and the combustion reaction between the air and fuel.

For a given total amount of air entering the cylinder on a single stroke, we have the option to vary the amount of fuel entering at the same time through the fuel injector pulsewidth or open time. The longer the injector is held open, the more fuel is added to this same air charge entering the cylinder, yielding a "richer" mixture. It has been established by our friends in the chemistry department that gasoline burns most completely when mixed with air at a ratio of 14.68 pounds of air for every 1 pound of fuel. This mixture allows for the best reaction between the hydrogen and carbon atoms in the fuel with the oxygen atoms in the air. The more complete this reaction is, the less leftover or wasted components we have at the end of the combustion event. The chemists refer to this balanced ratio of components as stoichiometric.

The exact balance depends upon what chemicals are being mixed. A

DESIGNING AND TUNING HIGH-PERFORMANCE FUEL INJECTION SYSTEMS 23 value of 14.68:1 defines the stoichiometric ratio for pure Iso-Octane (2-2-4 Trimethyl Pentane). The gasoline that most of us purchase at the local station is actually a cocktail of many chemicals that each contribute to the combustion mix, and thus, slightly alter the balanced stoichiometric point. It's not uncommon to see the stoichiometric point for gasoline listed as 14.56:1, 14.64:1, 14.68:1, or 14.7:1. The reality is that any of these could be right on a given day for a particular blend of fuel, detergents, additives, and contamination. To further complicate things, blending alcohol with the gasoline can make significant shifts in the stoichiometric mixture. Just a 10% mix of ethanol (commonly sold as "E10" at stations across the country) shifts the stoichiometric point down to 14.2:1.

It has become increasingly popular for stations to offer E85 fuel, an 85% ethanol blend originally intended as a more environmentally friendly fuel choice. Performance enthusiasts have embraced this fuel as of late due to its high octane rating and relatively low cost. Additional benefits also arise from the fuel's tremendous cooling capacity as it evaporates. The large amount of alcohol blended into this gasoline mix yields a stoichiometric point of 9.85:1. At a glance, this looks extremely "rich" to the average petrolhead, but one must realize that this is actually the same as 14.68:1 with pure gasoline, as far as the cylinder is concerned. A delivered ratio of 11.0:1 with E85 fuel is actually quite lean.

To further complicate things, what is commonly labeled as E85 is not always precisely 85% ethanol. Many stations in colder regions shift the blending during winter months as far as E70. The added gasoline volume increases the fuel's ability to evaporate in cold temperatures at startup. There is no reason why any performance enthusiast couldn't use ethanol-blended fuels, but this dramatic change in stoichiometric point shift must be accommodated to maintain proper air/fuel ratio control as the blend changes. Many enthusiasts have success with saving multiple tune files for the same engine to account for the shifted stoichiometric point as stations change from summer to winter fuel supplies and back.

One other concern with alcohol blends is their corrosive nature toward rubber and aluminum. OEM vehicles that are flex-fuel capable are typically equipped with stainless-steel fuel lines and Viton seals or O-rings to avoid this.

The Great Equalizer

Given that the stoichiometric mixture for the fuel may change depending on the exact mixture, a measurement of what balance the cylinder really "sees" would be very useful. A more useful number than actual air/fuel ratio might be something that indicates how far from stoichiometric the current combustion conditions are. It is helpful to know an excess air ratio more so than absolute air/fuel ratio. That way, if the actual stoichiometric mix changes with a different fuel, one can still use the same units of measure for "rich" and "lean." Most of the time an engine is running, the proper target air/fuel ratio is stoichiometric anyway. This means that an excess air ratio would instantly indicate exactly how far from this ideal mixture the engine is currently oper-

Fuel Type	Lower Heating Value kJ/kg	Octane (R+M)/2	Density kg/l	Stoichiometric Ratio kg/kg
Gasoline				
Regular	42.7	87	0.740	14.8
Premium	43.5	93	0.755	14.7
Iso-Octane	44.8	100	0.690	15.2
Diesel	42.5	25	0.835	14.5
Methanol	19.7	104.5	0.790	6.47
Ethanol	26.8	104.2	0.790	9
E85	29.19	101.6	0.783	9.87
Propane	46.3	104.5	0.510	15.67
Hydrogen	120	130	0.090	34.3
Methane	50	120	0.720	17.2
Kerosene	43	15	0.800	14.5
Benzene	40.2	115	0.880	13.3
Toluene	40.6	114.5	0.870	13.4
LPG	46.1	110	0.540	15.5

Internal combustion engines can operate on a wide range of fuels. The key is to make sure that the ECU is calibrated to the proper stoichiometric ratio before making adjustments based on wideband feedback.

COMBUSTION BASICS

The annual Woodward Dream Cruise along Michigan's legendary "Musclecar Boulevard" draws over a million visitors and the anger of environmentalists. Adding electronic fuel injection (and a high flow catalytic converter) to your classic car can contribute to cleaning up the emissions and improve performance as you enjoy actually driving the vehicle with fellow entusiasts.

ating. In essence, the excess air ratio is the current error from chemically ideal or stoichiometric conditions.

Engineers have long since recognized this need for a quantifiable excess air ratio and established a unit for it: lambda (λ). Lambda is defined as your current air/fuel ratio divided by the stoichiometric ideal ratio:

$$\lambda = \frac{\text{(Current AFR)}}{\text{(Stoichiometric AFR)}}$$

Equation 3.1

A delivered air/fuel ratio of 14.64:1 with gasoline has a lambda value of 1.00:

$$\lambda = \frac{(14.64)}{(14.64)} = 1.00$$

A richer mixture, such as 13.0:1 with gasoline, would have a lower lambda value. This indicates the excess air ratio of less than 1:

$$\lambda = \frac{(13.0)}{(14.64)} = 0.89$$

In this case, we only see 89% of the necessary air with the delivered fuel, an 11% rich condition compared to stoichiometry. If the goal is to run at stoichiometry, an adjustment of −11% to the fuel would bring the engine back to the target of 14.64 with gasoline. Conversely, a reduction in the calculated airflow by a factor of 0.89 at the same actual airflow point would yield a lower calculated fuel delivery that would coincide with the target ratio. One quickly starts to see the usefulness of this relative ratio expression. We will discuss this in more detail later.

AFR and Torque

While there is no argument that burning fuel in an engine helps create torque output, cylinder pressure is really the focus here. If only the relative ratio of air to fuel within a cylinder is changed, one can observe several other changes. Holding engine speed, load, throttle angle, and temperatures constant, the nature of air/fuel ratio can be seen in terms of instantaneous torque output.

When all other variables are held constant, one can see that the measured torque peaks between

E85 isn't always 85% ethanol year round. During the colder months, the blend is reduced to only 70% ethanol to aid in starting.

CHAPTER 3

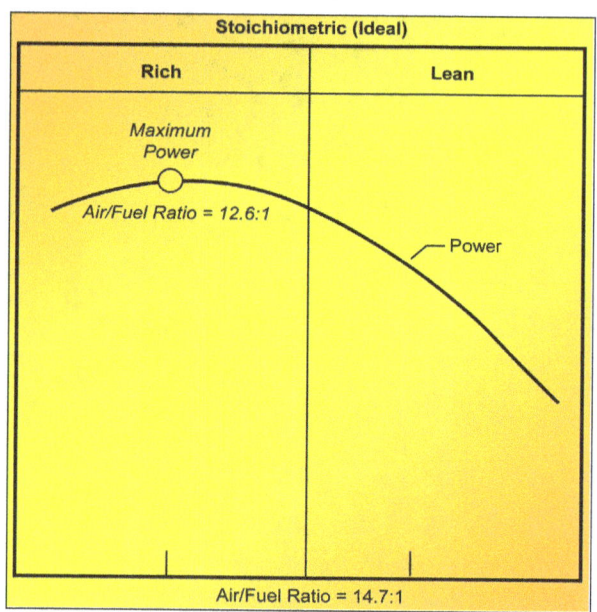

A mixture slightly rich of stoichiometry will generate better power and torque as the engine makes best use of all available oxygen in the cylinder. There is no single best air/fuel ratio for maximum output for all engines, but there is a range that gets close to optimal for most applications.

lambda=0.84 and lambda=0.92. In this region, there is relatively little change in engine torque as the air/fuel ratio is adjusted. The left edge of this torque plateau is referred to as "RBT" or Rich Best Torque. The right edge of the plateau is known as "LBT" or Lean Best Torque. Both RBT and LBT air/fuel ratios produce very similar torque outputs from the same engine at the same speed load. Straying too far either rich or lean from the plateau shown in the chart above can begin to quickly lose torque output. The actual width and shape of this curve is unique to each engine, but the general trend remains the same.

This begs the question, "Why does torque change with air/fuel ratio?" The answer lies in the speed of the chemical reaction. The actual rate at which the fuel and oxygen combust varies with concentration. A slightly rich mixture provides the best possible conditions for the flame to propagate from one set of molecules to the next. If the combustion event is started at the same time (ignition angle has not changed), a faster burn rate will lead to quicker buildup of pressure within the cylinder as the gases attempt to expand with the rising temperature. This is compounded by the fact that the piston is usually still working to compress the mixture immediately after ignition when spark is measured in degrees before top dead center (TDC). The rapid rise in pressure coupled with the higher overall pressure results in more force upon the piston immediately after TDC, where the largest amount of useful work can be extracted.

What's important here is to recognize the rate at which this reaction occurs. Effectively, pushing the mixture toward a faster reaction rate has the same net effect as advancing the ignition timing as far as cylinder pressure is concerned. Many OEM systems will have tables that intentionally adjust the spark advance with respect to lambda. A closer look at these adjustments shows a minimum of advance applied near the peak reaction rate and more advance added as the mixture becomes either excessively rich or lean. The faster reacting mixture can be timed to deliver this pressure at more useful times within the cycle to optimize torque output. If the piston does not have to fight against an expanding mixture, there is less effort wasted during the compression stroke in order to get the same effective pressure during the expansion stroke. (The timing of cylinder pressure peak versus TDC will be discussed in more detail later when we take a look at ignition angle.)

Fuel Economy and Emissions

While many performance enthusiasts could honestly care less about the emissions output of their racecars, there's no reason to intentionally pollute. The beauty of this situation is that good emissions can blend nicely with high power output. The general principle is to avoid wasting anything. This means either fuel or airflow. Running an engine rich of the stoichiometric balance results in progressively greater carbon monoxide (CO) and hydrocarbon (HC) emissions.

The rich condition can progressively inhibit fuel molecules from finding oxygen molecules during the combustion process. Going too far in

A world class sportscar is nothing without a powerful engine. One key to making the most of any engine is the precise control of the air/fuel ratio that an EFI system can provide.

---

26 DESIGNING AND TUNING HIGH-PERFORMANCE FUEL INJECTION SYSTEMS

COMBUSTION BASICS

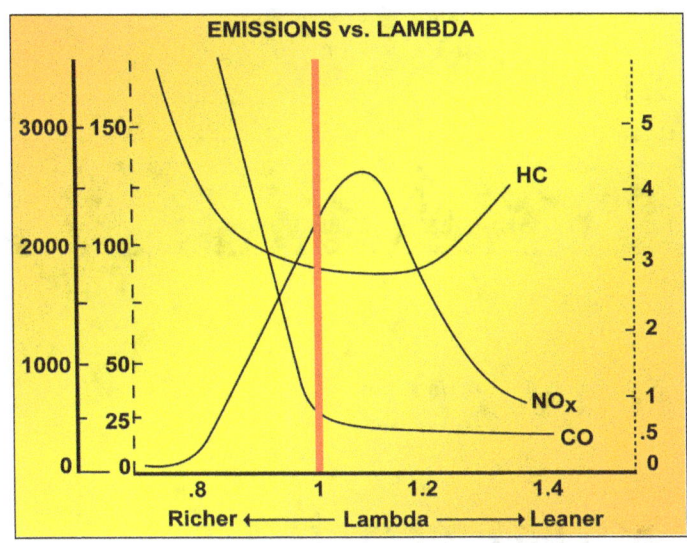

A stoichiometric mixture yields the best compromise for raw engine emissions. The addition of a catalytic converter will allow many of the leftover components to react afterward as well.

run in search of fuel economy. Unfortunately, this can be just as bad for fuel consumption as running rich, with the added penalty of torque loss. Running too lean can also lead to an increase in HC emissions as the engine begins to exhibit lean misfire events. Suddenly, operating at lambda=1.00 doesn't look so bad. Oh, and the catalytic converters (if they're installed) work much better near stoichiometric conditions too.

Over 400 hp on pump gas and emissions compliance? No problem for this supercharged Mustang GT after proper ECU recalibration. Making good power doesn't mean ignoring emissions when you have the level of control that modern EFI systems afford.

the rich direction leads to a misfiring condition due to the lack of available oxygen and shows up as raw HC emissions that are literally unburned fuel. Nothing can be worse for fuel economy than injecting fuel that never even gets burned!

It has become common for many people to notice that there is a peak in fuel efficiency with a slightly lean mixture. The peak flame temperature is found just lean of the stoichiometric mixture. The slightly lean mixture develops a high-temperature flame front, increasing the thermal efficiency of the cycle. While this is technically true, the actual gains are less than revolutionary. Most engines see less than a 5% decrease in steady state fuel consumption with lean burn conditions. Just as with torque, there is a "plateau" for fuel economy where one can get close to optimum by running within a certain window of air/fuel ratios. Dropping too far off either side of the plateau significantly reduces fuel economy.

Many inexperienced tuners make the mistake of attempting to see just how lean they can make an engine

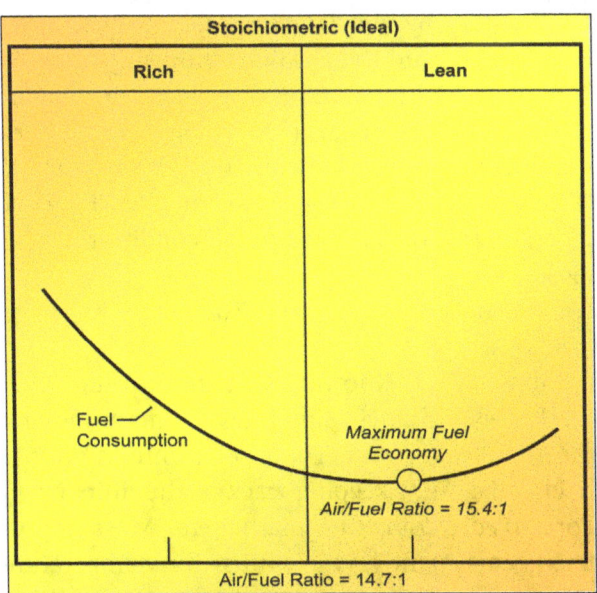

If better fuel economy is the goal, the biggest concern is to avoid running rich. Notice how there is almost no difference in raw fuel economy between stoichiometry and leaner mixtures. Running too lean can actually hurt fuel economy, as lean misfires occur.

As emissions standards tightened significantly in the late 70s and early 80s, manufacturers turned to EFI for improved precision of fuel metering compared to carburetion. This 1984 Corvette with its Crossfire injection system was one of the earlier mass-production examples of this new technology.

DESIGNING AND TUNING HIGH-PERFORMANCE FUEL INJECTION SYSTEMS

CHAPTER 4

VE Equation and Airflow Estimation

"Someone told me that each equation I included in the book would halve the sales." — Stephen Hawking

Whenever the engine is running, the primary job of the EFI system is to properly administer the injection times. The actual injection time is dependent upon two things, the flow rate of the injector and the desired fuel mass per shot. If flow rate is known, this leaves the determination of fuel mass per shot as the primary calculation. To go one step further, the fuel mass required has direct correlation to the aircharge (measured in units of air mass) on a given cylinder event as a function of the desired air/fuel ratio. Thus, for a given injector flow rate and air/fuel ratio, the injection time is directly proportional to the aircharge delivered to the cylinder on each intake event.

Finding the aircharge on the fly is the most important job the ECU has. Almost every other function is dependent upon aircharge either directly or indirectly. Many OEM controllers simplify this task by including a MAF sensor that directly measures the instantaneous airflow. This airflow is then input directly to the ECU control algorithms for further processing. In the absence of a MAF sensor, the values generated by the MAF sensor must be calculated by some other means. The speed density principle does this calculation based largely upon Boyle's Gas Law.

In 1662, physicist and chemist Robert Boyle stated that, "For a fixed amount of gas kept at a fixed temperature, P and V are inversely proportional (while one increases, the other decreases)." This, along with a few later works combined to give us the Ideal Gas Law of 1834 that we learned in chemistry class:

$$PV = nRT$$

Equation 4.1

In this equation, Pressure (P) multiplied by Volume (V) is equal to the number of moles (n) multiplied by the Universal Gas Constant (R) and the absolute temperature (T). In this equation, the units for pressure are Pascals (Pa). Volume is measured in cubic meters (m^3), and temperature in degrees Kelvin (K). The value for R is fixed for all conditions:

$$R_{air} = 287.05 \, J/kg - K$$

Knowing that the R value never changes simplifies the math moving forward. The most common error is not keeping track of the units when doing the math here. Most importantly, the units for temperature

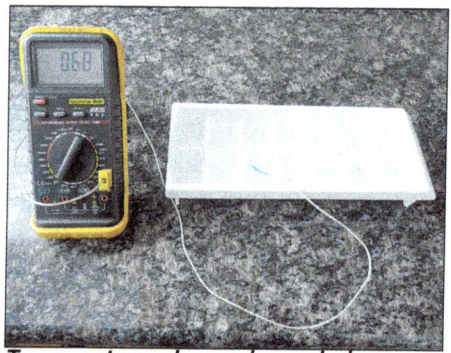

Temperature plays a key role in determining airmass in speed density systems. Acquiring an accurate temperature measurement can be critical to proper calculations.

must be observed. It is a common error to attempt this equation with the incorrect temperature scale units.

More careful examination of *Equation 4.1* shows some interesting relationships. If the amount of gas (n), and temperature remain constant, then the "nRT" portion of the equation remains constant. Thus, we confirm Boyle's Gas Law where P x V equals some constant number. If one increases, the other must decrease. With some simple algebra, the equation can be rewritten to show what happens with a constant volume:

$$V = nRT / P$$
Equation 4.2

Here, we can imagine a snapshot of what happens during combustion near TDC. The volume is fixed along with the amount of gas and Universal Gas Constant. In order to obey the Ideal Gas Law, temperature divided by pressure must also remain constant. So as temperature increases, pressure also increases by the same ratio. If burn temperature is kept the same, repeating this process with a larger amount of gas present in the cylinder also increases the resulting pressure. This is where the force (pressure multiplied by area) acting upon the top of the piston comes from for the power stroke. Either higher temperature or more complete cylinder filling will result in an increase in cylinder pressure.

More to the point of ECU functions, this relationship needs to show more than just the basic working principle of a piston-driven internal-combustion engine. The Ideal Gas Law can be used to calculate the quantity of a gas present if all other variables are known. To do this, more algebra is applied and the equation is solved for "n":

$$n = PV / RT$$
Equation 4.3

Here, one can see that predicted aircharge (measured in moles) can be calculated based on pressure, a reference volume, and temperature. Pressure can be measured directly with a MAP sensor while temperature is measured with the IAT sensor. The reference volume remains the biggest unknown. Since the engine

Manifold pressure is acquired by a MAP sensor in order to complete the volumetric efficiency equation. This sensor has been remotely mounted on the firewall with a rubber vacuum line connected to the intake manifold plenum.

Kelvin and Rankine Scales

The "T" in the Ideal Gas Law equation is absolute temperature and not simply Fahrenheit or Celsius. A reading of zero degrees on both of these scales represents something other than "no temperature," so a different scale must be used. An absolute scale that depicts temperature as a magnitude similar to the way mass is commonly shown is used. The Kelvin and Rankine scales do just that and satisfy the mathematical requirements for using the Ideal Gas Law. Think of Kelvin as an absolute Celsius scale and Rankine as an absolute Fahrenheit scale. Zero on either the Kelvin or Rankine scale represents absolute zero, the coldest possible temperature. Each is merely a fixed offset from their common counterpart. Kelvin uses the same scaling as Celsius, with an offset of –273.15 degrees. Rankine uses the same scaling as Fahrenheit, with an offset of –459.67 degrees. Therefore:

Temperature (K) = (Temperature °C) – 273.15
Temperature (°R) = (Temperature °F) – 459.67

It is still possible to convert between Kelvin and Rankine, similar to how conversions between Celsius and Fahrenheit are done:

Temperature (K) = (Temperature °R) x 5/9
Temperature (K) = (Temperature °F + 459.67) x 5/9

Temperature (°R) = (Temperature K) x 9/5
Temperature (°R) = (Temperature °C + 273.15) x 9/5

CHAPTER 4

A closeup of this stack injection system shows the fuel injector located on the inboard side where it is aimed toward the intake valve. Also notice the twin plug ignition system on this Hemi where each coil fires a pair of plug wires per cylinder simultaneously.

GM has been using a blended airflow model that includes both speed density MAP based estimation and MAF based direct measurement. The model favors the MAP based calculation at low flows where there is a lot of reversion and the MAF at higher flow rates that are more steady.

does not always completely fill the cylinders, even at WOT, some sort of volume scaling is required to allow this equation to output an accurate aircharge. This volume scaling is done with what is called volumetric efficiency (VE). When a factor is applied to the known cylinder volume, a corrected relative volume can be input to the Ideal Gas Law equation in order to solve for "n." All that is needed is some method to accurately predict the volumetric efficiency as the engine is running.

The corrected relative cylinder filling volume (V_{rel}) can be described as the product of the actual cylinder volume and the current volumetric efficiency.

$$V_{rel} = V_{cyl} \times VE$$

Equation 4.4

Since there is no such thing as a volumetric efficiency sensor, the value

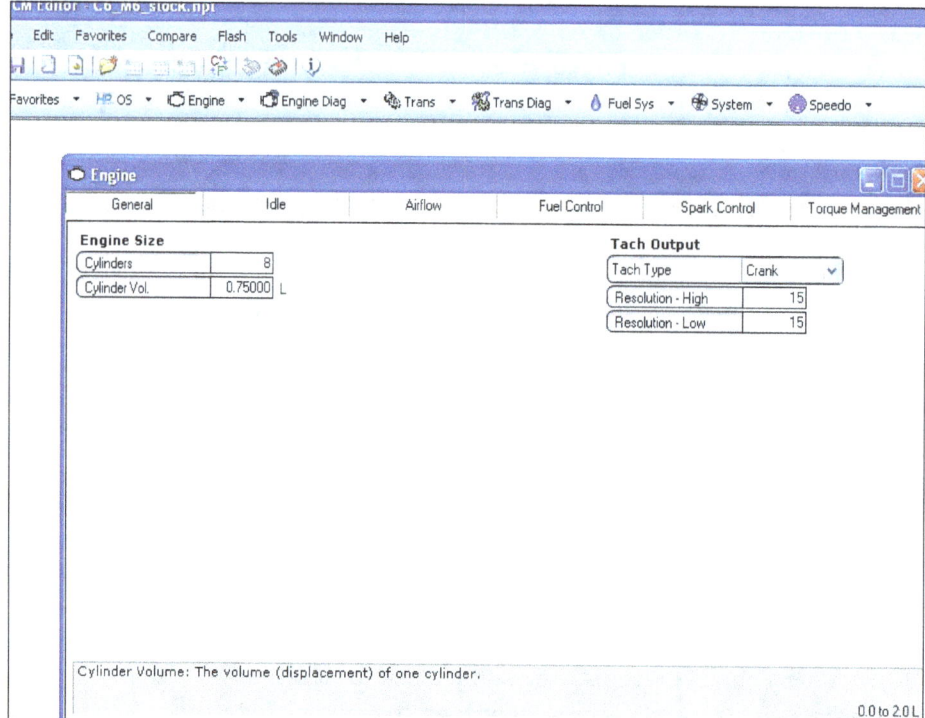

The GM speed density model for dynamic air calculation uses a single variable for cylinder displacement. This is the reference volume that will be adjusted by the volumetric efficiency to find the effective volume used in the speed density calculation. This particular snapshot is taken from a 6.0 L V-8 using HPTuners software.

for VE must be inferred from some other ECU function. It is known that cylinder filling is a function of engine load. So taking a sensor input that varies with respect to load is the first step toward finding volumetric efficiency. Intake manifold pressure has exactly the kind of relationship with load that is needed here. As pressure within the intake manifold increases, more air flows past the intake valve on each opening event. The relationship does not have to be completely linear, just predictable.

The other contributor to filling efficiency is intake and exhaust tuning. The standing waves within the manifolds vary in intensity and timing as engine speed changes. The ram tuning of an intake is not limited to a single frequency. There is a center point with peak amplitude and a range on either side of the tuning frequency where some positive influence is still exhibited.

The bandwidth and magnitude of this resonance range changes with intake runner dimensions such as area and length. The resonance range is further influenced by air density, temperature, and velocity. Frequency in the case of an engine is simply rotational speed because the valves open and close a fixed number of times per revolution. This gives a changing contribution to filling efficiency as the engine passes through various resonance points speed range. Thus, engine speed is used as another input to the volumetric efficiency estimation.

Alpha-N

Some systems forego the MAP sensor input for a different load estimator. Throttle position can also be used to estimate engine load. As throttle angle increases, restriction on the intake side is removed and cylinder filling is increased. This type of control system is known as "Alpha-N" from the common engineering abbreviations for throttle angle (Alpha) and engine speed (N). While the relationship between throttle angle and actual engine load is less precise than that between manifold pressure and load, it results in a simpler system with one less sensor.

Alpha-N systems actually work surprisingly well on "stack" injection systems where no common intake plenum is available for monitoring. In these individual runner installations, a relatively small change in throttle angle delivers a very large change in pressure upstream of the intake valve. This is part of what gives these systems their characteristic great throttle response as the driver touches the gas pedal. Unfortunately, most of this pressure change happens over a very small range of throttle angles and the idle vacuum is numerically less than most common plenum intakes. This makes it difficult to base load estimations on manifold pressure with stack injection systems.

While some individual runner layouts have been released with a connecting tube or hose between each intake runner and a central chamber and MAP sensor, this often leads to a noisy MAP signal, as each runner feeds a strong pulse to the sensor. Increasing the volume of the central chamber to which the MAP sensor is mounted decreases the signal noise level, but with quickly diminishing returns. It is almost always easier to simply abandon the complex mechanical averaging system in favor of a simpler Alpha-N control logic.

This Roush crate engine features a stack-type intake system with eight individual throttle bodies linked to a common cable wheel in the center. Since the individual intake tubes are fed directly by atmospheric pressure, a MAP sensor is not reliable and an Alpha-N control algorithm is preferred.

Transplanting a highly modified 4.3 L turbocharged V-6 from a GMC Syclone into a newer body S10 pickup made a great application of a standalone EFI controller. The all-wheel-drive transfer case from an Oldsmobile Bravada was also used to help melt all four tires evenly off the line.

The F.A.S.T. standalone controller in this turbocharged S10 is mounted under the passenger side of the dash where the wiring can be conveniently hidden. Since this vehicle does not use a CAN or serial bus network, the swap to a standalone system was relatively simple. The F.A.S.T. controller is actually significantly more precise and much faster than the 1980s vintage original ECU for the Syclone.

Provided that the volumetric efficiency correction factor is properly estimated, the Ideal Gas Law delivers aircharge as number of moles, "n." This must be converted to a more useful number that the ECU can work with. By multiplying the number of moles of air by the known molar density of air, one can solve for airmass.

$$n_{air} = 0.02897 \text{ kg / mol}$$

This calculation results in one of the most critical numbers the ECU generates: aircharge in units of mass. Even if the desired unit is not grams, it's simple to convert to kilograms, or pounds for display or further processing. From here, the required fuel mass can be calculated as a function of desired air/fuel ratio. Remember that air/fuel ratio is really a comparison of masses. All that is needed to obtain that exact desired fuel mass is a good injector model. Any errors in the calculated aircharge mass or fuel injector flow rate will result in an air/fuel ratio different than what was commanded by the ECU.

Going back to *Equations 4.3* and *4.4*, a clearer description of predicted aircharge can be made in terms of relative volume (V_{rel}), MAP, absolute temperature, and Universal Gas Constant:

$$\text{Airmass} = V_{rel} P / RT$$

Equation 4.5

All that is needed at this point is some helpful unit conversion factors to allow the inputs typically used in EFI systems to be used while delivering an output that is easy to work with. Ideally, it would be arranged to accept typical metric EFI input units of liters of displacement, degrees Kelvin, kilopascals of pressure, and decimal volumetric efficiency yielding an

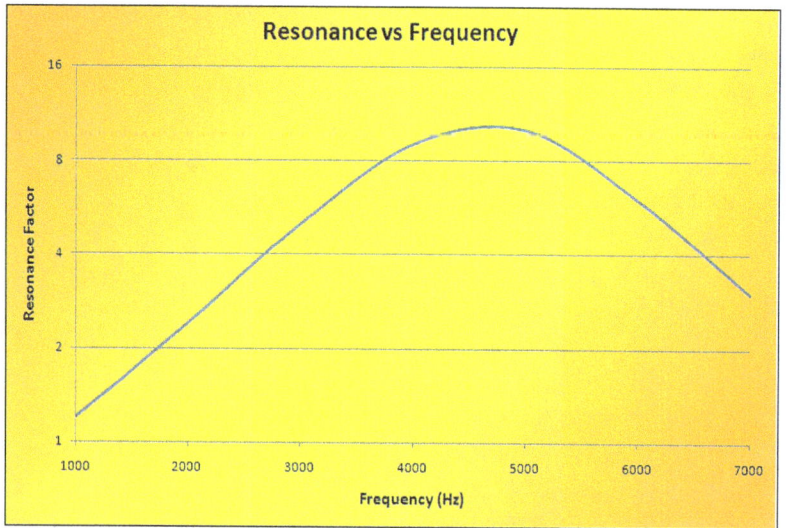

An open pipe will resonate at a fixed frequency based on the cross-sectional area and length of the pipe. As the excitation frequency of the pipe (engine RPM) approaches this point, the pipe will amplify the excitation and actually work to help fill the cylinder.

VE EQUATION AND AIRFLOW ESTIMATION

output in grams of airmass. Doing this requires that the decimal place gets moved several times in order to display the proper units. A revised version of the Universal Gas Constant for air is used:

$$R_{air} = 0.28705 \text{ kPa-L / g-K}$$

Plugging this revised value into *Equation 4.5* shows a revised version that can be used on the fly by the ECU:

$$\text{Airmass (g/cyl)} = \frac{V_{rel}(L) \times P \text{ (kPa)}}{(0.28705) \times T \text{ (K)}}$$

Equation 4.6

Alternatively, it can be expressed with the ECU parameters for cylinder displacement and VE (which is pulled from the VE table on the fly) included:

$$\text{Airmass (g/cyl)} = \frac{V_{cyl}(L) \times VE \times P \text{ (kPa)}}{(0.28705) \times T \text{ (K)}}$$

Equation 4.7

Some systems will not have a cylinder-specific displacement variable available for calibration. In these cases, the displacement is that of the entire engine and another variable must be included to indicate how many cylinders are in the engine. Unless you're Smokey Yunick, it should be safe to assume that all cylinders are of the same size in the engine. The result is that the ECU must perform some quick math to find cylinder volume and then use *Equation 4.7*:

$$V_{cyl}(L) = \frac{V_{engine}(L)}{(\text{\# of cylinders})}$$

Equation 4.8

Again, this can be combined with the earlier *Equation 4.7* to show airmass as a function of VE, engine volume in liters, number of cylinders, MAP in kPa, and temperature in degrees Kelvin. The final result is:

$$\text{Airmass (g/cyl)} = \frac{V_{engine}(L) \times VE \times P \text{ (kPa)}}{(0.28705) \times T \text{ (K)} \times (\text{\# of cylinders})}$$

Equation 4.9

An example would be a 6.0 L V-8 engine operating at 50% (0.50) VE, 60 kPa and 100 degrees F (311 degrees Kelvin) would have a current cylinder airmass of 0.25 g/cylinder. *Equation 4.9* is the fundamental operating equation for almost every true speed density EFI systems produced today. The most important job of any ECU is to determine the cylinder air filling. Total airflow and required fuel flow are derived from the airmass calculation, so it is imperative that this math is done correctly.

Airmass is an easier unit to work with when moving on to fuel mass requirements. Using airmass gives the "air shot" to each cylinder event so that calculating the "fuel shot" is simply a matter of desired air/fuel ratio. The chemistry tells us that air/fuel ratio is a comparison of masses of compounds entering the reaction. Knowing the mass of one and a target air/fuel ratio leads to a target fuel mass:

$$\text{Fuel mass (g/cyl)} = \frac{\text{Airmass (g/cyl)}}{(\text{Air/fuel Ratio})}$$

Equation 4.10

Once the target fuel mass is known, the ECU can look to the injector data to calculate the necessary pulsewidth to deliver that mass. This is basically just a matter of comparing flow rate against desired total mass, but it will be covered in more detail later. What is important here is to note how the ECU goes from sensor measurements (manifold absolute pressure, charge temperature, crankshaft speed) and reference values (volumetric efficiency, engine displacement, R_{air}) to calculated airmass and consequently, desired fuel mass. The sensor values are subject to change as engine conditions change. Reference values for engine displacement and Universal Gas Constant are fixed. Volumetric efficiency will also change as engine conditions change, so there is a calibrate-able table built into the ECU controls that must be populated in order to properly calculate the airmass. (The actual calibration of this VE reference table will be discussed later.)

Airmass may not seem like a very intuitive number to work with for the casual tuner. Many tuners prefer to see airflow in a more familiar format such as grams per second or pounds per minute. Making the conversion from airmass to total airflow can be done by sampling the frequency of airmass events in addition to the magnitude of each event as done earlier. The frequency of airmass events is determined by engine speed and number of cylinders. The more cylinders in an engine and the faster they are cycled, the more total opportunity for airflow there is. Therefore, an eight cylinder engine operating at 2,000 rpm can have the same potential airflow as a four cylinder engine at 4,000 rpm, provided the volume of each cylinder in these engines are the same. Mathematically, the airflow as a function

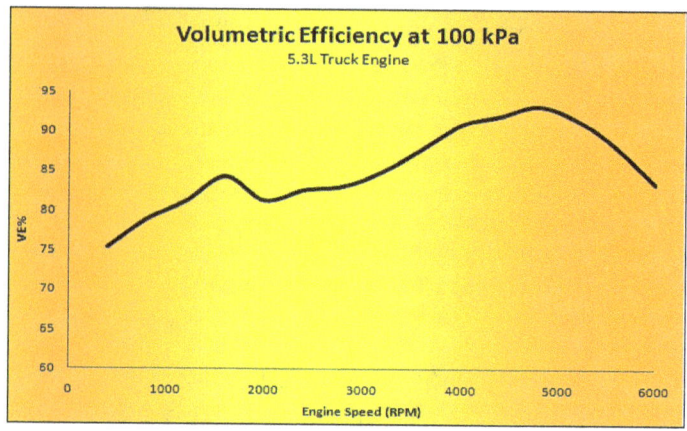

At 100 kPa, the volumetric efficiency curve closely resembles the WOT torque curve of the engine. The speeds where the engine is more efficient at pumping air show up as higher cylinder loading and result in higher torque production.

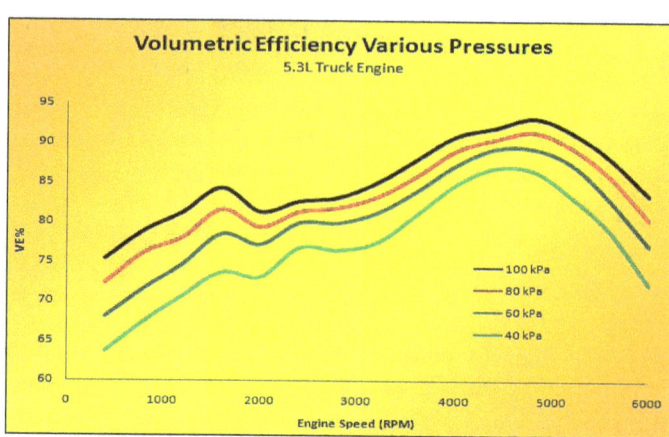

When additional pressure lines are plotted along with the WOT curve, one can see that the lower manifold pressures follow the same trends of improved pumping efficiency around the same RPM points as the WOT curve, but at a lower overall magnitude.

of airmass is shown by *Equation 4.11* below.

Taken a step further, *Equation 4.9* and *Equation 4.11* can be combined to show total predicted airflow as a function of total engine displacement, volumetric efficiency, MAP, engine speed and charge temperature. See *Equation 4.12* below.

Required fuel flow in terms of volume per unit time (liters/hr) is determined from the current airflow as found in *Equation 4.12* using the same ratio division as *Equation 4.10*. This becomes useful in sizing fuel pumps and lines when selecting the necessary hardware for an application. Most fuel pumps are rated in terms of volumetric flow rate at a rated pressure. A little bit of unit conversion is used to convert seconds into hours and an average fuel density of 750 g/l for gasoline can assumed. By taking the calculated airflow at maximum power along with the desired air/fuel ratio, the required fuel flow is found. See *Equation 4.13* below.

Taken a step further to incorporate *Equation 4.12* and *Equation 4.13*, fuel flow rate is expressed in terms of engine size, VE, MAP, inlet temperature, RPM, and air/fuel ratio. See *Equation 4.14* below.

Engine Load

Volumetric efficiency is a good indicator of how much pumping work is being done by the engine at any point, but it is often useful to know relative cylinder filling in another metric. Percent engine load looks at cylinder filling on a mass basis rather than volume. Finding this is relatively simple once the airmass is known. Percent engine load is expressed as the ratio of current airmass charge to theoretical airmass charge. The theoretical airmass charge is simply the swept volume of the cylinder times the density (ρ) of air under standard conditions, 1.168 grams per liter:

$$\text{Theoretical Airmass} = V_{cylinder} \times \rho_{STP}$$
Equation 4.15

Continuing the earlier example, the 6.0 L V-8 engine has a cylinder

$$\text{Airflow (g/s)} = \frac{\text{Airmass (g/cyl)} \times \text{RPM} \times (\text{\# of cylinders})}{120}$$
Equation 4.11

$$\text{Airflow (g/s)} = \frac{V_{engine}(L) \times VE \times P\,(kPa) \times RPM}{(34.446) \times T\,(K)}$$
Equation 4.12

$$\text{Fuel Flow (l/hr)} = \frac{V_{engine}(L) \times VE \times P\,(kPa) \times RPM}{(\text{Air/fuel Ratio}) \times T\,(K)}$$
Equation 4.13

$$\text{Fuel Flow (l/hr)} = \frac{V_{engine}(L) \times VE \times P\,(kPa) \times RPM}{(7.1763) \times (\text{Air/fuel Ratio}) \times T\,(K)}$$
Equation 4.14

VE EQUATION AND AIRFLOW ESTIMATION

volume of 0.75 L. The theoretical airmass of this 0.75 L cylinder would be (0.75 L) x (1.168 g/L), or 0.876 g. This represents the mass of air that would fill this cylinder to 100% of its capacity under standard temperature and pressure conditions. Percent engine load is calculated as the ratio of actual to theoretical airmasses:

$$\text{Engine Load (percent)} = \frac{\text{Current Airmass}}{\text{Theoretical Airmass}}$$

Equation 4.16

The previous airmass calculation at 50% VE, 60 kPa, 311K showed 0.25 g/cylinder. Dividing this by the theoretical airmass at STP of the 0.75 L cylinder shows an engine load of (0.25 g)/(0.876 g) or roughly 29%. This falls right in line for a typical engine load during cruising conditions. Idle loads usually work out to be about 10 to 20%. Most naturally aspirated engines will show approximately 80 to 90% load at WOT even though they show 100 kPa of manifold pressure. It takes a very efficient and properly matched intake, camshaft, and cylinder head combination to hit 100% load on a naturally aspirated engine, but it's certainly possible on race engines or more modern production engines near their tuning peak. It is perfectly normal to see calculated engine loads well in excess of 100% with boosted engines under full load. Engine load is closely tied to torque output.

Manifold pressure is proportional to engine load and airflow. While 100 kPa does not equal 100% VE or 100% engine load, one can still infer approximate engine loading based on MAP. There is a linear relationship between MAP and airmass over a large range of pressures. If one were to plot the VE table values for a single engine speed, the linear relationship becomes apparent. Between 50 and 100 kPa, most engines show a similar relationship for each speed breakpoint. The slope and intercept of this line will change with engine speed.

Some OEM speed density applications even use this relationship as the fundamental operating principle instead of using a VE reference table. This replaces a series of points in the large table array with just a pair of values for the slope and intercept that describe the linear conversion from MAP to airmass.

VE and Torque

Since we can now see how engine load and volumetric efficiency are related, it's time to draw another conclusion. Both load and VE are measures of relative cylinder filling. It stands to reason that the more the cylinder is filled with air and fuel on a cycle, the bigger bang can be expected after ignition. This bigger bang that comes from a higher cylinder loading translates directly into more pressure on the piston, and more importantly, more torque at the crankshaft.

Plotting WOT engine load (or VE) against RPM shows a familiar curve to those who have been around engines for a while. The resulting curve in the left-hand chart on page 34 looks very much like a dynamometer report for engine torque across RPM. In fact, the same can be repeated for a series of lower load points. Plotting VE across the entire RPM range, but at only 80 kPa instead of 100 kPa (WOT for a naturally aspirated engine) show a curve of almost identical shape and marginally lower magnitude. Repeating once again at an even lower man-

The number of cylinders does not directly change the VE equation math since you are usually solving for grams of air per cylinder. Adding more cylinders simply increases the frequency with which this calculation must be executed and the total mass of fuel to be delivered.

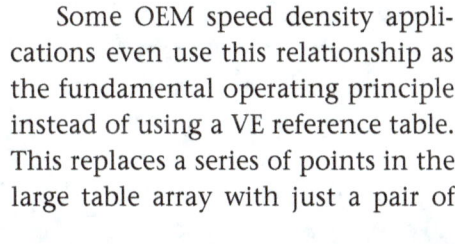

Changes to the engine's pumping efficiency due to a new low restriction air intake or higher flowing exhaust should be accompanied by ECU calibration changes in order to make the math model in the controller match the new higher physical volumetric efficiency of the engine. Harley Davidson offers the Screaming Eagle ECU recalibration tool to modify their controllers, which are just a simple speed density system.

ifold pressure of 70 kPa will continue to follow the trend of a similarly shaped curve of scaled-down magnitude. The right-hand chart on page 34 shows a series of tests where VE is recorded across the RPM range, each series taken at a constant manifold pressure.

By taking the VE values at various MAP points at a single RPM, we can once again see the linear relationship between MAP and VE for a significant operating range. This proves that MAP is a valid measure of engine load, just not a completely normalized one that makes for easy comparisons between engines. However, it's safe to say that increasing manifold pressure will increase both engine load and torque output at the same engine speed as long as no other major changes are made to the engine's operation such as camshaft position, lambda, or spark angle relative to optimum.

More importantly, the best way to increase engine torque output is to increase the volumetric efficiency. The whole goal of the performance game is to increase engine torque and power. Any hardware change like a bigger camshaft, ported heads, or free-flowing exhaust that has a measurable increase in torque will show a corresponding increase in volumetric efficiency. The ECU must know the current value for VE based on RPM and MAP if it is to calculate the correct airmass and consequently fuel mass or injection time. Speed density EFI systems require recalibration of the VE table after any significant hardware change in order to preserve this level of precision and control.

MAF Based Systems

Although this book focuses very heavily on speed density systems, it wouldn't be complete without some mention of mass airflow (MAF) based systems. These systems include a sensor that directly measures the airmass entering the engine on a time basis. The MAF sensor literally counts molecules of air per unit of time and returns a signal to the ECU that is proportional to this flow. The MAF sensor output can be either analog voltage similar to most 0- to 5-volt MAP sensors or a digital square wave that varies in frequency. The ECU must have an accurately tuned table that translates this output back to physical units of airmass. This is a critical statement. Any modification to either the sensor itself or the air ducting near it has the potential to shift the output signal of the MAF sensor at the same physical airflow rate. The factory goes to great lengths to ensure that the calibration tables in the ECU match the hardware installed in the vehicle. The reference tables are generated by putting the entire induction system on a flow bench and measuring airflow versus output signal. The resulting curve is then entered into the ECU calibration data and production inlet systems are built to close tolerances to retain this accuracy.

If the MAF sensor is properly configured and the corresponding ECU table matches the physical system characteristics, then *Equation 4.11* is already solved. In fact, the MAF sensor measurement can be plugged into the same equation to work it backward to solve for airmass (g/cyl) based on current measured airflow (g/s), engine speed, and the number of cylinders:

$$\text{Airmass (g/cyl)} = \frac{\text{Airflow (g/s)} \times 120}{\text{RPM} \times (\text{\# of cylinders})}$$

This is the shortcut that OEMs like GM and Ford employ in their MAF equipped controllers. As long as the reading from the MAF sensor is consistent, a weather-corrected airmass number can be easily reached with a minimum number of steps. The engine's airflow is usually fairly consistent at cruising and WOT conditions, so the MAF-sensor-based algorithm excels here. However, some engines with larger camshafts or fewer numbers of cylinders may have large pulsations in the intake air flow that can confuse the MAF sensor's reading. In these cases, a speed density airflow estimation is usually more accurate. GM has gone so far in many of their vehicles as to include both MAF-based and speed density airflow models to be used under the conditions they're each most useful.

For more information on MAF based systems, check out my other book: *Engine Management: Advanced Tuning* (CarTech, Inc.), where I cover the sensor itself and the control logic in more detail.

CHAPTER 5

FUEL INJECTOR BEHAVIOR

Before getting too deep into making adjustments to the running air/fuel ratio of the engine, it's a good idea to take some time to understand exactly how the fuel injector works and is controlled by the ECU. In Chapter 4, we examined how the ECU determines the instantaneous airflow of the engine. The next step is to take the calculated aircharge and correctly convert this to the matching fuel charge. Fundamentally, this means calculating the pulsewidth, or time of injection for a single shot from each fuel injector. Not only must the ECU decide how long to leave the injector open, but it must also decide when to begin or end this cycle relative to the crankshaft position. Timing of the fuel charge delivery against intake valve opening time can have a noticeable effect upon engine torque, fuel economy, and smoothness.

First, let's take a look at the window of opportunity to get the fuel into the engine. It takes some amount of time to flow a fixed mass of fuel through an open injector. The actual time required depends upon the flow rate of the injector and the pressure in the fuel rail that's trying to push this fuel through the injector. We can also look at the engine's cycle and know that the intake valve opens once every other revolution for the intake stroke. The faster the engine is turning, the more often the intake valve is opening or, more appropriately, the less time there is between intake events.

The time available to get all of the necessary fuel into the cylinder along with the aircharge is equal to the cycle time for the engine. Cycle time is how long it takes for the engine to make two complete revolutions, with a single intake valve opening event per cylinder. The maximum available window of opportunity for fuel injection is therefore determined by the engine speed:

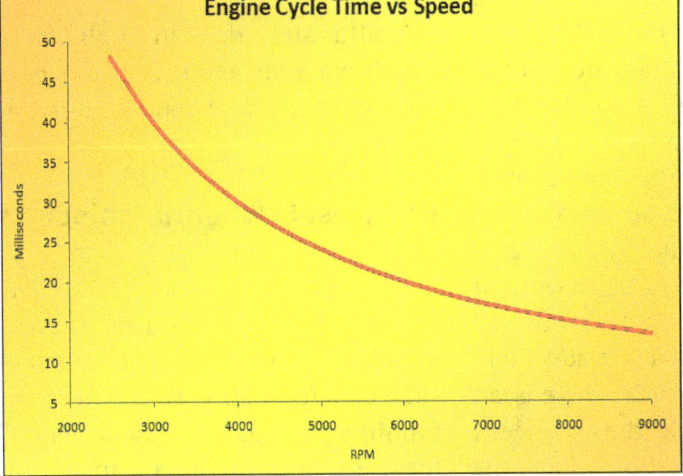

Cycle time for the engine decreases exponentially with speed, leaving less time for the injection event near redline. At idle, the cycle time is relatively large, so injector duty cycle is almost always a very small fraction.

Cycle Time (milliseconds) =
120,000 / RPM

Equation 5.1

If the available cycle time for the engine is known, then the injector "on time" can be compared against it to find out just how much of the injector and driver capacity is being used at any given time. The injector duty cycle is defined as the ratio of on

DESIGNING AND TUNING HIGH-PERFORMANCE FUEL INJECTION SYSTEMS

CHAPTER 5

time to cycle time, usually expressed as a fractional percent:

$$\text{Duty Cycle} = \frac{\text{Injector Pulsewidth}}{\text{Cycle Time}}$$

Equation 5.2a

$$\frac{\text{Duty}}{\text{Cycle}} = \frac{\text{Injector Pulsewidth (ms)} \times \text{RPM}}{120{,}000}$$

Equation 5.2b

For example, an engine operating at 3,500 rpm has a cycle time of 120,000/3,500, or 34.3 milliseconds (ms). If the ECU calculates an injector pulse of 6ms, then the duty cycle can be calculated as 6/34.3, or 17.5%.

An important note here is that there is no way for the ECU to execute pulsewidths that are greater than the cycle time. If a pulsewidth of 22 ms is commanded at 6 000 rpm (where the cycle time is only 20 ms), the result can only be an actual 20 ms pulse that is immediately connected to the following 20 ms pulse without any "off time." Since there is no way for the ECU to magically add more time to the engine cycle, there is no such thing as 101% duty cycle in actual injector operation. The ECU may request it, but the physical speed of the engine dictates that the window is only so big and the most that can be done is continuous operation without interruption.

This is bad for two reasons. First, the necessary fuel is not being completely injected on each intake stroke. The result is a leaner air/fuel ratio than the operator desires and the ECU intends to deliver, which may lead to knock or more severe engine damage under high load. Second, the electrical transistors on the board of the ECU are being driven at 100% of their capacity without any rest. This puts a lot of current

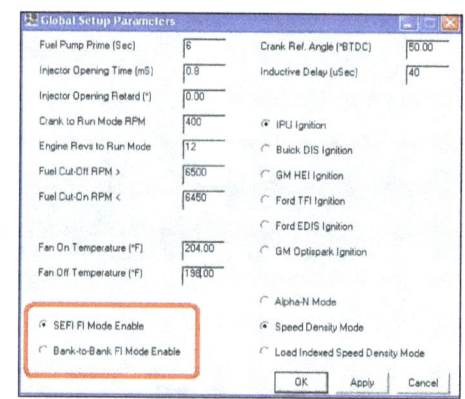

Many standalone controllers are offered in either batch or sequential injection configuration. The more advanced units like this F.A.S.T. are able to select either configuration from a menu as highlighted here.

and ultimately heat through them, which may damage the drivers over the long term and render the ECU inoperable.

Batch vs. Sequential Injection

The ECU must time the injection events to the engine's rotation somehow. There are two primary strategies for doing this. The most primitive method is called "batch" fuel injection. A more advanced system known as "sequential" injection is the industry standard today. Each

Marine engines are often equipped with central injection systems that are configured for batch injection. Boats are almost the ideal candidates for standalone EFI systems due to their simplicity in layout and wiring.

strategy has its own merits and limitations to either the ECU manufacturer or engine calibrator.

Batch fuel injection is the simplest form and easiest to implement with regard to software and ECU hardware design. With batch injection, groups of fuel injectors are all fired simultaneously for equal amounts of time. The groups usually consist of an entire engine bank of cylinders, so some manufacturers refer to this as "bank to bank" injector timing. However, the groups may be split across actual engine banks if the firing order of the injectors and cylinders are mixed. A four-cylinder engine with batch fuel injection will fire all of its injectors simultaneously while a V-8 engine will be split into two groups of four that alternate injection events. Actual injection time on a single batch or bank of injectors is typically split in two to provide one injection per engine revolution, but the total need only be calculated every cycle (two revolutions).

Batch injection simplifies the tasks to be performed inside the ECU since only one injection command must be calculated for each group of injectors on an engine cycle. The lower frequency of injection event time calculations means that a less powerful ECU can control the same engine to the same speed. On the other hand, a much higher revving engine can be controlled in batch fire since the processor load is greatly reduced. Additionally, ECU hardware costs are reduced since there are fewer required injection drivers on the board in order to control the same number of total fuel injectors.

The timing of the actual injection event on any given injector is not precisely aligned to each individual intake valve opening event.

FUEL INJECTOR BEHAVIOR

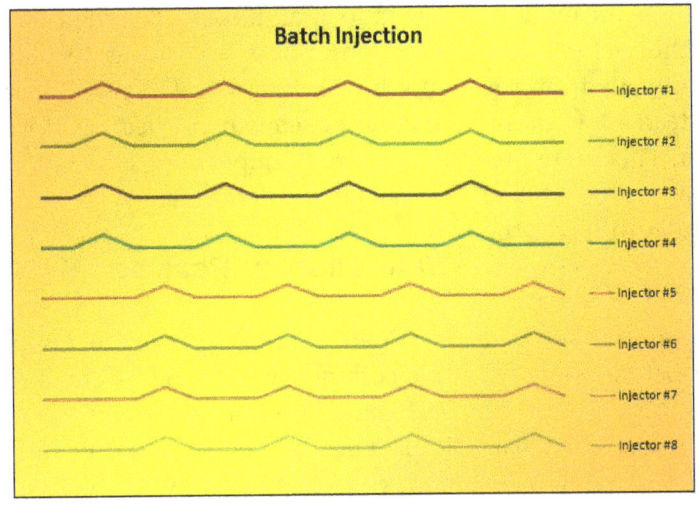

Batch fuel injection fires each injector once per crankshaft revolution as part of a group. Because the injection events are more frequent, the actual injection time is individually smaller and the timing of each event is not necessarily ideal.

As such, there is no need to have precise camshaft-to-crankshaft-location detection. Fuel injected in batch firing is simply added to the intake manifold where it is allowed to freely collect upon port walls and evaporate as airflow and temperature dictate. In most cases, fuel is being added to the intake manifold at the same rate it is being consumed by the intake valves and cylinders, so a constant flow system is established. Occasionally, some cylinders will get slightly more or less fuel than desired, but on the average, desired conditions are met by the fuel delivery.

Batch fire systems do not require that the fuel injector be installed close to the intake valve. It is common to see this strategy used in central-port-injection configurations that often look much like an electronic carburetor. If a system such as this is installed on the vehicle, batch injection is actually the preferred method of control.

The main drawback to batch injection is the lack of transient fuel control. If a rapid change in throttle angle is performed by the driver, the sudden increase of airflow will evaporate a larger part of the wall film of fuel that has been established by the system. Since the cylinder is depending on this wall film for a very large part of the total fuel mass delivery, the cylinders may exhibit a momentary lean condition. Much like a carburetor, a large accelerator pump function must be built into the software to offset this. The opposite is also true during a throttle closing event, usually leading to an excessively rich condition that may load up the engine if left unchecked. Tuning this transient fuel delivery can be tricky since the amount of correction needed changes with temperature and airflow.

Sequential fuel injection breaks down the timing of injection to a cylinder-by-cylinder chain of events. The ECU is given a specific order in which to fire the injectors, which is identical to the firing order of the engine. A single pulse is calculated for each injector that is timed to end at a specific interval before the intake valve opens. This allows for much more precise metering of the fuel being delivered to a given cylinder cycle.

The ECU must be properly equipped to handle sequential injection. Truly sequential operation requires a single driver for every injector as well as some method of detecting engine position and phase. Recognizing engine speed is typically done with a crankshaft sensor, but a camshaft sensor must also be installed to distinguish between TDC events for intake and power strokes on a given cylinder. Without this, the best the ECU can do would be a blended "staged sequential" operation that fires pairs of opposed injectors once per revolution. While mildly better than batch fire, it still lacks the precision of a true sequential setup. Sequential injection also uses more processor time to run the engine as each injection event is calculated. All things being equal, this

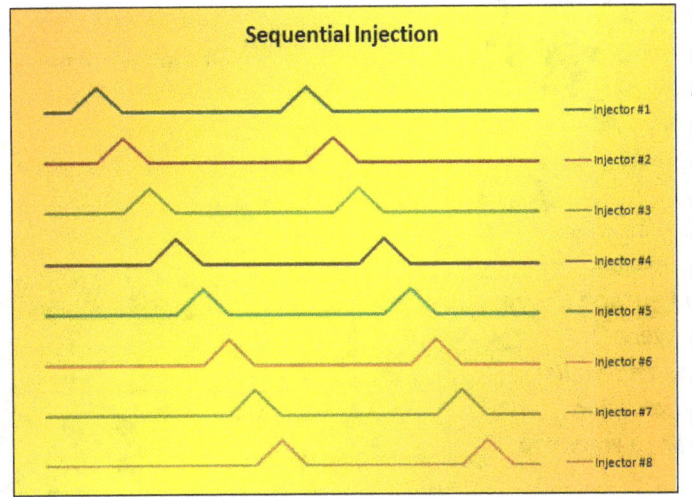

With sequential fuel injection, each injector fires only once per engine cycle (two crankshaft revolutions). The order of the injectors can be mapped to the firing order of the engine to make each injection event precede the intake valve opening on that cylinder.

DESIGNING AND TUNING HIGH-PERFORMANCE FUEL INJECTION SYSTEMS

CHAPTER 5

Dedicated race engines that operate at high RPM and airflow rates are better suited to batch injection. If the injection pulsewidths are large, the starting and ending point of each event get closer together.

requires a faster processor to operate the same engine at the same maximum RPM, which may increase the cost of the ECU. Fortunately, it's not hard to come by very affordable processors with sufficient speed for sequential fuel injection operation these days. The real trick is having the necessary software and board outputs to execute the strategy.

Sequential fuel injection requires that the injector be installed relatively close to the intake valve for best results. The small amount of

If idle stability and emissions are priorities, sequential injection timing can help. Just about every OEM system today includes sequential injection, which only helps the aftermarket performance when the modifications start.

"wet" intake port area means that a larger percent of the fuel entering the cylinder comes directly from the injection event instead of evaporation of the wall film. This more precise control of total delivered fuel mass on each intake event gives the ECU better control during transient throttle conditions.

The injection event can be timed so that it ends just before the valve opens. This reduces the chances of the fuel that was meant for that particular cycle going anywhere else. By injecting against a closed intake valve, most of the fuel is quickly evaporated and a cloud of fuel vapor is available for intake immediately as the valve opens. This promotes good mixing of the fuel charge within the cylinder and allows more of the fuel to burn closer to the desired ratio. Unevaporated fuel can lead to pockets of richness and leanness within the cylinder that burn unpredictably and poorly. The combination of properly timed injection events and smaller "wet" intake port area leads to a significantly reduced need for pump shot or acceleration enrichment. Individual cylinders can even be tuned to offset airflow differences in the intake manifold so that each cylinder operates at the desired air/

fuel ratio at all times. OEM engineers have long recognized these benefits and it's the reason why every car today uses sequential injection from the factory to improve emissions and overall engine performance.

Saturation vs. Peak and Hold

There are two types of fuel injectors commonly used today. The biggest difference between them is the impedance of their internal circuits and, consequently, how the current is applied to the coil.

Most OEM vehicles today use high impedance (12 to 16 Ω) injectors. According to Ohm's Law, the higher resistance dictates that the current will remain low. Low operating current means less heat in the wires and ECU board traces that power the injector, which is good for durability. The ECU signal that opens the injector looks like a square wave function that discretely switches on and off.

High impedance injectors are often referred to as "saturation" type injectors. The name comes from the electrical function of the driver. High-impedance injector drivers simply turn on and stay on for a predetermined amount of

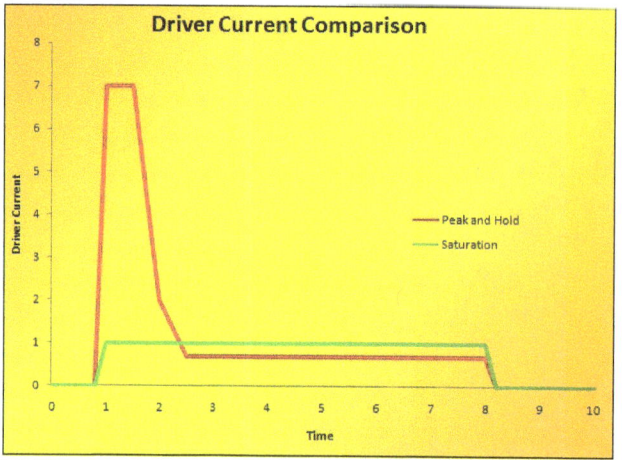

The difference in current profiles for high impedance (saturation) versus low impedance (peak and hold) is significant. If low impedance injectors are installed with a saturation driver in the ECU, the current will remain high for the entire injection pulse, which may damage the ECU.

FUEL INJECTOR BEHAVIOR

time. Once turned on, it takes a small amount of time to completely energize the coil inside the fuel injector. Naturally, this time delay between initialization of current flow and actual fuel injector pintle movement must be taken into account by the ECU. Although it is not a tremendously large amount of time, it is still significant, especially when compared to the desired flow times at idle. The fuel injector coil is driven to saturation, and held under this condition for as long as the ECU intends the fuel to be flowing.

Upon completion of the desired flow time, current through the injector driver is shut off. Because the coil is still saturated (there is some amount of inductance), the injector does not close until the field can collapse and the force holding the pintle open disappears. Again, this is a very small slice of time that must be accounted for by the ECU.

The difference between the opening delay and closing delay is known as the injector offset. The injector offset is the value that the ECU will add to whatever desired flow time is calculated for the injector on a given shot. If this time offset is not used, the actual fuel delivery would be lower than desired, resulting in a lean condition. Since the time offset is relatively small, this is most noticeable at low pulsewidths near idle where this offset represents a significant percent of the total open time. Most high impedance injectors have a combined injector offset of approximately 0.4 to 0.8 ms at normal vehicle operating voltage. If a total idle pulsewidth of 2.0 ms is calculated based on airmass and injector flow rate and the offset is 0.5 ms, we can see that 25% of the energization time of the circuit is just dedicated to getting the pintle open in the first place. This can be the difference between a lean misfire condition and an engine purring at an idle fuel mix of lambda=1.00.

The injector offset is a function of available voltage. Higher voltage means more energy available to quickly saturate the injector coil and open the pintle. The relationship between available voltage and injector offset times for a typical high impedance injector can be seen above. Although the changes to injector offset are relatively subtle at and above normal operating voltage, any time voltage drops, a significant adjustment can and should be made to injector pulsewidth to compensate for the change in offset. Something as simple as a weak battery during cold cranking that only has 9 volts available can require an entire extra millisecond of additional on time for the injector just to get the same fuel mass delivery as seen under normal conditions. Further, you don't want a failed alternator, which results in low system voltage,

Injector opening time varies with system voltage and can differ significantly compared to normal idle pulsewidths. This table is not accessible for recalibration on all ECUs, but it should at least exist in the background.

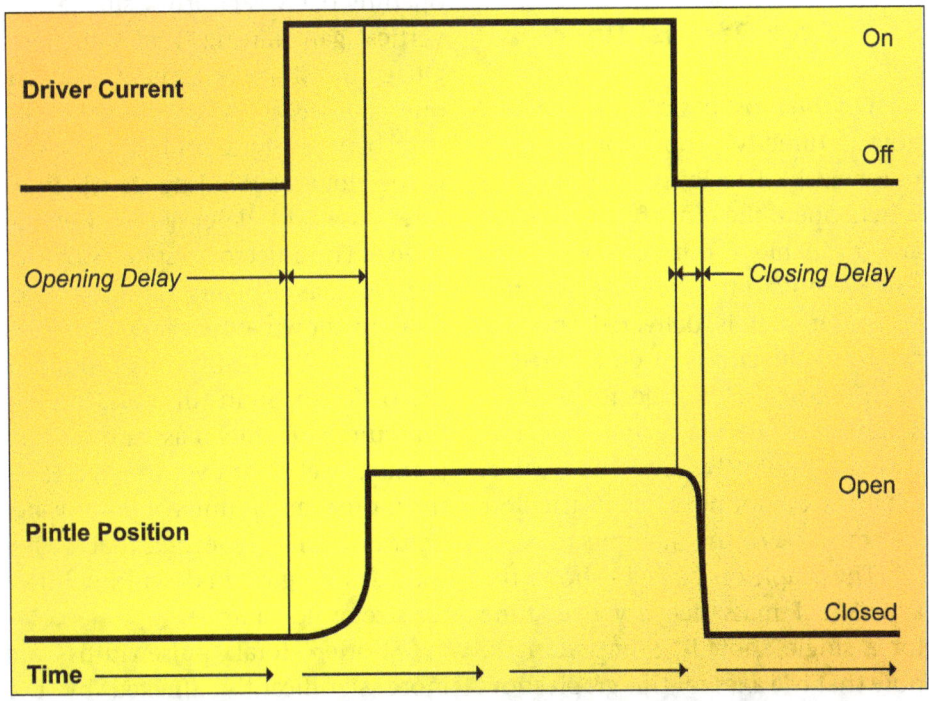

It takes a small amount of time for the electrical energy from the ECU to overcome the resistance of the injector's closing spring and fuel pressure before actually opening for fuel flow. This delay time varies with injector design and can represent a significant portion of the idle pulsewidth.

to render the engine immobile due to an excessively lean condition. If the injector offset is properly compensated for a wide range of system voltages, at least the delivered fuel mass will remain on target if other unfortunate circumstances arise.

The other common type of fuel injector is the low impedance or "peak and hold" variety. These injectors have a significantly lower internal impedance of approximately 2 to 6 ohms. As expected, the lower impedance of these injectors leads to a generally higher operating current, so the proper changes must be made to the ECU injector driver hardware prior to using these.

The name "peak and hold" comes from the function of the injector driver used to control these low impedance units. The low resistance coils are easily excited to full field potential and do not require as much energy to maintain this field throughout the remainder of the injection pulse. Once the field has been established and the injector is open, current through the coil is reduced to a nominal amount and held there until the end of the injection event. Closing times are also much shorter since there is less inductive energy to dissipate after the driver is shut off. Typical injector offset time for a low impedance unit is approximately 0.2 to 0.4 ms.

The primary advantage of the low impedance fuel injector is the significantly shorter injector offset times that are possible. Shorter and more consistent injector offsets mean that the ECU can reliably control much shorter pulsewidths. This becomes extremely helpful when the static flow rate of a fuel injector is relatively high. The higher the static flow rate, the shorter the pulsewidth needed to supply the same amount of fuel. If the flow rate is too high, it may become impossible to deliver a short enough pulse to deliver the small fuel amounts required at idle. Low impedance fuel injectors alleviate this problem by giving the ECU more control in this range.

Most OEM applications can be satisfied with fuel injectors whose flow rate is low enough to allow the use of high impedance injectors and still maintain sufficient idle control. As such, there is no reason to justify the added expense of the peak-and-hold drivers. Luckily, most aftermarket ECUs are built knowing that there is a good chance the user will attempt to make more power than the typical OEM application. Stand-alone ECUs are typically equipped with peak and hold injector drivers that can handle almost any port fuel injector out there.

Flow Rate vs. Time

On the most basic level, total fuel flow is directly proportional to the pulsewidth. The longer the injector is held open, the more fuel is injected and available for intake when the valve opens to the cylinder. The rate at which fuel is delivered through the open injector is often referred to as the "size" of the injector, such as 42 lb/hr. Since many fuel injectors are mechanically interchangeable, what is really of note here is the flow rate or slope of the fuel injector.

The graph on page 43 shows the actual fuel mass delivery over time for a single shot. It is important to note that the axes for this graph show fuel mass and time. Earlier, I noted that the ECU works in terms of airmass and fuel mass. The relationship shown in this chart is what the ECU

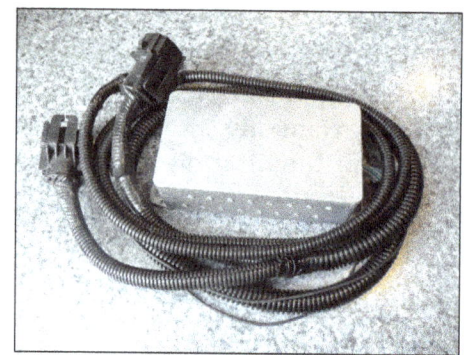

Most factory ECUs are equipped with saturation drivers that can only operate high impedance injectors. Using an external driver box like this one allows the ECU to still see the proper load while operating the low impedance injectors from its own power supply based on the signal from the original controller.

uses to convert from the calculated fuel mass desired to go with the airmass into an injection time that will be passed to the driver circuits. The opening delay is clearly visible as the vertical gap starting from time zero. Once the pintle is actually opened, one can see a straight-line relationship between time and fuel mass. It is the slope of this line that is most often used to describe an injector "size." The injector's upper slope of the fuel mass delivery is more appropriately known as the static flow rate. The algebraic definition of slope is rise over run. So in this case, the rise is accumulated fuel mass and the run is time. Fuel mass over time gives us the more familiar units of pounds per hour or grams per second that we are used to seeing when describing injector size or flow rate.

Shorter total pulsewidths are more significantly affected by the nonlinear flow rate that comes with a pintle that is only partially open for a significant amount of the total injection time. During the split second of injector opening, pressure differential across the tip of the injector is at its highest. Once flow is established, the local pressure immediately behind the pintle relaxes slightly and the flow rate settles into the previously discussed static flow rate. The slope during this short window of high injector flow is known as the dynamic flow rate and can be approximately 10 to 15% higher than the static flow rate.

In a way, fuel injectors behave just like the average garden hose. Water is turned on at the faucet with a nozzle attached to the end of the hose. The hose itself behaves like the fuel rail in an engine, retaining some pressurized reserved supply that can be delivered by opening a valve at the end. Opening the nozzle on the hose is similar to the ECU triggering the fuel injector. Immediately upon opening, the water stream shoots the longest stream possible and quickly recedes to a lower, but still very sizable, flow. The distance at which the water lands from the user holding the nozzle is proportional to the available water pressure. Since the flow area of the nozzle is constant when completely open, it is safe to say that this increase in water pressure has delivered an increase in water flow rate. Flow rate is then represented by the landing distance of the water stream. The longer initial distance is proof that the flow rate was temporarily greatest immediately after opening the nozzle. The same happens each time an injector is fired. A slightly higher flow rate is realized for a very short duration before static flow is established.

The best control systems will have more elaborate injector flow modeling capabilities that can accurately represent this phenomenon. This can be done by either shifting the desired pulsewidth of the injector based on some reference table or by providing

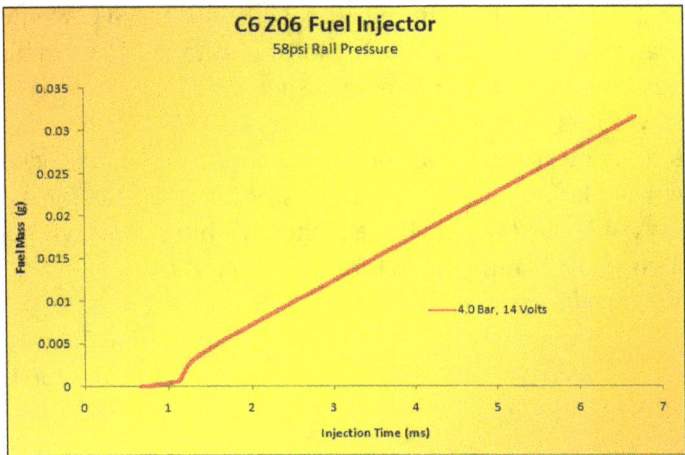

The actual fuel delivered over time for one particular injector. This unit stabilizes to a slope of 5.26 grams per second or about 41.7 lbs/hr.

Ohm's Law and Fuel Injectors

$$V = I \times R$$

Ohm's Law states that voltage in a circuit is the product of current (measured in amps) and resistance (measured in ohms). If the voltage available in a circuit remains constant, then current must increase as impedance decreases to satisfy the equation. In the case of fuel injectors, the ECU operates with roughly 12v available. If we have a fuel injector with an impedance of 14 ohms, the current is then found by:

$$I = V / R$$

Or: $I = 12v / 14\Omega = 0.857$ amps, which is a fairly low current that is easily handled by most injector drivers.

If a 2Ω low impedance injector is exchanged into the same 12v circuit, we find that the current increases significantly: $I = 12 v / 2\Omega = 6.0$ amps, an increase of 600% over the previous level. Since current flow is the primary contributor to heat and ultimately failure of these circuits, it becomes apparent that low-impedance-injector drivers built to handle these conditions are required. Running low impedance injectors on a standard (high impedance) driver will almost always lead to thermal failures, a damaged ECU, and a stranded vehicle. Always check to ensure what kind of injector drivers are included with the ECU before attempting to run the engine. If the ECU is not equipped to run low impedance injectors, an outboard injector driver box may be employed to avoid damage to the internal drivers of the ECU.

two different injector slopes for static and dynamic flow rates. If neither compensation strategy exists in the ECU, any fuel delivery errors in the low flow range will simply be "baked in" to future airflow calculations in order to maintain a stable air/fuel ratio near idle and light load conditions. In a speed density system, this would show up as slightly increased values for volumetric efficiency in the low load region, even though the actual flow may be lower.

Choosing an Injector

The static flow rate of a fuel injector can be used to estimate the maximum power that can be supported. It is also possible to decide what size injector is necessary based on how much power is expected. Both calculations are tied to air/fuel ratio and engine efficiency. The common measure of this is brake specific fuel consumption (BFSC), expressed in terms of grams per kilowatt hour or pounds per horsepower hour. Since most fuel injectors are listed in units of lb/hr, it makes sense here to depart from the metric system for an example.

Most naturally aspirated engines consume fuel at WOT with a brake specific fuel consumption somewhere between 0.3 and 0.5 lb/hp-hr. Supercharged engines, which run richer under high load, will be slightly higher at 0.55 to 0.7 lb/hp-hr. Using this basic efficiency unit, one can simply multiply the target maximum horsepower by anticipated BSFC to show total engine fuel delivery needs:

$$M_{ff} \text{ Total} = BSFC \times Power$$
Equation 5.3

For example, a 500 hp supercharged engine operating at an anticipated 0.6 lb/hp-hr BSFC would need 300 lb/hr of total fuel flow. This represents the fuel being delivered to all cylinders combined, so it can be split across any number of available injectors. With one injector per cylinder, the minimum individual injector flow is found by:

$$\text{Min Injector Flow} = \frac{(M_{ff} \text{ Total})}{(\text{\# of injectors})}$$
Equation 5.4

In this example, a 500 hp V-8 engine using 300 lb/hr of total fuel flow would need an absolute minimum of 37.5 lb/hr static flow rate from each individual injector. Some may stop here and go out to purchase injectors for their 500 hp engine. This would be a mistake because the injector drivers in the ECU should not be run at full capacity on a continuous basis. Doing so will often overheat the transistors that drive the fuel injector from the continuously high current flow. To avoid this, some safety margin should be used to give the injector drivers a rest between shots. A 20% safety margin will usually be sufficient to prevent the overheating of the injector drivers. The safety margin is applied to the minimum injector flow rate. See *Equation 5.5* below.

To continue our 500 hp V-8 example, the introduction of the 20% safety margin yields a corrected injector flow requirement of 46.9 lb/hr. This would mean that even at the engine's maximum power output and fuel enrichment, there is still room left over for some extra flow. Combining *Equations 5.3, 5.4, and 5.5* gives a single comprehensive equation for estimating injector size based on anticipated power and fuel consumption rates. See *Equation 5.6* below.

The added safety margin comes in handy when the car may be occasionally run in cold weather where air density is higher, power is increased, and total fuel requirements are slightly higher than the original calculation assumptions. Otherwise, a car that is equipped with injectors that are barely adequate may run lean in cold weather, possibly leading to engine damage. A little extra safety margin here can save thousands of dollars and countless hours of later aggravation.

Fuel Pressure

By now, it should be fairly obvious that increasing fuel pressure will increase the flow rate of any injector. Even better, it has been established that this relationship between pressure and flow is predictable. Because fuel injectors are effectively a fixed orifice for fuel flow when open, they follow the Bernoulli equation for pressure and flow rate:

$$\text{Corrected Injector Flow} = \frac{(\text{Min Injector Flow})}{(100\% - \text{Safety Margin \%})}$$
Equation 5.5

$$\text{Corrected Injector Flow} = \frac{(BSFC) \times (Power)}{(\text{\# of injectors}) \times (100\% - \text{Safety Margin \%})}$$
Equation 5.6

FUEL INJECTOR BEHAVIOR

This Nissan GTR requires significantly more fuel injector flow capacity to match the increased airflow capacity from the twin turbos. Turbocharged engines typically operate at richer air/fuel ratios than their naturally aspirated counterparts, which further drives the need for large fuel injectors.

$$Q_f = Q_n \times \sqrt{P_2 / P_1}$$

Equation 5.7

Here flow is represented by the engineering shorthand "Q," where Q_f is the final flow rate and Q_n is a nominal or reference flow rate. Reference pressure is P_1 and final pressure is P_2. This equation can be used to compensate for changes in fuel pressure setting that are different from the rated flow pressure of a known fuel injector. Many fuel injectors are listed with static flow rates as tested with 3 bar (43.5 psi, 300 kPa) reference pressure. If this injector is used in an application where the static fuel pressure is different, it is imperative that the flow rate values entered into the ECU are adjusted. Failure to do so will result in skewed injection time calculations and often lead to improper adjustments to the airflow models and VE tables during the calibration procedure.

An example of the practical use of the Bernoulli equation would be the installation of a set of Bosch "green top" fuel injectors in a late model GM fuel system. The Bosch specification for these injectors is 42 lb/hr of static flow at 3 bar (43.5 psi). The GM fuel system is internally regulated to a pressure of 4 bar (58 psi), so one can naturally expect some increase in the flow rate. The new static flow rate is found by using *Equation 5.7*:

$$Q_f = 42 \text{ lb/hr} \times \sqrt{(4 \text{ Bar} / 3 \text{ Bar})}$$
$$= 42 \text{ lb/hr} \times \sqrt{(1.333)}$$
$$= 42 \text{ lb/hr} \times 1.155$$
$$= 48.5 \text{ lb/hr}$$

In order to give the ECU the best control of actual fuel delivery at this elevated fuel pressure, it's a good idea to use the new value for injector flow rate of 48.5 lb/hr instead of 42 lb/hr. There is a 15% shift between the two, which can be the difference between starting out right on the target of 14.6:1 air/fuel ratio and 12.64:1 when first targeting lambda=1.00 at cruise. It is imperative that the fuel injector flow rates are correct, since they will be used as one of the key assumptions when calculating airflow corrections. The more accurately the injector flow is represented in the ECU, the more precise the calibrator can be later on when making changes to the VE table or other airflow calibrations.

The relationship between fuel pressure and flow can be used to the engine builder's advantage. If a set of fuel injectors is just slightly undersized to support the desired engine power level and flow requirements, a calculated increase in rail pressure can be used to effectively increase the injector flow rate.

Our theoretical 500 hp V-8 engine requires a static injector flow of approximately 46.9 lb/hr. If the vehicle is equipped with a set of "green top" 42 lb/hr injectors, we can see that the engine runs the risk of running lean or overheating the injector drivers in the ECU. The fuel rail pressure can be adjusted upward to recover the safety margin. Using the above example, the 42 lb/hr fuel injectors effectively become 48.5 lb/hr injectors when the pressure is raised from 3 bar up to 4 bar. This 15% increase in flow capacity translates directly into an additional 15% more horsepower that can be supported at the same air/fuel ratio. More importantly, the increase in fuel rail pressure has brought the static flow rate above the corrected injector flow that correlates to our desired 20% safety margin even at the 500 hp level. This engine should have no trouble delivering the required fuel mass even under the most extreme conditions.

The fuel-pressure-correction math works both ways though. The pressure used in this equation is not absolute or even gauge pressure. It is really pressure drop across the injector itself. The measurement is usually taken with atmospheric pressure acting on the regulator's diaphragm. This usually means either disconnecting the vacuum line from the intake manifold briefly or taking the measurement when the fuel pump is running and the engine is not. Most mechanical fuel pressure regulators will automatically hold a constant pressure differential between the reference side and the rail pressure itself. If the reference side is connected to the intake manifold by a vacuum line, the reference pressure will decrease when the engine is throttled at idle or cruising conditions. This lower reference pressure results in a similar decrease in rail pressure, keeping the pressure drop, or "delta," across the injectors constant even as MAP changes. This is what ensures that the static flow rate of the fuel injector remains at the same value that the ECU is using for its own injection time calculations.

Even better, these mechanical regulators will almost always work when positive manifold pressure is applied. Each pound of manifold boost from a supercharger or turbocharger should be met with one pound of rail pressure increase to maintain a constant injector flow rate. As long as the fuel pump has the capacity to maintain this increased pressure at the necessary flow rate, everything works just fine. However, if for some reason rail pressure does not increase 1:1 with manifold boost, the flow rate of the injector is decreased. This drop in rail pressure delta may be a symptom of inadequate fuel pump supply or undersized feed lines and rails. Unfortunately, this is usually under high load and flow rate conditions, just when it is needed most.

This adjustable fuel pressure regulator makes it easy to effectively change the flow rate of the fuel injectors. The vacuum line is connected to the intake manifold, allowing the regulator to maintain a constant pressure drop across the injectors even as intake pressure changes with throttle movement.

Continuing to use our theoretical 500 hp supercharged V-8 engine, let's take a look at what happens if we make 10 psi of boost, but only see 40 psi on a fuel pressure gauge. Earlier, we intentionally moved the target rail pressure up to 58 psi delta. This delta is the difference between manifold and rail pressures. The addition of 10 psi of manifold boost means that we should really see 58 psi plus 10 psi, or 68 psi total guage pressure at the rail if we are to maintain the target flow rate. Since we effectively have a drop in available pressure across the injector, we can calculate exactly how much the flow rate has reduced as a result using *Equation 5.7*. In this case P_2 (40 psi from the gauge) is actually lower than P_1 (58 psi target), which will work out to give us a lower flow rate:

$$Q_f = 48.5 \text{ lb/hr} \times \sqrt{(40 \text{psi} / 58 \text{psi})}$$
$$= 48.5 \text{ lb/hr} \times \sqrt{(0.690)}$$
$$= 48.5 \text{ lb/hr} \times 0.830$$
$$= 40.3 \text{ lb/hr}$$

It becomes clear here that the reduced injector flow rate that results from the lower fuel pressure delta is lower than the original 42 lb/hr that did not have sufficient safety margin. In fact, it's only slightly higher than the 37.5 lb/hr absolute minimum requirement at 100% output. Although this particular engine probably won't drift lean under load, it still doesn't have very much reserve for cold weather, high barometric conditions or other unforeseen load increases.

The solution here should be to investigate the cause of the dropping fuel pressure. This may be as simple as a clogged fuel filter that hasn't been changed in a while. It may also

In a supercharged application, it's important to consider intake manifold pressure as well as fuel rail pressure when determining injector flow rates. This Ford Mustang's factory ECU is equipped with a sensor that measures the delta pressure across the injectors directly by sampling both fuel and intake pressure across the same diaphragm.

be a sign that the fuel pump just can't keep up with the flow requirements of the engine and injectors. A higher flow aftermarket pump will usually fix this at a modest cost penalty. Keep in mind that a fuel pump's maximum flow capacity varies with total pressure. A fuel pump's energy can be used to generate high pressure or high flow rates, but usually not both. It must trade one for the other at maximum output, so it pays to verify that the pump can support the necessary flow rate at the pressure needed to maintain the desired injector delta pressure.

If the pump being used is advertised as being capable of supporting the flow rates in question, it may be time to look a little deeper at the vehicle hardware. On an otherwise stock vehicle, we may find that the relatively small diameter feed line between the pump and engine may be causing the restriction. Even though the fuel rail may be operating at 60 psi, there may be additional pressure drops between

FUEL INJECTOR BEHAVIOR

the rail and pump from the line and filter restrictions. Upgrade as necessary before attempting to fix any of this with ECU calibration adjustments.

Multiple Injector Arrays

Some aftermarket ECUs have the ability to control more injectors than the engine has cylinders. The simplest way to accomplish this is by simultaneously firing two equally sized injectors. The fuel mass is split evenly between both injectors on the same cylinder. This effectively doubles the power capacity of the fuel supply as long as the pump can keep up. The only drawback to this is that it also doubles the minimum amount of fuel that can be injected. This may make it difficult to control the small fuel mass requirements at idle and light loads.

If the ECU is able to discretely control two injectors per cylinder and time them independently, they can be configured so that only one injector fires per cylinder at low loads. At higher loads, where the single injector would be quickly running out of capacity to support the necessary fuel flow, a second injector on the same cylinder is triggered to share the fuel delivery. This is known as staged injection. The onset of the second injector contribution can be triggered by injector duty cycle, total instantaneous flow rate, or manifold pressure.

A clear advantage to staged injection is that the primary fuel injectors do not need to be tremendously sized in order to support a large amount of total engine power. The smaller primary injectors will then have correspondingly larger pulse-

The fuel filter is often one of the more neglected parts on a vehicle's maintenance schedule. A clogged or damaged fuel filter can reduce delivered fuel rail pressure at high load, leading to a lean condition that may damage the engine.

widths at idle and low rates. This longer pulsewidth makes it easier for the ECU to make very fine adjustments to total fuel mass deliveries. It also means that the injector offset represents a much smaller percent of the total on time during idle pulses. Again, this reduces the variability of air/fuel ratio control just when it is most critical. The end result is an engine system with tight control of delivered lambda and ultimately cleaner burning, better emissions, rapid throttle response, and superior fuel economy.

The only real downsides to staged injection are cost and complexity. Staged injection almost always required some rather exotic modifications to the intake manifold to provide the additional injector locations as well as fuel rails and lines to feed them. The ECU must also be manufactured with the additional output drivers and be programmed with the necessary code to divide the fuel mass delivery across two different injector groups. There are only a handful of OEM applications that allow for multiple injectors per cylinder for just these reasons.

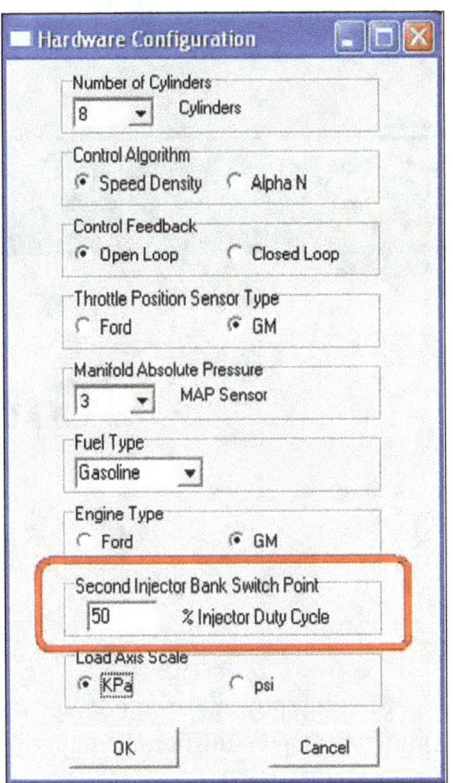

The BigStuff3 system allows the user to determine the turn-on point for the second set of fuel injectors. Here it is set so that once the first set of eight injectors reaches 50% duty cycle, the fuel mass will get split evenly across all 16 injectors to increase capacity at high loads.

Staged fuel injectors allow for better control where a single injector per cylinder is used for most light duty operation. This engine has a second fuel rail that feeds another pair of fuel injectors per cylinder for a total of three injectors per cylinder. That's a lot of fuel to go along with those two huge turbos.

CHAPTER 6

IGNITION ANGLE AND CYLINDER PRESSURE

Making power, or more appropriately torque, ultimately depends upon cylinder pressure. It is the pressure generated by the combustion process that pushes down on the top of the piston and ultimately turns the crankshaft. The more pressure available to push the piston down the bore, the more turning force is applied to the crankshaft. Torque times speed equals power, so making more power still means making more cylinder pressure. Any way you look at it, cylinder pressure is the key to making both torque and power.

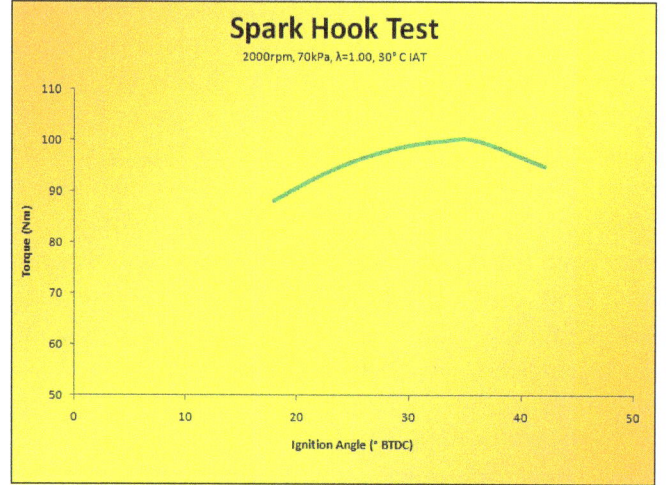

The results of a spark sweep test are plotted against ignition angle to display the hook curve for a single operation point of the engine. Note the relatively gentle slope of the plateau in torque output near MBT and the measurable loss of torque from excessive advance.

Timing the pressure to the engine's rotation angle can have a very pronounced effect upon net torque output as well. The cylinder pressure increases and decreases in a repeating cycle with each rotation of the engine. There exists a point of peak pressure in each combustion cycle where the available energy is at its maximum. Both before and after this maximum, there is still a significant amount of energy contained in the cylinder and the air/fuel mixture. Getting the most useful work out of this energy release is a matter of harnessing the expansion pressure during the power stroke of the engine. The more pressure available throughout the entire power stroke after TDC, the more energy can be transferred to rotational work by the crankshaft. Energy released to the piston by the burning air/fuel mixture during the compression stroke before TDC is actually negative work that is subtracted from the net total crankshaft work on the cycle. While it's impossible to avoid this negative work during compression, a balance between negative compression work and positive expansion work can be found, applying the maximum amount of net work to the crankshaft as a result of combustion on any cycle. The timing of the combustion and rotation cycles is what determines how efficiently the pressure is converted to rotational work. Think of ignition timing as controlling the mechanical efficiency of the combustion cycle. Applying the pressure at the right time in the cycle

IGNITION ANGLE AND CYLINDER PRESSURE

makes the most out of the combustion that's already happening.

The timing of the engine cycle is fixed based on engine speed, but the timing of the combustion cycle can be controlled and predicted. The ignition event controls the start of the combustion cycle. Shifting the phase of the combustion cycle is as simple as timing the spark event to a certain crank rotation angle. This phase shift of the combustion cycle often includes compensation for anticipated rates of pressure rise within the cylinder. This pressure rise is dependent upon the effective compression ratio, engine speed, and burn rate of the mixture. Timing of the ignition can and should be adjusted to compensate for changes in any of these contributing factors. Making more torque from the engine can be simplified down to just making more torque at the most useful point in the cycle.

Driving down the road, the engine does not need to make maximum torque to maintain a legal speed. In this case, total load (which is really cylinder filling, remember?) is controlled by throttle angle. Opening and closing the throttle blade will change the amount of air available to enter the cylinders. The reduced airflow at part load and corresponding fuel delivery sets the potential maximum energy available for the cycle. It is up to the ignition control to start the chain reaction of combustion at the right moment so that as much of this potential energy is transferred to the crankshaft as useful work. If everything is working correctly at cruise, the throttle angle has controlled airflow to just the right amount to deliver the necessary power to maintain speed while ignition timing is selected to most efficiently burn the air/fuel mixture.

Performing the spark hook test requires a dynamometer with some form of load control and torque measurement. This Mustang dynamometer uses an eddy current retarder to provide resistance to the rolls. The reaction force is measured by a load cell at a fixed distance on the arm, giving a direct measurement of instantaneous torque.

Spark Hook Test

So, with all the variables that can affect necessary ignition lead, how does one find the ideal point? In almost all cases, the answer is to pick the point with the most mechanical efficiency. Peak mechanical efficiency can be found by testing for actual torque output across a series of ignition angles at the same airflow and engine speed.

Finding this point is a matter of controlling the variables during testing. Since the majority of an engine's life is and should be spent at a stoichiometric air/fuel mixture, that's the best place to start. Additionally, most of the engine's operation occurs in a fairly narrow coolant temperature range around 82 to 100 degrees C (180 to 212 degrees F) when the thermostat and radiator are working as intended. Air temperatures can vary widely with conditions, but it's safe to assume that a "normal" inlet temperature of about 27 to 32 degrees C (80 to 100 degrees F) for most cases. Certainly, there are times when these conditions aren't present, but to get started, let's look at only the relationship between spark angle and torque.

With nominal conditions set for the engine, a test can be run where we sweep ignition angle at a single engine speed and load. The first measurement is taken with a fairly low spark advance value and the torque is read from a load-bearing dynamometer in real time and recorded. This process can be done on either an engine or chassis dynamometer. All that is important is that conditions are held constant and accurate, so repeatable measurements can be made. Without changing operating temperatures, lambda, or airflow, spark is advanced by a few degrees and a new torque measurement is taken. This second torque value is higher than the original because more of the combustion is taking place at a time in the cycle when the pressure is able to do more useful work to the crankshaft. The new torque value is recorded and the spark angle is again advanced by a few more degrees.

This process is repeated across a wide range of ignition angles for the same engine speed, load, temperatures, and lambda. At some point, the torque measurements will no longer increase with ignition angle. Going further, delivered torque will actually decrease as spark angle is added. This is a sure indicator that the crankshaft is having to work harder during the compression stroke to fight the early combustion before TDC. Continuing to advance timing from this point will further decrease measured torque output. If timing is advanced far enough, audible knock will appear and delivered torque will drop off sharply.

Taking the data from this string of measurements, one can plot the torque against spark angle. The resulting plot shows a hook-shaped characteristic with a maximum torque value at some point. This is where the term "spark hook test" is coined as we see the complete timing response curve at a single speed-load point for the engine. The point at which torque is maximized is MBT, representing the peak mechanical efficiency point for ignition timing at this particular combination of engine speed, load, lambda, and temperatures. The process can be repeated for every speed-load point in the ignition map to determine best efficiency across a wide range of operating points.

Increasing engine speed will generally increase the amount of spark advance necessary to reach MBT. As the speed increases, there is less and less time available for each cycle. Just like the time available for fuel injection is decreased with speed, so is the time for combustion. If the burn rate of the fuel remains relatively constant, then the process must be started earlier just to get to peak pressure at the right time in the cycle. Much like hitting a fastball, a faster moving target requires an earlier swing to make contact at the desired point. Don't be surprised when spark hook testing reveals that high engine speeds have very high spark values for MBT. Values of 40 to 50 degrees of spark advance for MBT are not uncommon at high speed and light loading on some engines.

Even motorcycles can benefit from the addition of electronic controls. This supercharged Harley Davidson features a control system that has unique VE and spark maps for each cylinder to accommodate the uneven pumping efficiencies between them.

As engine load is increased, it will take even less ignition lead to reach MBT. Increasing engine load means that more air and fuel are present within the cylinder. Once lit, this mixture will have a more rapid release of energy and the rate of pressure rise within the cylinder will be increased. To offset this, the process is simply started later so that too much of the energy is not released during the compression stroke, but rather during the expansion stroke where it is useful. The combination of low engine speed and high load may yield MBT values of very low advance angles. Many modern engines have negative spark advance values (actual degrees ATDC) for high load below 1,500 rpm. It just so happens that the combination can work out to be a negative number.

OEM engineers perform the spark hook test for every single combination of speed and load in the base spark advance map. Admittedly a very time-consuming process, but necessary if one wants to squeeze every bit of fuel efficiency and throttle response out of an engine. In

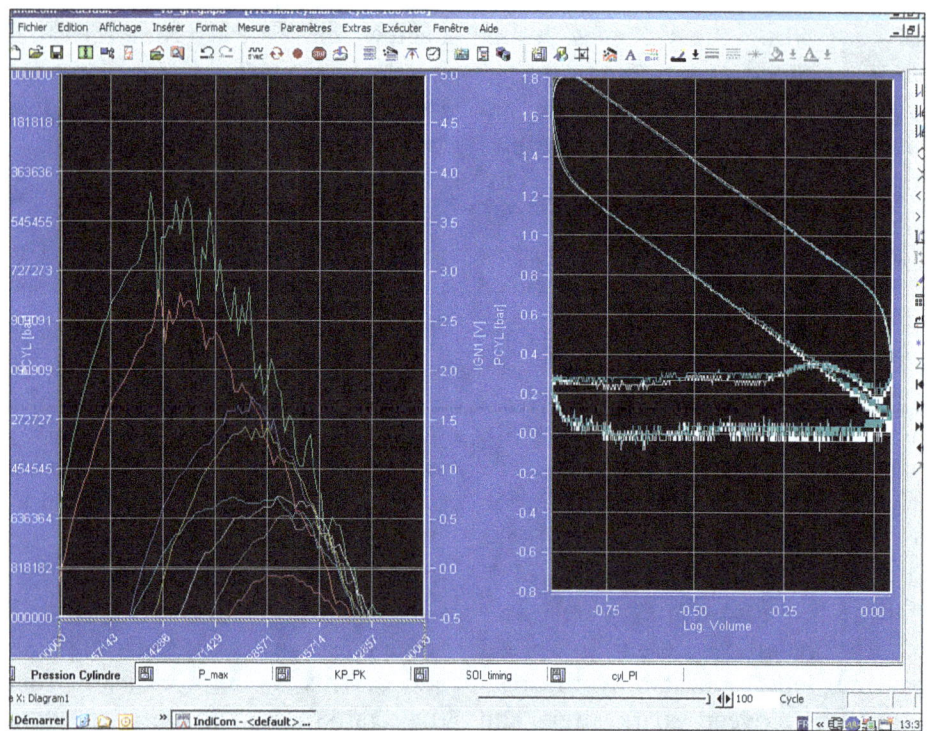

A closer look at the actual pressure trace during knock shows the telltale jagged peaks as opposing flame fronts collide within the cylinder. This recording was made with very sensitive pressure transducers, but the noise becomes plainly audible if the knock intensity is high enough.

IGNITION ANGLE AND CYLINDER PRESSURE

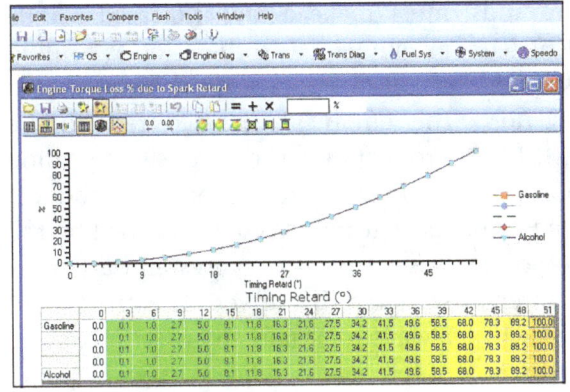

A torque reduction estimation from a factory calibration is seen here using HPTuners software. This table allows the ECU to correlate degrees of spark retard from MBT to a percent reduction in instantaneous engine torque output that can be used for traction control or transmission requests to smooth shifting.

today's competitive car market, manufacturers just can't afford to ignore this crucial step in the development process. While some racers may not justify the time spent to perform this test at every point, it can be very worthwhile to find MBT at the points where the engine will spend any significant amount of time while driving. Remember that improving mechanical efficiency also goes a long way toward getting the most energy out of every drop of fuel, so mileage is also impacted.

Knock

If the pressure generated by combustion is exerted upon the crankshaft at the wrong time, the downward force on the piston may not be efficiently converted into turning effort on the crankshaft. In a worst case scenario, the downward force applied may happen at a time when the crankshaft is trying to drive the piston upward. The result is two opposing forces that are each working to compress the air/fuel mixture, piston, wrist pin, connecting rod, and bearings. If this compressive force exceeds the capacity of any system component, the resulting damage usually makes for some interesting conversation pieces.

The knock that can be heard is more intense than most engines will usually tolerate for any extended period of time. If the "marbles in a can" noise is present during testing, it's time to quickly retard timing, reduce load, or both before a mechanical component failure results. This is especially true during WOT testing where working pressures are at their highest and the potential for mechanical failure is greater.

During spark hook testing at light loads, knock is usually found at spark advance values well beyond MBT timing. At these points, torque has already begun to drop off from excessive compression work before abnormal combustion begins. At higher loads, knock can happen much earlier, though. Near the engine's torque peak, combustion is very rapid. Over-advancing the timing here can quickly lead to knock, often before MBT is reached. This is particularly true in forced induction applications where raw cylinder pressures and temperatures are significantly higher than their naturally aspirated counterparts.

Even though the objective is to get the most mechanical efficiency out of the combustion process, the presence of knock trumps the hunt for efficiency. If knock is encountered prior to reaching the MBT point during a spark hook test, the knock threshold effectively becomes MBT since that is the highest allowed torque value for that particular speed and load combination.

If knock is found prior to reaching what would otherwise be MBT, it stands to reason that engine performance could be improved by moving the knock threshold. The easiest way to do this is to increase the fuel octane. The increased octane of the fuel moves the point at which it will begin exhibiting abnormal combustion upward. If the knock threshold is moved further up the hook curve, more torque can be safely extracted from the same engine hardware as we move toward MBT timing. If the engine is already able to operate

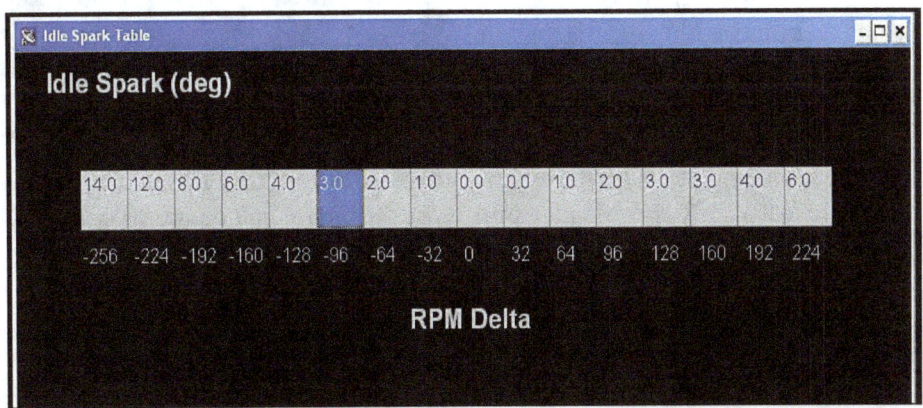

Good standalone control systems will include a table to adjust spark advance based on idle speed. This BigStuff3 table displays a raw spark advance adder based on the error between current and target idle speeds.

at MBT at full load, increasing the fuel octane will not do anything to aid torque output even if timing is increased. In some cases adding high octane fuel actually loses torque, especially if timing is not advanced to offset the slightly slower burn rate of some racing fuels. In short, choose the fuel octane first and tune the engine to run the lower of either MBT or the knock limit for best torque output.

Torque Control

During the spark hook test, it was revealed that the engine's output torque depends heavily upon spark angle. This relationship can be exploited by engine controllers to manage instantaneous output. It is sometimes helpful to be able to momentarily reduce engine torque during launch, transmission shifts, or other events. Since spark advance is calculated and delivered by the ECU on an exceptionally fast recurrence rate, changes to output torque can be executed in very short order. Most ECUs with torque reduction strategies can implement changes on a cylinder-by-cylinder basis as quickly as the next TDC event. As such, it is often labeled the "fast path" to torque control. The "slow path" is load control, which requires changes to throttle angle of IAC position that take significantly longer to make a difference in the cylinder.

The spark hook tests for the engine usually reveal a fairly close relationship between torque reduction and degrees of spark retard. The relationship is more closely tied to percent torque reduction than absolute foot-pounds of change. Although not linear, it is predictable and fairly consistent across a wide range of speeds and loads. If the ECU knows the general relationship between degrees of spark retard and percent torque reduction, a calculated reduction can be applied at any time.

There is a special case of normal engine operation where MBT is not desirable. At idle, it is helpful to maintain a torque reserve to ensure that the engine can quickly respond to changes in resistance. By intentionally operating the engine with less than MBT timing, the ECU knows that it could increase the engine's torque almost instantaneously by adjusting back toward MBT. The ECU can also instantaneously retard timing to reduce engine torque in cases where less is needed for a brief period. The gap between delivered ignition timing and actual MBT at idle represents the torque reserve that is held for unforeseen changes in engine loading later on.

Idle control is fundamentally torque control at a delicate balance of zero net flywheel torque. All frictional, pumping, accessory, and transmission forces are effectively negative torques applied to the crankshaft. At idle, the engine

The individual coil packs on each spark plug of this Chrysler V-6 engine can be seen between the intake runners. Since each coil has two engine revolutions to recharge, more energy can be delivered on each strike to the plug, improving lightoff characteristics during the early part of combustion.

must make a raw indicated torque exactly equal to these losses to hold a constant speed. If the losses exceed the engine's indicated raw torque production, speed drops and stalling is possible. If the engine produces more torque than is absorbed by the losses, speed increases and a flare is seen by the driver. The trick is to always maintain the precise balance of losses and indicated raw torque so that the resulting rotational speed remains stable. The torque reserve at idle allows the ECU to quickly adjust raw engine torque to offset any change in idle loading such as a gear shift from park to reverse, turning on the air conditioning compressor, or turning on the power steering and loading its pump.

Changing from neutral or park into gear has a significant impact upon engine loading. During the initial gear change, the momentary increase in torque is handled by the fast path torque reserve from ignition angle. However, it's still possible that the driver may further load the engine by later turning on the air conditioning, turning the power steering near lock in a parking lot, or adding electrical alternator loads from the defroster, stereo, headlights, and heater blower. To avoid having the stackup of all these losses overwhelm the torque reserve, the ECU begins to shift the source of the torque from spark to airflow. The IAC or throttle blade is slowly opened to allow more airflow while timing is dialed back from MBT again. Effectively, timing is traded for airflow while net torque is held near zero. This allows for a torque reserve to be maintained even after pulling the vehicle into gear and avoids a possible stall from additional loads.

CHAPTER 7

VE TABLE ZONES

Among the most common of questions asked about fuel injection systems is, "How do I know where I'm at in the table at any given time?" The answer is, of course, "It depends." Fortunately, the main tables usually use a common set of axes. The most common is speed in engine RPM and load in either kPa of manifold pressure or percent filling. The combination of speed and load tells the ECU a lot about what the engine is being asked to do.

To make this easier, let's break the base maps down into "zones" and explore what's going on in each of them. The chart on this page shows a typical volumetric efficiency map divided into several zones. This could just as easily be demonstrated with a spark advance or commanded air/fuel ratio map, but we'll discuss all three as we walk through the different zones. The zones may overlap slightly, and boundaries shown are not absolutes for all engines.

By dividing the VE map into several zones, we can get a better idea of what's going on with the engine. Each numbered zone represents a different operating condition for the vehicle and will have its own priorities for fueling and spark.

Zone 1

The first zone is the idle region. Centered around the target idle speed and nominal idle vacuum, it represents the lowest running speed of the engine and a point where most engines spend a great deal of time. Air/fuel ratio is typically held around lambda=1.00 for both emissions and fuel economy. Within this zone, the engine speed and load may vary slightly as the vehicle is pulled into gear without yet moving or as accessories like air conditioning and power steering are cycled. Through all of this, stalling is not allowed and measures must be taken to prevent it at all costs. Smooth control of idle speed is executed by adjusting both airflow and spark advance in an effort to deliver smooth, consistent opera-

DESIGNING AND TUNING HIGH-PERFORMANCE FUEL INJECTION SYSTEMS 53

CHAPTER 7

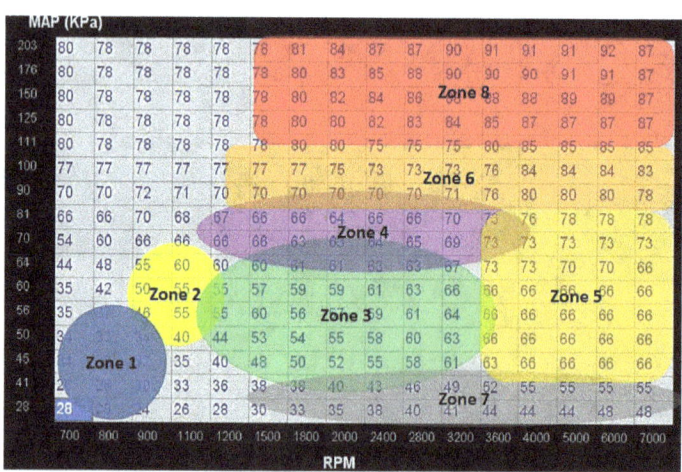

Zone 1 is the engine's normal idle range. Throttle is closed and timing is manipulated to maintain a steady torque output equal to the sum of the losses in the system at the target speed.

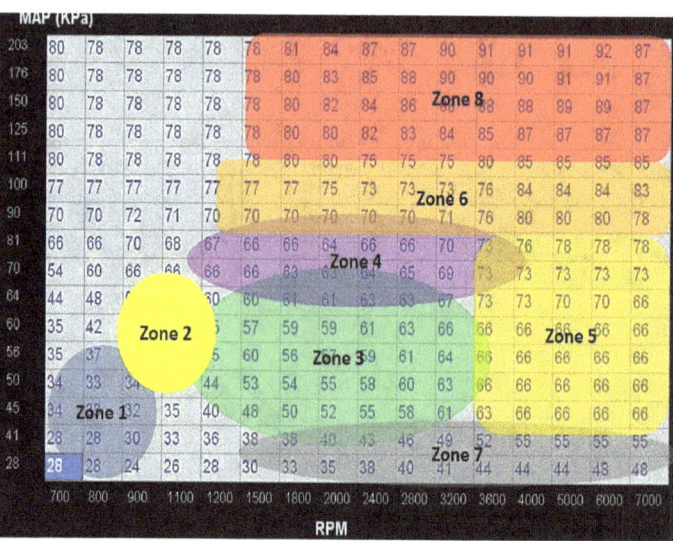

Zone 2 is the tip-in range. Drivers cross this zone frequently and tend to be very critical of throttle response here.

tion. Ignition timing is fairly low at idle on purpose in an effort to provide a torque reserve for sudden changes.

Zone 2

Zone 2 represents the tip-in area. After idle, this is the next point drivers will experience with the engine. Air/fuel ratio should remain at lambda=1.00, even as this zone is entered in a transient condition. Doing so requires two things. First, the airmass estimation in this region at steady state must be correct. The steady state airmass at each cell within this zone represents the target airflow. If this target airmass is not clearly defined, it's almost impossible to get the fuel mass there on the fly with any accuracy. Second, the transient fueling corrections must be sufficient to cover the changes in actual cylinder fueling compared to fuel added directly at the injector. There are usually a set of additional tables to compensate for transient fueling, but having the Zone 2 VE table values correct in the first place makes tuning the transient fuel tables later that much easier. Ignition timing in these cells should be set to MBT to provide maximum torque response as the driver performs a tip-in.

Zone 3

Zone 3 is the cruise area. Engines will spend a lot of time here, especially when driving at a relatively steady speed with minimal road grade. Within this zone, the cylinders are typically only being filled about 20 to 30% of their maximum

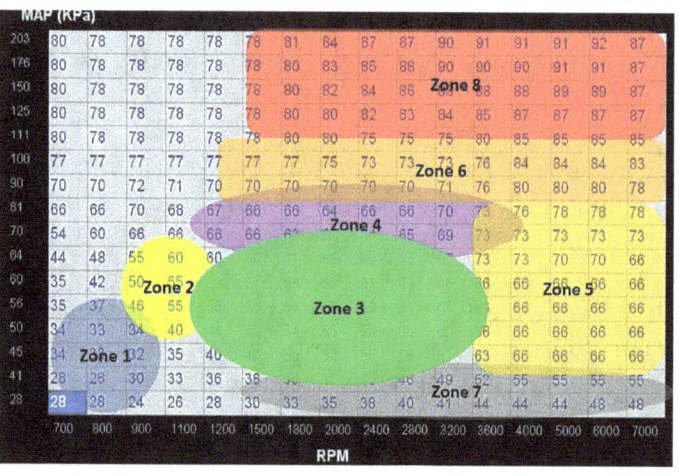

Zone 3 is the cruise region. Most engines spend a great deal of time here and should be calibrated to operate at lambda=1.00 within this range to improve fuel economy and emissions.

Strapping a car to a chassis dynamometer lets the operator replicate just about any driving condition seen on the road. This allows the calibrator to hold the engine in one condition almost indefinitely without worrying about traffic, pedestrians, or police stopping his progress.

54   DESIGNING AND TUNING HIGH-PERFORMANCE FUEL INJECTION SYSTEMS

VE TABLE ZONES

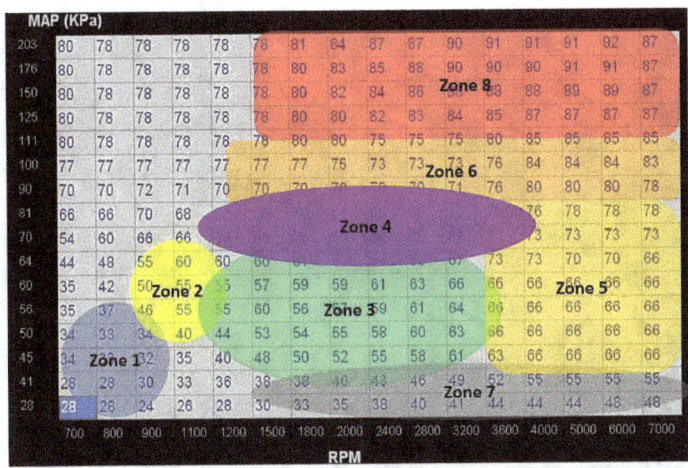

Zone 4 shows moderate acceleration or driving against an increased load such as on a grade or when towing. Output torque and engine cooling become a greater concern here.

On this chart, Zone 5 is an area of high speed and relatively light load. Protection of engine components is the primary concern here, so some extra fueling is commonly added.

on a mass basis, fairly light load. This zone should get a lot of attention during the calibration process since it has such a profound impact upon the "feel" of the car as well as the fuel economy and emissions. Air/fuel ratio is set to lambda=1.00 throughout this region to promote good emissions and decent fuel economy. Spark knock is usually not a concern in this zone.

Timing should be carefully tuned to MBT at as many of these points as possible to improve the mechanical efficiency of the cycle. By running at MBT at each of these points, the engine delivers the most torque possible for the same amount of air and fuel being burned. If this torque is more than the driver needs, he will instinctively reduce the pedal position, which in turn reduces the cylinder load and fuel consumption to a lower point. This lower point should also be similarly optimized for timing and torque so that, at any given point, the driver is only burning the minimum amount of fuel necessary to generate the desired torque needed to push the vehicle down the road.

This goes a long way toward improving fuel economy and should get the appropriate amount of attention during the calibration process.

Zone 4

Zone 4 correlates to a region of moderate acceleration on level roads to steady driving on a grade. The cylinder loading and delivered torque are both slightly greater than Zone 3, but not yet high enough to warrant a full power strategy. Air/fuel ratio remains at a target of lambda=1.00 and timing is still set to MBT as long as knock is not present. With a properly engineered engine system, component temperatures should not be an issue yet.

Zone 5

Zone 5 lies in an area where most drivers hopefully don't spend very much time. It is an elevated engine speed, but with only moderate loads such as leaving the engine in a lower gear on purpose. Most automatic transmissions will not allow the engine to operate here unless the driver has specifically selected the lower gear. Road racers may spend time here as they heel-toe downshift or hold a lower gear through a long, sweeping corner. In this condition, the added engine RPM can contribute to higher component temperatures, so some cooling strategies may be set in motion. Exhaust valves, catalysts, and exhaust manifolds in particular will be subject to high temperatures if the engine is run here continuously at lambda=1.00, so some enrichment is typically added to help bring combustion and exhaust gas temperatures down. Values of anywhere between lambda=1.00 and lambda=0.85 may be necessary to control temperatures, depending on the system.

Ignition timing should still be significantly advanced in Zone 5. The lighter load and higher speed both point to the need for numerically larger spark advance values. Don't be afraid to use what looks like really high ignition timing values here as long as no knock is present. Overly retarded ignition timing in this zone will have a large amount

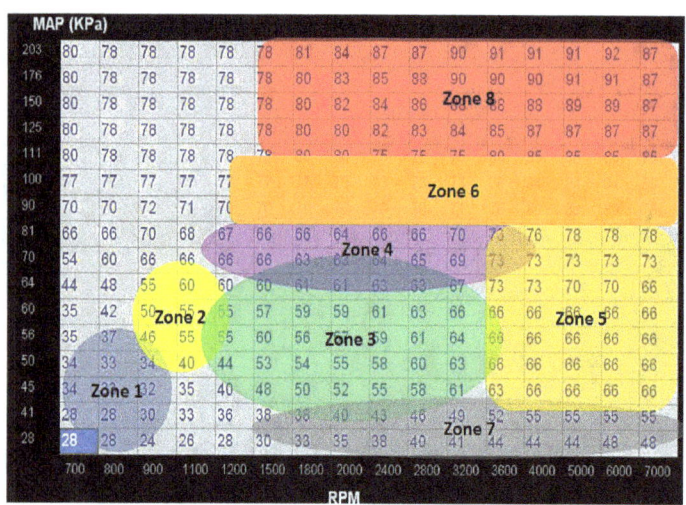

Zone 6 is the WOT region for naturally aspirated engines. Boosted engines may also operate here at part throttle, but should still target the right air/fuel ratio for the conditions.

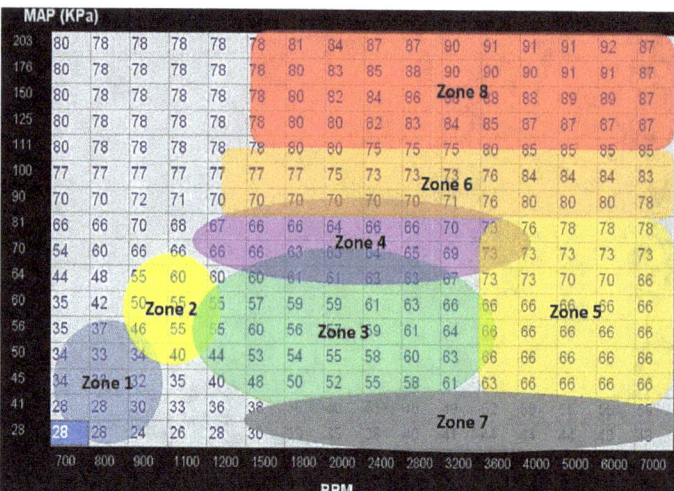

Zone 7 represents heavy deceleration with engine braking. Many ECUs employ a deceleration fuel cutoff while in this zone.

of fuel burning late in the exhaust stroke and as it travels down the runners, releasing the heat to the sensitive exhaust components instead of to the water-cooled cylinders, where it would otherwise be better absorbed. Too little timing here can quickly overheat and fail even the best exhaust components.

Zone 6

A naturally aspirated engine will travel through this zone at WOT. Manifold pressure may be slightly lower than atmospheric pressure if there is some restriction in the intake system plumbing and filter. Remember that at higher altitudes, this zone may include MAP values as low as 70 kPa since that's all that is available from the atmosphere at WOT. The only way the engine gets here is by application of full throttle, so the objective is maximum output. Achieving this is aided by some amount of fuel enrichment, usually to lambda≈0.87 so the most effective use of intake oxygen is made. The additional fueling also helps to control exhaust component temperatures as seen in Zone 5. Timing is set as close to MBT as possible without getting into knock.

Boosted engines will also pass through Zone 6 at part throttle on their way to full load. Within this zone, the engine doesn't know that it's supercharged and can be treated just the same as if it were a naturally aspirated version of itself for both spark and air/fuel ratio. If the engine is a low compression variant, this typically means that volumetric efficiency and torque output within Zone 6 are lower than the higher compression naturally aspirated equivalent.

Zone 7

Whenever the throttle is abruptly lifted, manifold pressure drops to its minimum and Zone 7 is entered. Getting into this zone requires that the throttle be almost completely closed. By getting here, the driver is basically requesting zero or negative torque output. He wishes to slow down as quickly as possible. If the torque request is zero (or less), it makes engine control very simple. In order to produce zero torque, zero fuel is required. Many OEM systems have strategies to recognize this set of conditions and employ what is known as deceleration fuel cutoff (DFCO) to assist in engine braking. Removing 100% of the fuel and engine torque production means that engine braking will be much more pronounced. This can be achieved by simply modeling the volumetric efficiency as zero within Zone 7. Zero VE means zero airmass, and at any ratio still equals a command of zero fuel mass delivered.

If deceleration fuel cutoff is not desired, the engine can be set to run at lambda=1.00 just like Zone 3 above it. Errors in the calculated volumetric efficiency are harder to notice here, since the engine typically sweeps through this zone pretty quickly.

Even though loads are exceptionally low in this zone, spark advance does not necessarily need to be that high. The same values as shown in Zone 3 above are a good starting point. Adding too much spark advance in Zone 7 may result in a "popping" noise in the exhaust.

VE TABLE ZONES

This turbocharged M3 is getting a healthy dose of Zone 7 operation as it enters a corner at Gingerman Raceway. It will pass through Zone 3 mid corner on its way to Zones 6 and 8 as it exits onto the next straight under boost.

Zone 8 is the boosted region for turbo and supercharged engines. It's often not possible to physically enter the boosted region at low RPM due to the boost curve of the supercharger or turbocharger being used.

Zone 8

Boosted engines have the ability to generate higher manifold pressures than their naturally aspirated equivalents. Whenever this happens, they leave Zone 6 and travel vertically into Zone 8. The cylinder loads become significantly higher in this zone as more air and fuel molecules are force fed into the same physical chamber volume. With this increase in pressure comes heat, which is further compounded by the additional heat generated by actually burning larger amounts of air and fuel in the same chamber. This added heat dumps more energy into the engine's cooling system as piston, valve, and cylinder head temperatures are all increased with the added heat release of a larger combustion event on each cycle.

The increase in heat means that flame speeds will generally increase and the knock threshold is greatly reduced. In order to maintain safe operation, extra fuel is added in Zone 8 for a mild cooling effect as well as increased knock margin. At moderate boost levels, a target ratio of lambda≈0.80 may be sufficient, but some non-intercooled applications may benefit from running ratios closer to lambda≈0.75 for added safety. Any time a close-coupled catalyst is used in a high output engine, brick temperature limits may require additional fuel for cooling of the exhaust gases. In some OEM applications, this can trump the typical ratios desired for clean combustion as ratios as rich as lambda=0.65 have been used to keep from melting what was once an expensive catalyst brick into what closely resembles moon rocks.

The Lysholm supercharger from Vortech on this truck engine will allow it to move past its previous limitation of Zone 6 into the boosted region of Zone 8.

Ignition timing strategy for Zone 8 closely follows the goals of Zone 6. The object is to run as close to MBT timing as possible without getting knock. The added cylinder load and temperatures of Zone 8 often mean there is a significant gap between the knock limit and MBT at most points. As such, the delivered timing is almost always a reflection of how close to the knock limit the engine calibrator is willing to run, or how much confidence he has in the knock sensor logic. This is a condition where higher octane fuels with their higher knock resistance can allow the engine calibrator to unlock more power from the same engine hardware if all else is equal with operating conditions. With most blends of pump gasoline, power is limited by how close to the edge the calibrator is willing to run the engine on an extended basis. Most experienced tuners will opt to maintain a significant safety margin for knock in Zone 8 instead of trying to eke out that last bit of horsepower.

DESIGNING AND TUNING HIGH-PERFORMANCE FUEL INJECTION SYSTEMS

CHAPTER 8

INTRODUCTION TO SETUPS AND CALIBRATION

Before trying to calibrate an engine or vehicle, it is helpful to become familiar with some of the tools of the trade. Engine tuning is more than simply looking at tables on a computer screen and saying, "I think this should be at this value." Collecting valid data is the most important part of the process. Without some indication of how a system is performing, it's very difficult to know what adjustments should be made to bring everything into operational harmony. Even worse than no data at all, is bad data. Making adjustments based upon the wrong assumptions can move progress backward in a hurry. The emphasis in this chapter is that the calibrator needs to understand what he is seeing and use that data to make the proper calculated changes moving forward.

Laptop

The most obvious piece of tuning equipment for any calibrator is his computer. Most tuners prefer this to be a laptop, but it's not absolutely necessary. Laptops just make a lot of parts of the tuning process much easier, particularly if it includes in-vehi-

The laptop computer has become the cornerstone of ECU programming. It's more important to make sure that the computer has the necessary connection ports to communicate with the ECU than it is to have the latest processor or the most RAM available. My touchscreen Panasonic Toughbook has proven to be a very reliable instrument in the field.

cle work. While I have been known to tune the occasional car with a 15-foot serial extension between the

INTRODUCTION TO SETUPS AND CALIBRATION

A simple way to make room for a wideband sensor is to weld in a new fitting on the exhaust. A simple M18x1.5 threaded jam nut can be used as long as one remembers to chase the threads after welding and cooling to avoid galling the threads.

ECU and tower PC, nothing beats just sitting in the car and seeing all of the vehicle's gauges along with the laptop screen.

Computer geeks will continue to argue as they always have about what constitutes a "good" machine for tuning. In all honesty, almost any modern laptop will get the job done. The ECU in the car is doing all the hard work, so there's surprisingly little processor power used by most calibration interfaces. Don't confuse the ability to run the latest online interactive game with capacity for recording data or editing a tuning map offline.

More important to me is the selection of ports on the laptop. Does the tuning interface require a serial connection? Many standalones still use serial interfaces, so it's better to actually have one on the laptop than to rely on a USB-serial converter. These converters are not all made equal and some may not have sufficient buffer capacity to transfer large data blocks without interruption. The best way to avoid the situation is to just have the proper interface on the laptop in the first place or ask the ECU or software manufacturer if a USB interface is available. Some newer, less expensive laptops have thrifted out the serial port, so it's definitely worth checking prior to any purchase.

Speaking of USB connections, how many does the laptop have and where are they located? Some software packages have a USB hardware key that must be plugged in to allow the program to run. These "dongles" come in many sizes and widths. Some of them may be wide enough to prevent plugging another USB device or cable into an adjacent port if the locations are too close. It may also be necessary to have more than two USB devices plugged in simultaneously if each needs its own port for flashing device, datalogger, hardware key, or network connection. In these cases, it may be helpful to purchase an outboard USB hub. Just as with USB serial converters, USB hubs are not all created equal either. Make sure that the hub can support the necessary current if any outboard devices are USB powered and that communication is not affected by the presence of the hub.

Another very helpful feature in a laptop destined for tuning use is a touch-screen interface. While not ideal when actually traveling on a bumpy road, it is a serious convenience when operating in the relative comfort of a stationary vehicle on a chassis dynamometer or sitting at a nearby workbench. Much of the calibration process consists of applying changes to regions of a two-dimensional map or wide sections of a single-dimensional table. The touch-screen stylus makes selecting these regions just that little bit quicker and more efficient. As a nifty bonus, there are a wide variety of double-duty pens that include a stylus either as a selectable tip or on the reverse end. These come in very handy when constantly switching between writing calibration notes on a clipboard and entering data in the laptop. Trust me, once you experience the convenience of a good touch-screen monitor while tuning, you won't want to go back.

Wideband Oxygen Sensor

Apart from computer access to the ECU and a working vehicle, the next most useful piece of engine calibration equipment is the wideband oxygen sensor. Often referred to as UEGOs (universal exhaust gas oxygen sensors), wideband oxygen sensors can return a valuable piece of information to the calibrator. Knowing the actual delivered air/fuel ratio during testing is absolutely critical to making the proper adjustments when working on the air models such as VE tables or MAF transfer functions. By taking a careful and accurate measurement of the currently delivered air/fuel ratio, calculated adjustments can be made instead of simply adding more or less fuel blindly until things fall in line.

Getting an accurate lambda measurement with the UEGO sensor starts with having good equipment. Not all UEGO sensors and controllers are built to the same standards. There are a plethora of affordable wideband systems flooding the market today and most of these are junk as far as the professional calibrator is concerned. First and foremost, any "wideband" that uses a standard four-wire binary sensor isn't truly a wideband and tells you absolutely nothing outside of the stoichiomet-

CHAPTER 8

ric region. Actual wideband sensors themselves are manufactured by NTK or Bosch with a minimum of five wires necessary to control the more complex Nernst cell and heater logics active in the sensor. There are varying grades of actual UEGO sensor sensitivity, but almost any will work well enough for basic calibration work as long as it is used in combination with a good controller.

The controller is the brains of the wideband measurement system. This is where the mediocre, low cost systems are separated from the good affordable ones further yet from the professional systems. Some controllers may have widely different outputs from the same sensor once conditions sway from stoichiometric or nominal temperatures. Many of the low cost widebands are pretty accurate around stoichiometric mixtures because that's the easy part. Output current of the pump is zero at a stoichiometric mixture, so it doesn't take very sophisticated equipment to detect a zero.

Moving further down the richness scale (as is necessary in supercharged or other high load applications), however, will show a different tale when comparing lesser units. The richer the gas mixture, the harder it is to correctly process the signal. Changes in the temperature of the sensing element can also significantly impact the signal returned to the controller. The best controllers are the ones that can consistently control sensor temperature and compensate accordingly instead of experiencing sensor failures or returning bad data. Ironically, it is during high load, high temperature operation that accurate measurement of the air/fuel ratio is most critical to engine survival.

Just because a certain wideband manufacturer has a large advertising budget and claims to be a standard of the industry doesn't make them so. Much like the world of truly high performance sports cars, the best rarely need to advertise. Don't be swayed by the "everybody's using them" argument in favor of any cheap wideband. They are cheap for a reason. Do a little research before purchasing to find out how many people have problems with a certain wideband controller before spending good money on one. Even if it's initially cheaper, is it worth the cost of wasted dyno time during a failure, or worse yet, an engine failure after bad data is used to make calibration changes? For the professional tuner, the answer is an unequivocal "No." The average enthusiast doesn't need to buy a $3,500 lab-grade controller, but it's not worth risking bad performance and possible expensive engine damage just to save $50 on equipment selection up front. Just think of how many tanks of gas it will take to equalize the price difference when precious tuning time is squandered on working around a cheaply built UEGO controller.

Equally as important as good equipment is collecting reliable lambda data; proper installation of the good equipment can make the difference between frustration and success. Location of the actual UEGO sensor is critical to long life and a reliable signal. The sensor should be installed so that the tip always points downward, preventing water condensation from collecting directly upon the sensing element. If there is liquid water present during warm-up (when most condensation occurs), the fragile ceramic element can crack and fail. It's always a good idea to have at least a 15 degree angle above horizontal for any UEGO installation.

Local pressure near the sensing element is also a significant concern. UEGO sensors are designed to work best in an environment with local pressures between 0.8 and 1.2 bar. If too much backpressure is present, it can make rich signals look even richer than they really are. This can be misleading to an inexperienced tuner, who may mistakenly reduce fueling thinking he has overshot the fuel delivery requirements when in reality that is not the case. The backpressure may be a result of insufficient muffler flow, restrictive catalytic converters, or even a properly functioning turbocharger's turbine section.

Bosch's own data suggests that for every 50 hPa (hectopascals) (0.7 psi gauge pressure) of pressure increase, there is approximately 1.3% shift in pump current out of the sensor. This change in pump current will in turn register as a change in displayed lambda. The magnitude of the lambda shift depends on how far away from stoichiometric the measurement is being taken and how much pressure is present. Specifically, if just 10 psi of backpressure is present, it can cause a shift in displayed lambda with a Bosch LSU4 UEGO sensor from 0.81 down to 0.78. With gasoline, this represents the difference between a good delivered mix of approximately 11.8:1 air/fuel ratio and a display of about 11.4:1. It's easy to see how some people may look at the indicated "11.4:1" ratio on the display and assume that the engine is operating too rich. The resulting adjustment would actually lean the engine out beyond what may be desirable.

Fortunately for the tuning enthusiast, most aftermarket performance

INTRODUCTION TO SETUPS AND CALIBRATION

exhaust systems include mufflers with relatively little backpressure even at maximum flow rates. Working around turbine backpressure is as simple as locating the UEGO bung on the downstream side of the turbine section. This will also go a long way toward preventing overheating conditions for the sensor, as the turbine has a significant temperature drop across it when functioning at full load. Factory catalysts can be another obstacle altogether. It is a Federal "no-no" to remove a properly working catalyst on a street-driven vehicle. If the converters are the source of the restriction, it's best to either take pressure measurements for lambda correction or measure WOT mixtures downstream of them and accept the signal latency. For racing applications, this is usually a non-issue.

To further reinforce the point of always collecting reliable data from the wideband sensor, it is important to note that oxygen sensors change as they age. Most UEGO sensors experience gain shift where the output current of the Nernst cell shifts slightly over time. The longer the sensor has been in service, the more critical it becomes to check and verify its calibration. The easiest way to accomplish recalibration of a UEGO sensor is to expose it to normal atmospheric conditions free of any fumes or hydrocarbons. Oxygen sensors are precisely that, devices that measure percent oxygen in a mix of gases. They are just used in automotive applications to measure relatively low amounts of residual oxygen molecules in exhaust gases. Since the Earth's atmosphere is always approximately 20.9% oxygen, the wideband controller can compare the instantaneous output of the sensor against this reference to get a calibration point very far along its

Engine Control and Monitoring

In the case of wideband control systems, ECM (Engine Control and Monitoring, Sunnyvale, California) is that standard by which all others are measured. ECM makes a wide range of UEGO controllers that fill every niche from in-vehicle testing to R&D facility emissions benches. Almost every dynamometer test cell in the big three is equipped with an ECM lambda sensor system for a reason; probably the same reason the EPA uses them for their test cells.

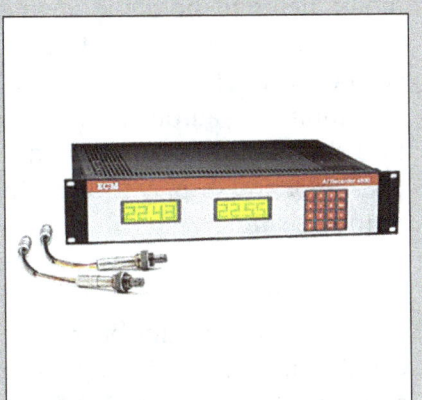

The ECM 4800r is probably the best wideband controller on the market today. This unit can be found in almost every engine dynamometer cell at GM, Ford, and Chrysler where accurate data is an absolute necessity. (Photo courtesy of ECM)

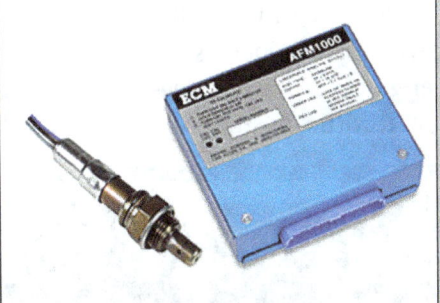

The AFM1000 can be found in almost every powertrain development vehicle at the GM, Ford, and Chrysler proving grounds. This affordable controller is also used by many professionals in the aftermarket because it has a 0 to 5v analog output that can be easily integrated into a dynamometer or other data acquisition system. (Photo courtesy of ECM)

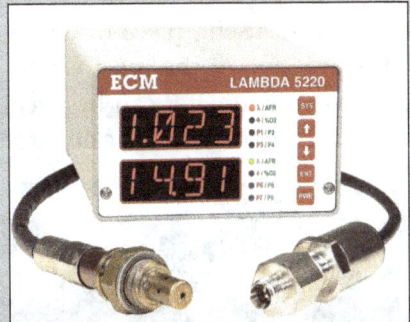

By integrating a pressure sensor with a laboratory grade wideband sensor, the ECM 5220 represents the latest in air/fuel ratio measurement. The raw measured lambda is automatically corrected for local exhaust pressure so that the calibrator can see a true corrected reading. (Photo courtesy of ECM)

DESIGNING AND TUNING HIGH-PERFORMANCE FUEL INJECTION SYSTEMS

operation curve. This makes for very accurate adjustments and correction with minimal question as to the validity of the signal.

The ability to recalibrate the controller for an aging or recently replaced UEGO sensor is critical to obtaining good data over the life of the wideband. Many newer vehicles come equipped with wideband UEGO sensors from the factory. Each of these vehicles' ECUs contains logic to recalibrate for sensor aging over the life of the vehicle. This is a very necessary operation if the emissions of the vehicle are to remain within allowable limits over its useful life. Recalibration of the UEGO sensor controller should be performed at the beginning of every tuning session for best results. Think of this task as an ongoing process that must be updated continuously.

Dynamometers

Beyond the laptop and wideband, the next most useful piece of equipment is also one of the most expensive. The dynamometer can be a real time-saving device for any calibrator who uses it wisely. For those who are simply looking for big numbers and bragging rights first, with drivability tuning to be done later, it is often their nemesis. Properly employed, the dynamometer will allow the calibrator to zero in on exact conditions that line up directly with breakpoints in the ECU calibration tables. What better way to find out exactly what the volumetric efficiency is at 2,000 rpm and 60 kPa than to hold the engine at exactly that point? The dynamometer can be used to do just that. There are two main categories of dynamometers: engine and chassis.

Engine Dynos

As the name implies, an engine dynamometer tests only the engine itself by attaching a resistance unit directly to the flywheel. This resistance may be either a water brake, eddy current brake, or an AC motor. The water and eddy current brakes are usually sufficient to get the vast majority of calibration work done since they can be adjusted to whatever load is necessary to hold the engine at a fixed speed, regardless of throttle position or power level, almost indefinitely. The operator has the ability to move from one speed and load setting to the next at will, working his way through the entire fuel or spark map. With the water and eddy current brakes, the engine dynamometer can hold steady at any point where the engine is making positive torque.

There are some cases where the engine's combustion efforts do not equal the frictional and pumping losses. At higher speeds and lower loads, the net output of the engine is actually negative torque that attempts to slow the engine down until some lower equilibrium speed is reached. In order to hold the engine to these negative net torque conditions, some assistance must be given. An AC motoring dynamometer has the ability to do just this by literally driving (motoring) the engine with electrical power through the flywheel coupling. The added rotational force from the electric motor helps to hold the engine at the desired speed so that readings can be taken. The controls of the AC dynamometer automatically recognize the negative reaction torque at the motor and display it accordingly to the operator.

In practice, it is not always necessary to completely map the negative torque region of engine operation. By definition, the driver is only applying a small, often zero, amount of gas pedal input in this region. If the airflow mapping is not precise here,

The highlighted section of this VE table shows the general location of the negative torque region. In this area, the energy from combustion is actually less than the friction and pumping losses which results in a net negative torque delivered to the flywheel by the engine.

INTRODUCTION TO SETUPS AND CALIBRATION

Engine dynamometers are tremendous tools for calibration that allow the operator to dial any combination of engine speed and load without working against the transmission or driveline. With the engine out of the vehicle, there is easy access to the valvetrain and intake system as well as an almost unlimited cooling capacity.

This engine dyno is set up in a portable environment inside of an enclosed trailer. Everything needed to operate the dynamometer is contained inside, even a separate control room behind the glass shield in the background.

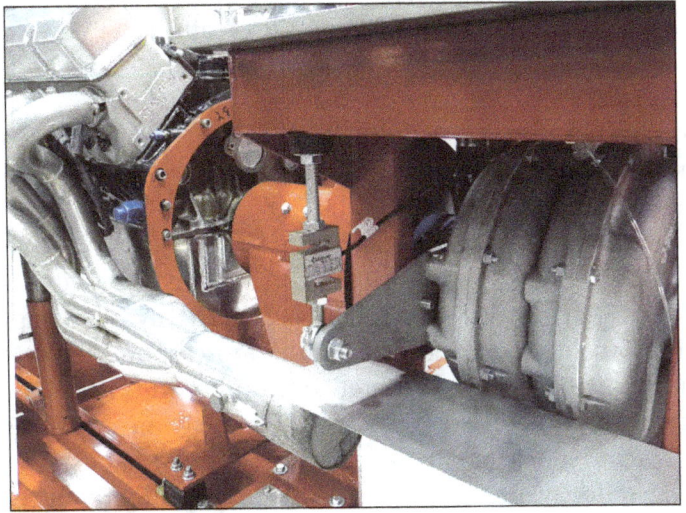

The business end of an engine dynamometer is shown here with the pair of toroids that form the water brake attached to a lever arm. The reaction force is measured with an "S" shaped load cell.

On an engine dynamometer, power is transmitted through a prop shaft to the load cell. A safety guard is also used to contain the prop shaft as an extra precaution.

many drivers never notice it from a "seat of the pants" perspective. Further, many ECUs completely cut all fuel delivery at high RPM and closed throttle. Since the driver is effectively asking for zero engine output at zero pedal position, the total fuel requirement to make no power is a nice, round number. This is referred to as deceleration fuel cutoff or "DFCO." Current airflow is not even necessary for a fuel calculation that gets cut to zero anyway. In the OEM environment, the ECU is tasked with maintaining precisely lambda=1.00 at all times (unless DFCO is active), so this area is actually mapped just as carefully as the rest. The engine must also smoothly transition into and out of DFCO at light loads without showing an increase in emissions, so this gets a fair amount of attention in a production calibration.

The ability to hold the engine

CHAPTER 8

This well-used Dynojet has seen countless cars over the years. With only inertial loading, WOT testing is common, but steady state loads are not possible on this particular unit.

Underneath the vented covers in the foreground lies an eddy current brake that is able to apply an infinitely variable resistance to the rolls of this Dynojet 224 xLC. This unit can be programmed for either steady state or continuously variable load control, allowing the calibrator to collect data under more controlled conditions.

at a steady speed and load allows the calibrator to concentrate on a single point in either the fuel map or spark map at a time with minimal influence from any other part of the table. By holding the engine at a steady state condition, any effects from wall film dynamics can be reduced to almost zero when calculating airflow based on measured air/fuel ratio. This assures the calibrator that any changes seen are a function solely of the base map instead of some transient.

The entire engine calibration can be performed on an engine dynamometer. This is how the vast majority of base engine calibration work is done at the OEM level. However, great care must be taken to ensure that testing conditions on the engine dyno closely match what will be seen on the vehicle. Most importantly, the entire intake and exhaust system from the air filter box to the tailpipe should be used whenever possible. Many engine dynos simply fix a set of headers to the engine and evacuate to a large-diameter stack. If this is not the intended layout for the vehicle exhaust, one can begin to see where some serious differences can occur. The addition of pipe length, catalysts, mufflers, and resonators adds restriction to the engine's breathing capability in the form of backpressure that changes with total exhaust flow. Increases in backpressure translate directly to a reduction of engine pumping effectiveness (volumetric efficiency) that is being estimated by the VE table in the ECU. The same holds true for intake systems. Testing with an open throttle body does not show the same intake pressure drop as an airbox, filter, and inlet tube. It is absolutely imperative that engine dyno measurements and calibrations be done with the same equipment that will be used in the vehicle. Failure to do so will result in an ECU calibration that works fine on the dyno (and probably makes really good power), followed by lackluster performance in the vehicle that exhibits a rich condition, poor fuel economy, and soggy throttle response.

Chassis Dynos

The second category of dynamometer, the chassis dyno, is rapidly becoming more popular in the aftermarket tuning world. The chassis dynamometer tests the engine as installed in the vehicle. Resistance is applied directly to the drive tires through a drum while the vehicle literally drives in place while restrained. The clear benefits to this type of testing are that it uses the exact hardware that will be driven on the road or track; and that it is much more time effective when the engine is already installed in the vehicle. Many modern engines and ECUs won't even run with proper communication to the rest of the vehicle's network. Also, it's not very practical to completely remove a

INTRODUCTION TO SETUPS AND CALIBRATION

fully instrumented and functioning engine from the vehicle just to perform testing.

Fundamentally, the same tests can and should be run on the chassis dynamometer as the engine dynamometer. This means performing steady state checks at as many of the ECU map cells as possible to confirm that the base tables are properly mapped. This exercise alone shows a clear difference between the two varieties of chassis dynamometers.

The most common type of chassis dynamometer in use for aftermarket tuning is the inertial dyno. These dynamometers are basically just a weighted drum with a speed sensor. They derive power by looking at the acceleration rate (first derivative of speed) for the known mass of the drum. The more power (force) applied to the drum, the greater the acceleration rate and consequently, calculated power. The catch is that in order to measure any power, the drum must be accelerating. Likewise, any power input results in a net acceleration of the drum. Without any additional input, it is impossible to perform steady state speed testing at anything other than the force equal to the frictional losses of the system. Positive loads result in positive acceleration, so speed increases any time the throttle is opened farther. As such, measuring dynamically across the WOT line of the fuel and spark tables is easy, but carefully tuning the majority of these maps requires additional equipment to be done right.

The second type of chassis dynamometer, which is rapidly increasing in popularity as tuners and consumers become more educated, is the load-bearing dyno. These machines still use a drum as the primary interface to the tire, but the weight of the drum is no longer the critical component for power measurement. Additional loads are added to the drum by either an eddy current or water brake. The actual load applied to the vehicle can now be precisely controlled by the dynamometer and varied infinitely just as with the engine dyno. By holding the transmission in a single gear, engine speed can be controlled as a function of wheel speed by the dynamometer. This opens the door for steady state testing with the engine installed in the vehicle. The calibrator can now hold the engine precisely at a single cell and perform the necessary calibration adjustments in steady state. Again, this helps reduce the confusion that may come with transient testing where rich/lean conditions may be a result of wall film influences or dynamic airflow changes. Even better, the tests are performed with the exact intake and exhaust hardware that will accompany the engine on the road and track.

While steady state testing is ideal on the chassis dynamometer, there are some unique concerns. First and foremost is engine cooling. Engine dynamometers are often equipped with a cooling tower and substantial reservoir that provide almost unlimited cooling capacity. Most vehicle cooling systems are not

At Diablosport's headquarters in Boca Raton, Florida, the R&D work is done on this Superflow AutoDyn eddy current equipped chassis dynamometer. The dyno is situated such that fresh air flows freely across the vehicle with open doors at both ends of the shop to aid in cooling and ventilation.

Having seen a melted strap on the dyno first hand, I can assure you that it's not something this author wants to repeat. The straps holding a truck to this Mustang dynamometer can be configured in a wide variety of angles to avoid any such issue. Adding redundant straps on high torque applications is also a good idea.

sufficient to keep up with the heat release associated with holding 4,000 rpm for twenty minutes straight at various loads. The radiator works best with the large airflow associated with driving down the road at 20 mph or more. Getting that level of airflow in an automotive chassis dyno test cell is expensive at best. Even with astounding amounts of airflow available to the radiator, all but the most robust road-racing cooling systems are incapable of keeping up with the heat rejection rates necessary under these conditions. The solution is to keep a careful eye on engine coolant and oil temperatures when performing steady state tests on a chassis dynamometer.

At higher speeds, it's often best to just bring the engine up to load on a single cell long enough to stabilize and take the necessary wideband or torque measurements and then let off the throttle while making the actual adjustments. In many cases, it will be necessary to allow "breathing time" between measurements to cool the heads, intake, and exhaust. Remember that the idea is to take consistent data under consistent conditions. Rushing here may result in a skewed correction due to increase temperature compensations that have not yet been optimized. The more consistent and precise you can be during this process, the more robust the core of the engine calibration will be, making many other subsequent tasks that much easier. Take your time and do it right!

On the subject of heat, the exhaust system deserves some attention at this point. Just like the radiator, the exhaust system was designed to be driven down the road when loads are high. Even with heat shields and adequate spacing, lots of interesting things can get hot on the chassis

Having access to a computerized flow bench, like the one at Diablosport, can greatly simplify the calibration process. Using this equipment, the calibrator can know the exact transfer function of a MAF, IAT, or MAP sensor before ever seeing the vehicle.

dynamometer. Catalysts, in particular, run exceptionally hot and without the convective cooling from vehicle movement, they can do a terrific job of heating things around them. Make sure that the underside of the vehicle has adequate airflow and cooling time during chassis dyno testing to avoid an inadvertent thermal event.

Ventilation

While most engine dynamometer cells do a good job of supplying fresh intake air and evacuating exhaust fumes, I have seen an alarming number of chassis dyno setups that seem to have forgotten this. Unfortunately, it has become common practice at many smaller tuning shops to simply put the chassis dyno in whatever space was available without concern for ventilation or recirculation. First and foremost, the safety and health of the dyno operator, calibrator, and whatever technicians are in the area should be considered. Carbon monoxide can and will kill you with only just a headache for symptoms. This alone should be motivation to make sure that a shop is properly ventilated.

From the engine's point of view, the presence of spent exhaust gases in the environment will alter the chemistry of the intake charge. EGR still works when it is allowed to travel from the tailpipe back to the air filter and the ECU has no idea this has happened. Continuing to tune in this environment (assuming you don't pass out) will result in unintentional reductions of the engine airflow estimation since fuel is only added to match the fresh-air fraction of the intake charge. An engine tuned in a polluted environment will run lean once brought outside to the normal world where there is once again 20.9% oxygen content.

Even worse, the effective EGR of the polluted environment will allow the tuner to add an otherwise improper amount of spark advance before reaching either MBT or the knock limit. Returning to a fresh-air environment yields an over-sparked tune that rattles and may risk engine damage. If you won't make sure there's fresh air in the test cell for the engine, at least do it for your own health.

Additional Equipment

While a laptop, wideband, and dynamometer cover the vast majority of calibration needs, it's also handy to have some additional tools to make sure things are really as they seem. I like to think of these as the "reality check" tools. These are tools used to make sure that the calibration values being entered into the ECU are actually performing as intended.

The first of these tools is the timing light. Before the advent of the ECU, the timing light was the primary tool for tuning. Today, it's still important because there still exists the potential for error in any system. Before spending hours on the dyno adjusting spark maps, it's always a good idea to make sure that the values in the table are actually what is being delivered to the plugs. Most ECUs have the ability to set timing to a constant value for diagnostic purposes. Confirming that 10 degrees BTDC is really 10 degrees BTDC goes a long way toward preventing some unregulated anger later on. The timing light is the most useful means of ensuring that the crank and cam sensor inputs are being properly registered by the ECU since spark delivery is directly tied to their inputs. Occasionally, a bad outboard ignition module can be diagnosed by a varying offset in delivered ignition timing. The point here is to make sure that the calibrator is really in control with the spark advance tables in the ECU. Remember that the delivered timing may be more than just the base spark table value once the adders (modifier values from other tables that are used to adjust the base table value) for temperature, air/fuel ratio, barometric pressure, and idle control are active.

A digital volt-ohm meter (DVOM) can be a very useful tool for diagnosing simple signal error and possible short or open circuits. It's a good idea to always check against a known value such as a good 12v battery to verify proper operation of the DVOM before taking other system voltage measurements.

The most flexible electronic tool is probably the DVOM, or digital volt-ohm meter. Every tuner should have one in his toolkit. Most sensors on the engine have voltage based outputs, so they can be checked with the meter independent of the ECU connection. A sensor with a short or open circuit can be quickly diagnosed using this simple tool. Likewise, variable sensors like the TPS can be swept through their range and tested for individual broken traces that would otherwise appear as random cutouts while driving. The ECU itself and harness can be tested to make sure that the 5v reference voltage is available at each sensor connection as well. Alternator output and battery voltage can also be real concerns when tuning, so don't overlook the simplest of uses. In a pinch, the test light serves as an even simpler check.

What dynamometer test cell would be complete without a few gauges? In most well-equipped test cells, the computer running the dynamometer also has multiple analog input ports that can be used to track additional sensors. Among these pressure sensors on both the intake manifold and fuel rail are the

CHAPTER 8

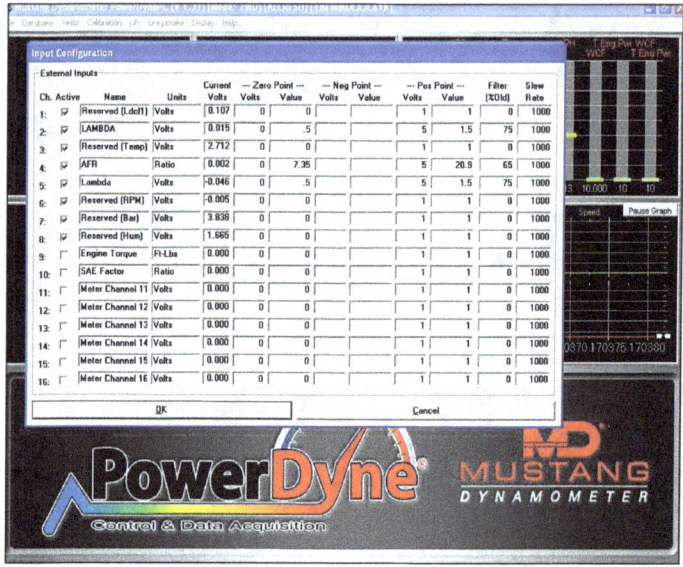

Most dynamometers have the ability to record data from additional analog input channels. Each channel name should be clearly labeled after the proper conversion units are entered.

It's a tight fit, but the EFI intake manifold only takes up as much room as most tunnel ram carburetor intakes do. The Ramjet 502 is available as a fuel injected crate engine from GM Performance Parts and many standalone controller companies have a base tuning file for it that can greatly reduce the time needed to get it running properly.

most useful. If the dyno control computer has the luxury of using standard 0 to 5v inputs on an analog board, this is usually the easiest and most effective solution. Since the majority of measurements will be taken in relatively steady conditions, the pressure sensors can be installed with a vacuum line tee into any other manifold pressure source. Fuel pressure sensors require more care and proper sealing to avoid a leak in a very dangerous environment.

Electronic pressure transducers can be sourced from many places and almost all of them will work sufficiently for most calibration tasks. The most precise (and expensive) are the professional-grade, certified units available from testing supply houses such as Omega Engineering. If a measurement is to be taken, chances are Omega has the equipment to do it. A less expensive alternative would be to use OEM engine sensors with the dynamometer. A 3 bar MAP sensor (P/N 12223861) can be ordered through just about any GM dealership and has the ability to measure about 30 psi of boost for a very meager price. Many gauge companies such as Autometer also offer their pressure sending units separately from their gauges. Do not use a MAP sensor for liquid (fuel) pressure measurement. There are specific sending units for this application.

MAP sensors can also be used to track exhaust backpressure. Exhaust backpressure measurements will help spot restrictions that may cost significant power, or determine proper turbocharger exhaust housing sizing. Installation of a backpressure sensor must have some separation and insulation from the exhaust environment's heat. The best method to do so is by using a small-diameter copper tube installed onto a pressure tap on the exhaust pipe or manifold. The metal tube can easily resist the heat of the exhaust gases and pipes. A length of about 2 to 3 feet of copper tubing should be sufficient to allow gases to cool before connecting to either a standard rubber hose or a fitting on the sensor itself. The sensor is mounted remotely to avoid direct exposure to the hot environment.

In the absence of electronic sensor monitoring, it's possible to use traditional analog gauges to gather information. Some vehicle owners have already opted to install boost and fuel pressure gauges, which can be used during the calibration process to verify that pressures measured by the ECU match reality. An outboard mechanical fuel pressure gauge always comes in handy during initial injector setup and will serve as a telltale indicator of insufficient fuel pump flow at high speeds and loads. A drop in rail pressure toward the tail end of a WOT run almost always points to insufficient pump flow or some other restriction.

DESIGNING AND TUNING HIGH-PERFORMANCE FUEL INJECTION SYSTEMS

CHAPTER 9

INITIAL SETUP

The very first step in any tuning process is to make sure you have the right software available. If you have purchased a standalone ECU, chances are that the box included a disk with the necessary software. Follow the manufacturer's instructions for installation on your computer and ensure that you are able to open, modify, and save files before connecting to your ECU or vehicle.

Assuming that you now have a working software suite, it's time to get into the actual tuning process. The best possible starting point is another tune for an identical engine using identical hardware. If someone else has already taken this test and got an "A," there is no shame in starting from a known good file. Most software systems that support reflashing a stock ECU will have the ability to download the stock calibration first, or at least provide you with a stock tuning file. Many standalone ECU manufacturers will provide known good tuning files for popular stock and crate motor applications. This starting file should be saved and never touched again. This will provide you with a fallback solution should the worst happen with your custom-tuning file in the future or if you unintentionally work yourself into a bad calibration. A copy should be made of the original tuning file with a unique name. The second copy will serve as your working file as you move forward with the calibration process. My personal preference is for the file name to include the client's name and project date. I sort tuning files within a folder structure based upon vehicle and engine type for easier location later.

One of the best parts about tuning stock engine controllers is that the majority of hardware setup options are already hard coded into the file. With a standalone controller, their flexibility can become a liability if great care is not taken upon initial setup. Once a file is loaded, the first thing to check is all of the hardware configurations. Since the standalone controllers often work with such a wide variety of ignition systems, crank and cam triggers, firing orders, MAP sensors, TPS sensors, and injector configurations, all of these items must be checked and validated as correct before starting the engine.

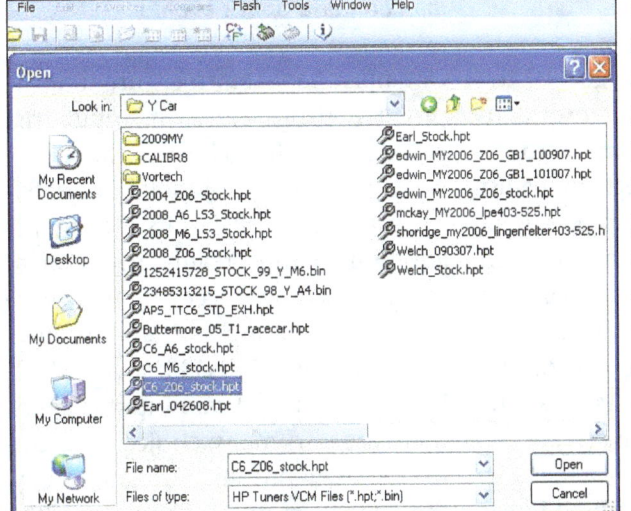

Whenever possible, it's a good idea to start from a known good calibration file. This is much easier when reprogramming factory controllers where you can read out a tune that has literally millions of dollars of development time behind it, but some standalone controller companies have good working files available for popular applications.

DESIGNING AND TUNING HIGH-PERFORMANCE FUEL INJECTION SYSTEMS

CHAPTER 9

This MSD crank trigger is a series of four magnets installed on a wheel behind the crank pulley. System phasing can be changed by sliding the pickup mount along the arc of the mounting bracket to properly align ignition and injection events with the crankshaft.

Newer EFI systems use a "60 minus 2" crankshaft target wheel that actually has 58 teeth and a wide gap for better resolution. The gap is located with a specific offset from TDC for cylinder number 1 to give the ECU a solid reference point for injection and spark events.

signal gets from the ECU to the spark plug as long as it gets there when he commands it with sufficient energy.

The purpose of this book is not to debate the advantages of the various trigger and output layouts, but rather to make sure that whatever system is chosen is properly implemented. It is important to verify that the selection shown on screen matches the hardware installed on the engine itself. If there is any mismatch here, the rest of the calibration process is doomed to failure and aggravation.

The best way to validate both trigger inputs and ignition outputs is to use a timing light and fixed ignition angle output. Set the timing to a fixed value and check against the balancer's marks. If for any reason there is a discrepancy between the commanded and delivered ignition angle, it's time to go back to square one with the trigger setup validation. Right now, 10 degrees commanded advance must equal 10 degrees delivered advance, or you are in for a long and unrewarding tuning experience moving forward.

A good place to begin is the crankshaft and camshaft sensor configuration. Most standalone controllers allow the user to select from a list of common OEM triggers and ignition outputs. Aside from the common OEM options, a custom system can also be defined. This is probably one of the trickiest propositions for the first-time user since there is no shortage of places for potential error.

If it is decided that a custom trigger definition is to be used, great care must be taken to ensure that the proper settings are used. Input triggers can be defined by a digital square wave, hall effect, or bipolar pulse (flying magnet). Each has its own merits and limits, but in reality any of them can be used to successfully operate an engine as long as they are properly installed and calibrated. Much like the crank and cam input triggers, there are also many choices for ignition system output. Fundamentally, the calibrator doesn't care how the

Engine firing order should also be defined at this point. Firing order will impact both ignition and fuel injection for sequential systems. Many engines use common firing orders for V-8, V-6, and I-4 engines, but with different cylinder numbering systems. Cylinder number 1 on a Chevrolet small-block is really cylinder number 5 on a Ford small-block. The Ford's cylinder number 1 is really the Chevy's number 2, and so on. In the end, this is more a matter of engine wiring layout, but it's a good idea for the calibrator to visually check where the number 1 plug wire goes and compare that to the firing order shown in the calibration data file. Sequential fuel injection systems also need to be properly defined in order to get

The single tooth on this distributor shaft is sufficient to provide the ECU with a reference between the intake and power strokes of the crankshaft. This makes sure that fuel is delivered at the proper time in a sequential injection system.

This Ford distributor shaft has multiple teeth so that it can act as both a cam and crank position sensor, but with lower resolution than most newer systems.

INITIAL SETUP

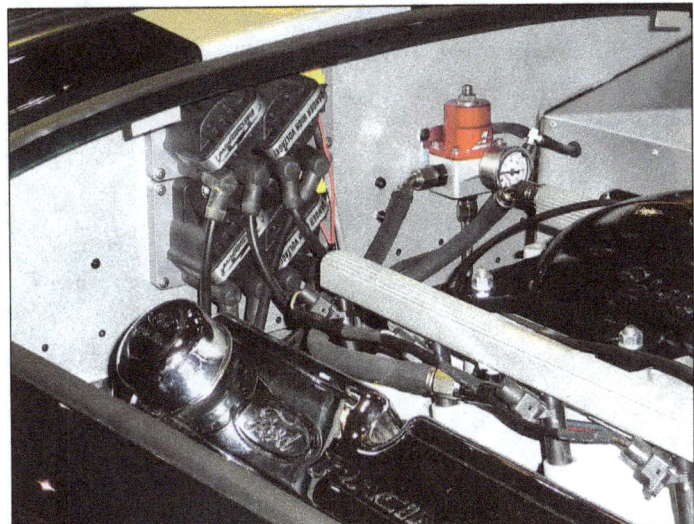

This Electromotive system uses two pairs of coil packs that are remotely mounted on the firewall. Each pack is wired to a pair of cylinders that are 360 degrees out of phase and fired at each TDC event.

Verifying delivered ignition timing is a critical step in the setup of any EFI system. Here, Dave from Nelson's Performance is using a dialback timing light to determine the exact offset angle of this system.

the desired evaporation characteristics with respect to valve opening events.

Once ignition triggers and output are clearly defined, we can begin to look at actual fuel delivery. Before defining flow rates of the injectors, fuel pressure must first be verified. Injector flow rate is heavily dependent upon rail pressure as evidenced by the Bernoulli equation earlier. Before typing in the flow rate of your injectors, check the pressure to verify that those 30 lb/hr injectors really are going to flow 30 pounds per hour. Adjust fuel pressure as necessary to achieve the injectors' rated pressure or recalculate the new flow rate if some other pressure is intentionally being used.

Injector offset should also be entered at this point. If the ECU does not support entry of the complete offset versus voltage curve, the value for offset at nominal charging voltage should be used, typically 13.6 to 14.0 volts.

A good-quality mechanical gauge is the best tool for setting fuel rail pressure. This system is being set to a nominal value of 40 psi with the vacuum port disconnected to match the fuel injectors' ratings.

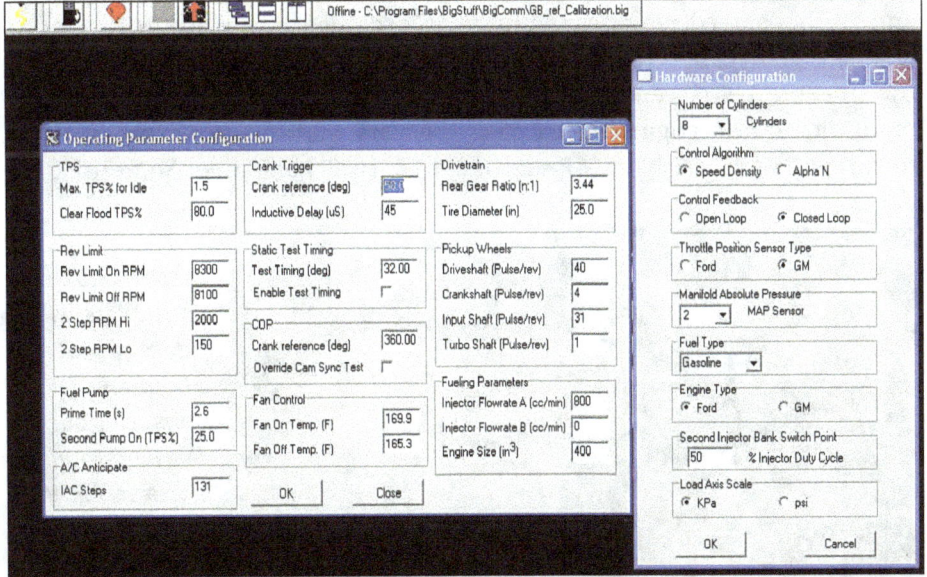

The BigStuff3 standalone system allows the user to change the fundamental setup to accomodate just about any crankshaft trigger, MAP sensor, or ignition system on the market today. Engine size and number of cylinders are also configurable so that actual airmass estimation is possible using the math from Chapter 4.

DESIGNING AND TUNING HIGH-PERFORMANCE FUEL INJECTION SYSTEMS

CHAPTER 9

Electric fuel pumps are driven by relays connected to ECU triggers. Some ECUs allow the user to trigger a second fuel pump based on TPS or MAP values to support higher flow without excess fuel heating at idle and cruise.

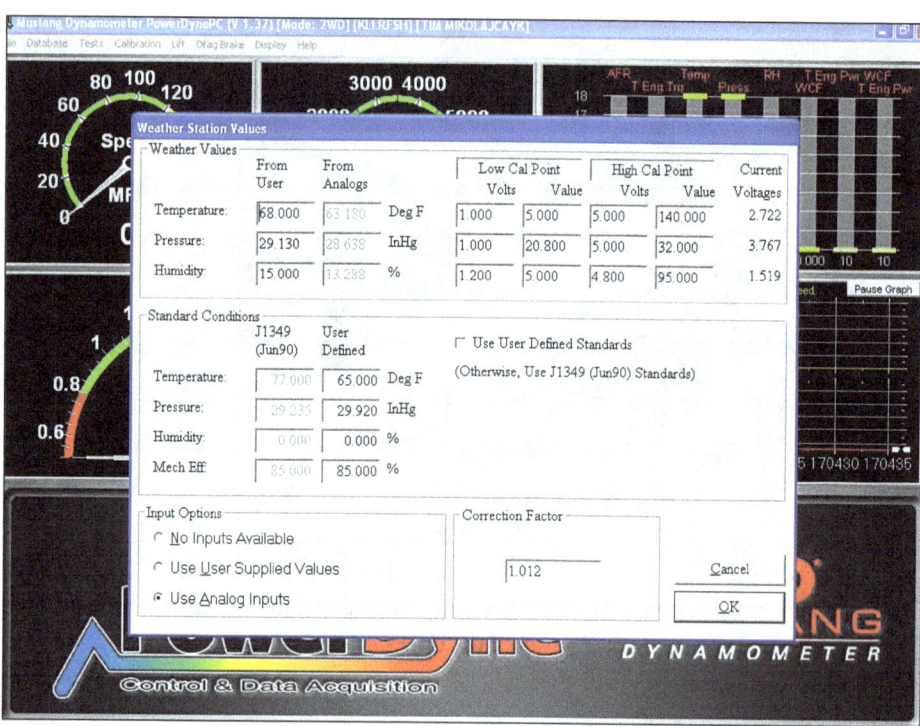

Just as important as vehicle setup is the calibration of the tools used for measurement. The weather correction factors shown here will help make sure that the data collected during this session can be compared to almost any other run later.

The initial setup phase should also include a cursory check of all other sensor inputs. Most prominently, the MAP sensor selection should be verified. Again, most standalone controllers will support a wide variety of MAP sensor options. Most naturally aspirated engines will simply use a 1 bar MAP sensor because they never need to measure beyond atmospheric pressure. Super and turbocharged engines require a sensor that can actually measure the pressure being generated in the manifold. If the engine is planned to run at 20 psi, a 2 bar MAP sensor is not sufficient and should not be used. If the input range of any sensor is exceeded, there is little hope of getting fuel charge calculations correct. Be cautious of some newer MAP sensors that are not simply in the 1, 2, or 3 bar range. Some of these are 2.4 or 2.6 bar sensors and have an output just different enough to operate poorly but continue running when an even-increment sensor configuration is used. Double-check the part number and manufacturer of the MAP sensor to confirm that the proper settings are used in the ECU.

Another important input to the airmass calculation is the engine displacement and number of cylinders. Chapter 3 showed how the ECU goes from measured manifold pressure and engine speed to cylinder airmass. A key part of those equations was the displacement of the cylinders. The ECU will have either a cylinder size variable that must be entered or both total engine size and number of cylinders. This is the time to input these values and not change them again during the calibration process.

Most standalone controllers will adapt to just about any TPS sensor through a learning routine accessed in the setup menus. This BigStuff3 application uses a Ford TPS sensor with a GM weatherpack connector.

72   DESIGNING AND TUNING HIGH-PERFORMANCE FUEL INJECTION SYSTEMS

CHAPTER 10

CREATING A VE TABLE FROM SCRATCH

Once the framework of the calibration has been established by properly setting up the sensor inputs, firing order, and injector constants, we can move along to what is arguably the most important table in the whole ECU calibration. The volumetric efficiency (VE) table is the ECU's reference for pumping efficiency across all engine speed and manifold pressure conditions. Adjustments to this table have an effect upon almost every other aspect of ECU and engine operation, so it is imperative that this table is calibrated in the most accurate way possible. As discussed earlier in chapter three, the volumetric efficiency value taken from this table is used to infer an effective working cylinder volume that is in turn used to calculate the current cylinder airmass. Although VE is not the only variable in the airmass calculation, it is one of the most dominant. Volumetric efficiency is a direct multiplier upon calculated airmass, so a 10% change in VE yields a 10% change in calculated airmass.

Collecting the data to populate the VE table is a tedious process. When working with a complete engine and wideband to solve for VE, there are several serious concerns. First, one must understand that there is a very strong assumption of accuracy in fuel delivery. When adjusting VE based on measured lambda error, we are basically saying that all of the delivered error in air/fuel ratio is a result of improper airmass estimation. In doing so, we rely upon the fuel injector to act as a metering device. Here is where we begin to realize just how important it was to be as precise as possible when modeling the fuel injectors' physical behavior in the ECU calibration. If the actual amount of fuel flowing through the injectors differs from what the ECU model shows, an error is introduced into the system. Left uncorrected, this error would get "baked in" to the VE table corrections. This error is usually most apparent at the low injection times associated with idle and light cruising conditions where some larger flow rate injectors have

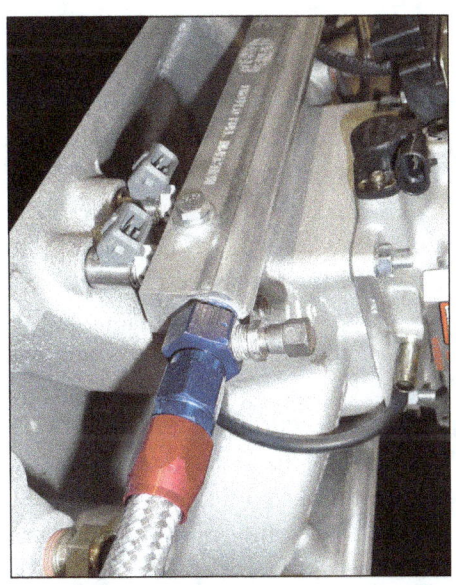

Before attempting to use a wideband to calculate corrections to an airflow model like the VE table, it is important to ensure that the injector characteristics are correct within the ECU. This also means verifying and carefully setting the fuel rail pressure to avoid errors due to the Bernoulli effect.

not yet reached the linear portion of their flow curves. The bigger the injector, the more likely this is to matter since their breakpoints

CHAPTER 10

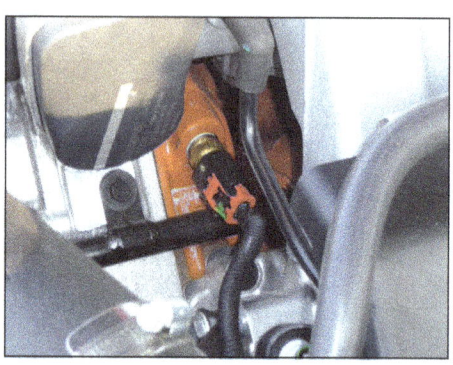

Monitoring engine coolant temperature is key during the population of the VE table. There are separate correction tables that can be used for extreme temperature compensation, so the VE table should be corrected only under normal operating conditions.

before reaching steady flow tend to be numerically higher in terms of fuel mass. Just as important is to make sure that the linear flow rate of the injector really is in line with ECU expectations. Remember that something as simple as a change in expected fuel pressure can lead to a whole series of incorrect calculations here. One can rapidly see where the earlier efforts to accurately describe injector function to the ECU make the job of calculating VE easier, regardless of fuel flow.

The second serious concern when working on a VE table calibration is consistency. Most notably, this means taking the data under the same conditions for all points in the map. The physics equations shown earlier that take us from PV=nRT to cylinder airmass are just as dependent upon temperature as they are upon volume. The 1/T function can skew the calculated airmass significantly if it changes during the course of testing. Since we are actually solving for relative volume in this case, it becomes necessary to hold temperatures as close to constant as possible. This means keeping a careful eye on both intake air temperatures and engine coolant temperatures. The actual temperature in question is the gas entering the cylinder, which is a function of both inlet temperatures and any heating or cooling that happens to the gases as they go through the intake manifold and cylinder head ports. If the engine is at normal operating temperature, the air entering the cylinders is almost certainly heated by some amount after it passes the throttle body. More sophisticated ECUs will even have a whole series of tables to describe the amount of aircharge heating as a function of engine coolant temperature and MAF rates. For simplicity, it's best to just plan on starting your VE table measurements and adjustments with everything at a "normal" temperature. In practice, this means letting the coolant and the rest of the engine get up to normal operating temperatures before attempting to adjust the VE table. This minimizes the impact of the temperature influence on our adjustments. You can come back later and modify the temperature-based compensation if needed for a cold engine.

So where does one start with VE table population? The values need to come from somewhere. The easiest starting point is another calibration for a similar engine that is known to operate well. If someone else has already done the homework here, it's a good idea to copy it in order to get a running start at what can be a very daunting task. Most popular engines have already been calibrated somewhere before, it's just a matter of digging a little to find an example. In many cases, the manufacturer of the ECU may have a selection of reference files from which to start. Even if you are not using that exact hardware combination, one of these files can at least give you something to work from as you make the first attempts at quantifying volumetric efficiency.

If you decide to start with an existing VE table, don't feel tied to the axis breakpoints or values shown. Remember that the key function of the VE table is to represent the physical pumping efficiency of this particular engine. Changes as subtle as muffler design, air filter housing, or header length can have significant effects upon the VE table in multiple places. Don't be afraid to move RPM breakpoints on the table if it is an option on your particular controller. The reference engine may have idled at 900 rpm, but a milder camshaft in your application may allow you to settle to 650 rpm. If this is the case, you will certainly want breakpoints in the VE table directly on, as well as just above and below, your final target idle speed. This will afford the ECU more precision in calculating the cylinder airmass during one of the most critical and customer-sensitive engine functions. You don't want a rolling idle to be exaggerated by inaccurate airmass calculations that could be prevented by increasing the table precision here. It is preferred to have breakpoints within no more than 200 rpm on either side of the warmed-up idle speed to give the best results.

On a similar note, make sure that the top values of speed in the VE table align with the expected RPM range of the engine. There is no use in having a VE table that extends to 9,000 rpm if the camshaft is only expected to perform up to 6,500 rpm. These extra cells of table resolution are better used at lower speeds where the pumping efficiency is more likely to change with speed. If, for some reason, the maximum engine speed in the VE table is exceeded, most ECUs will take the last value seen at the table maximum and continue using it until the engine returns to the table's prescribed range. As long as the final engine speed breakpoint was beyond the torque peak of the engine, the result is usually only an overestimation of cylinder airmass and a rich fuel condition. This is definitely better than underestimating airmass (which would lead to a lean fuel condition at high speed), but is still not desirable. In short, make sure that the ECU tables match the engine hardware's capabilities.

Remember what you just read about engine speed range in the VE table? The same goes for manifold pressure. Engines with large-duration camshafts will not typically have a very strong idle or cruising vacuum. As such, there is really no need to provide a whole array of MAP breakpoints below idle vacuum if the engine simply can't get there. This resolution is once again better spent above idle MAP points where more precision can be given to tip-in conditions that are very sensitive to the driver. If the engine is boosted, it is absolutely critical that the VE table include breakpoints above 100 kPa to calculate the proper cylinder airmass. If the engine runs more than 14 psi of boost, the same holds true for exceeding the 2 bar MAP limit of 200 kPa. Just like with RPM, the ECU has no choice but to use the last known value for VE if measured MAP goes above the last breakpoint in the table. The potential results here are more concerning than just going beyond an engine speed breakpoint since adding boost typically increases relative airmass and any air/fuel errors at this level can be very costly.

If you simply don't have any reference calibrations available to look at and copy, you're in for a slightly more challenging time while calibrating. This doesn't make it impossible by any stretch, just a bit more time consuming. In an absolute-worst-case scenario, the entire VE table would start out populated by the same number in every single cell, perhaps around 60% to begin. We know that the finished table will be anything but constant, but you have to start somewhere.

With some sort of values entered into the volumetric efficiency, an attempt can be made to run the engine. To begin, we will set the desired air/fuel ratio to a constant value across all speeds and loads. This will make the calibrator's life much easier since he is no longer trying to hit a moving target. Stoichiometric operation should be the goal to begin, so set the entire table to lambda=1.00 or approximately 14.64:1 for gasoline. By doing this, the delivered lambda measurement from the wideband will represent the exact correction factor we need to apply to the VE table value in question. In the beginning, we will only be checking moderate loads, below 100 kPa, so no significant fuel enrichment is required. Later on, we can change the target air/fuel ratio for full load to a richer setting.

When the engine is first started, initial operation may be quite rough and unpredictable. If this is the case, the best course of action is to apply enough throttle to hold the engine at a higher speed. Approximately 2,000 rpm is usually sufficient to avoid stalling and help get the engine up to operating temperature quicker. Idle is actually very difficult

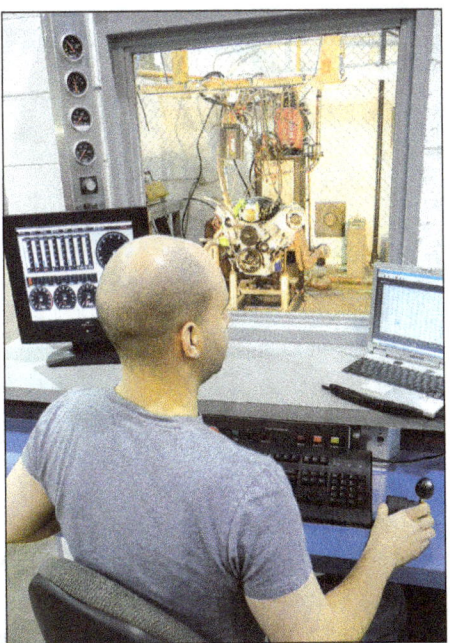

The engine dyno is the best tool for developing a VE table because the operator can simply dial-in whatever combination of engine speed and load he desires. Large cooling systems allow the engine to operate for long durations under conditions that would otherwise overheat a conventional radiator or vehicle cooling system.

for an engine to do properly and requires a fair amount of coordination between aircharge estimation, fuel delivery, and spark advance to hit a moving target while warming up. By skipping this step completely for the time being, one can focus on the easier task of quantifying part load VE where the engine is far more forgiving of delivered air/fuel ratios and timing changes. In reality, most engines will at least continue to operate at light loads and moderate speed even if the delivered air/fuel ratio is as rich as lambda=0.61 (9.0:1 AFR) or as lean as lambda=1.36 (20:1 AFR).

If, during the initial checkout, a wideband reading of extremely rich or lean is consistently seen, it's a

CHAPTER 10

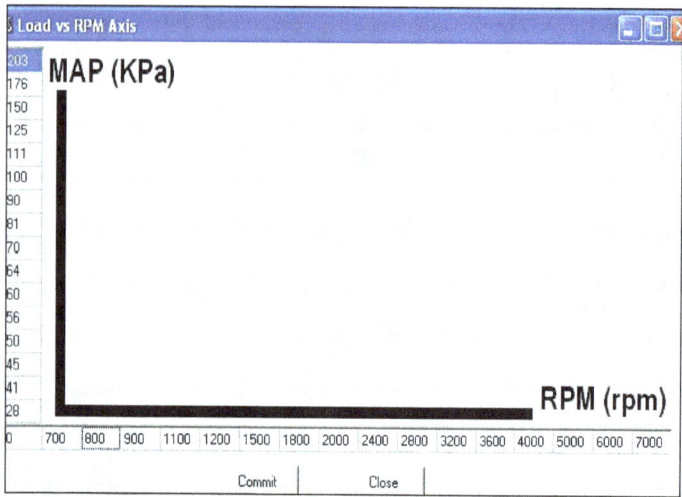

Carefully choosing the breakpoints for the VE table before starting can make the final calibration much more robust. Having more resolution at low speeds gives better idle control and tip-in behavior while upper RPM points can be spaced farther apart without much compromise.

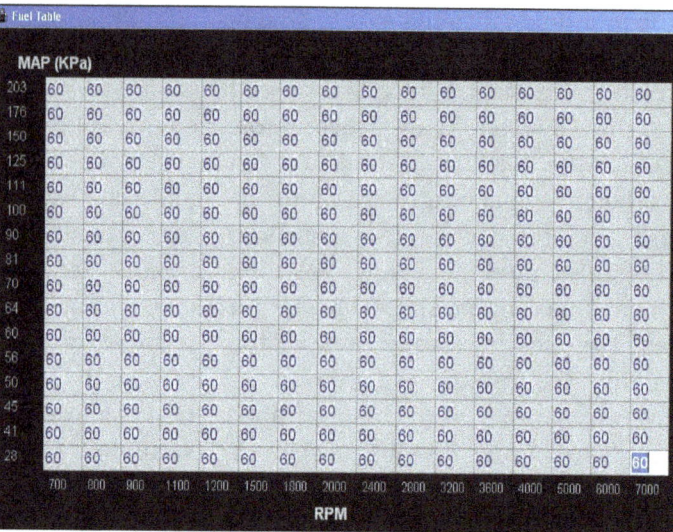

If you're building a VE table from scratch you have to start somewhere. A constant value is set just to get the engine running long enough to gather some data at part throttle and make some calculated corrections.

good idea to make a global change to the entire VE table as long as there are no other mechanical problems such as air leaks or fuel delivery issues. Don't be afraid to make what appear to be very large changes here. It's not uncommon to need to make 30% or greater shifts when first tuning a new combination. In these preliminary steps, the changes are applied to the entire VE map since it is often difficult to tell exactly which cells are being used to calculate the current volumetric efficiency and airmass. Chances are, whatever physical changes to the engine that require a local change in VE, also require similar changes at higher speeds and loads. You will still get a chance to fine tune individual cells later if this first global shift proves too aggressive.

Getting Moving on the Dyno

At this point, the dynamometer should be configured to perform a constant speed test. Ideally it would be set to control to engine RPM, but a constant wheel speed test will also work. Vehicles with a manual transmission are easier to operate on a chassis dynamometer for this testing since they have a single fixed ratio between engine and wheel speed for each gear. Just pick a gear and drive the vehicle under moderate load on the dyno and allow the load absorber to control speed. Third or fourth gear usually works best since there is less gear multiplication and a more direct connection between the engine and driveshaft speeds. You will see that it's easy to move between VE table load cells by simply moving the gas pedal. Applying more throttle angle will increase MAP and move vertically within the table at the same engine speed.

With an automatic, it can be a little trickier to control. Below the stall speed of the torque converter, you have a variable slip rate that can make engine speed difficult for the dynamometer to control. If the vehicle is equipped with a lockup torque converter, now would be the time to engage it, once the wheels are moving. Again, third gear usually works well here. If the vehicle does not have a lockup torque converter, steady state high-load test data cannot really be gathered below the stall RPM of the torque converter. Concentrate first on the areas of the map that can be logged in steady state before dropping down to these lower load points. You will often find that adjustments made at a single engine speed can be applied as a percent all the way down to minimum MAP.

The first task is to begin correcting the VE able at a single moderate engine speed. With the dynamometer controls set up to hold a constant speed of approximately 2,000 rpm, use your right foot to maintain a stable load. Also make sure that the engine coolant and air inlet temperatures have stabilized. This is extremely important since aircharge temperature has a significant influence upon calculated airmass. You do not want to perform corrections to the VE table based on varying charge temperatures, so try to keep these temperatures as consistent as possible throughout this exercise. Once both MAP and measured lambda are stable, you are ready to take a valid measurement. Take note of any error in delivered lambda. Since your target is lambda=1.00, a displayed ratio of anything else represents the exact correction factor that should be applied to (multiplied by) the existing VE value in the table.

In a perfect world, individual measurements would be taken at each cell in the VE table. This can prove very time consuming, only to get an initial string of test data that all indicate very similar errors or follow the same trends. To improve the speed of this exercise, it's possible to take the corrections seen in part of the VE table and apply them to others. Starting at 2,000 rpm and a moderate load of 60 kPa or so, global changes can be made as before in the initial checkout. Moving up in load to perhaps 70 kPa, the changes applied in the 2,000 rpm column can also be applied as a percentage to all speeds at the same 70 kPa load and above. This makes the assumption that if the engine's pumping efficiency is slightly better (or worse) at 70 kPa, it will continue to be better (or worse) as manifold pressure is increased. Again at 80 kPa, the correction is applied to all speeds at loads of 80 kPa and above. This process can be repeated going downward in measured MAP as well, where corrections found at 50 kPa are applied across all speeds for loads of 50 kPa and below. Again at 40 kPa (if possible, depending on your camshaft selection) the changes are carried downward across all engine speeds as a percentage.

Even at this moderate speed, you may not be able to go all the way up to 100 kPa load on the engine in steady state without fear of knock or high temperatures. Don't worry, we'll come back to this later after filling in more of the VE table. For the time being, just go as high as you are comfortable taking the engine with a stoichiometric mixture in steady state.

If, at any point during the volumetric efficiency mapping, spark knock is heard, it must be addressed. Do not continue to operate at a knocking condition for extended periods as engine damage may result. Whenever knock is detected during this exercise, return to the spark advance table and remove timing locally until no further knock is present. Mild knock may only take 2 to 3 degrees to remedy, but don't be afraid to take more for the time being. You can always add it back in later, after the fueling is dialed-in.

By applying the percent changes seen near 2,000 rpm across all speeds for the same load, the general trend of the engine's pumping efficiency is more quickly established. After the first corrections are applied at 2,000 rpm, it's time to move to another speed. Next up should be a slightly higher speed of perhaps

Knowing what fuel is in the tank is critical before diving into the ECU calibration. If you're buying racing fuel, it's a good idea to check with your supplier to find out the fuel properties before tuning to an incorrectly assumed stoichiometric air/fuel ratio.

Setting a constant target of lambda=1.00 (14.6:1 for gasoline) makes the math easier as you begin calculating individual corrections in the VE table cells. A stoichiometric target means that the instantaneous lambda equals the current correction factor and greatly speeds up the calibration process at part load.

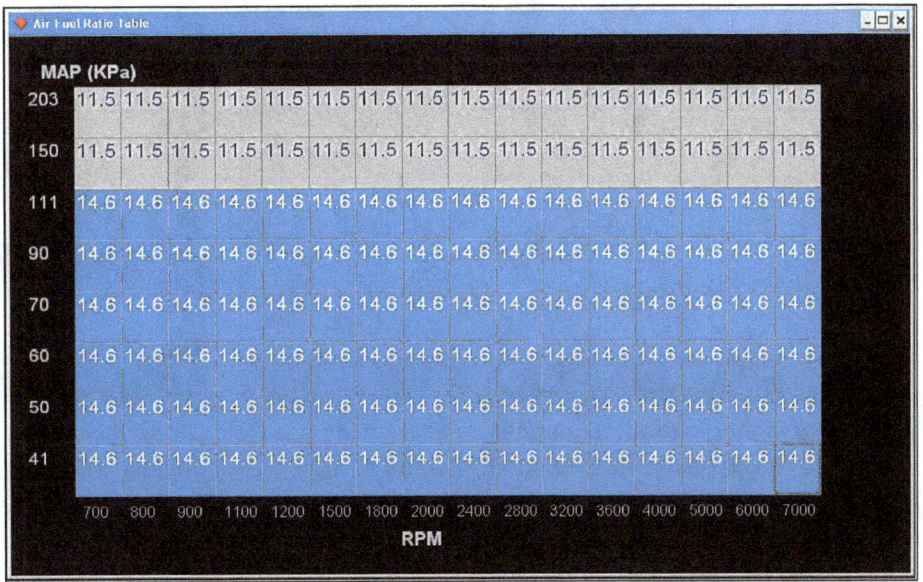

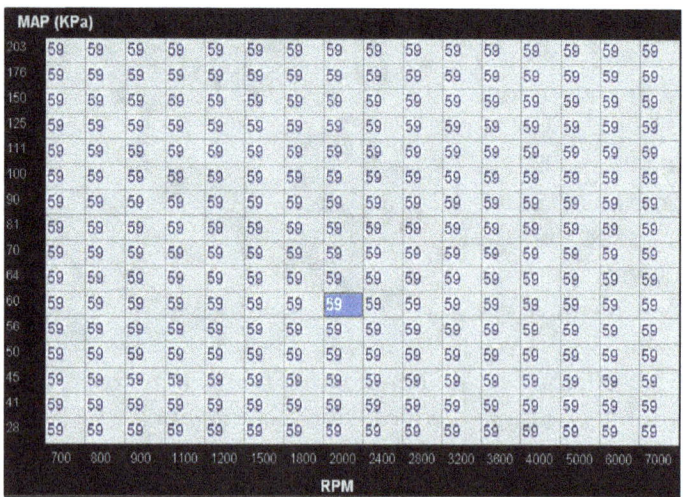

If the engine stabilizes to a delivered lambda of 0.98, this value is used as the correction factor for the entire table for this first adjustment. Multiplying the previous volumetric efficiency value of 60 by the 0.98 correction factor rounds to a new table value of 59 that is used everywhere initially.

Moving to a higher load/kPa value, the delivered lambda was noted to be about 1.07 in steady state. A 107% correction is then made to all speeds and loads ≥ 70 kPa, resulting in a new value of 63% VE.

2,400 rpm or so. Your breakpoints don't have to be exactly 2,000 and 2,400 rpm, just consider these examples for the time being. Even if you started with a completely flat VE table before making the corrections at 2,000 rpm, you should now have some form of linear or curved trend for VE against MAP. The only thing that has really changed now is valve excitation frequency as a result of engine speed. Depending on the cam and intake combination, you may now see slightly higher filling efficiency at 2,400 rpm than was seen at 2,000 rpm. Begin by once again taking a stable reading of lambda error at a moderate load. Apply this correction to the entire column of 2,400-rpm VE points as well as the rest of the VE table for speeds above

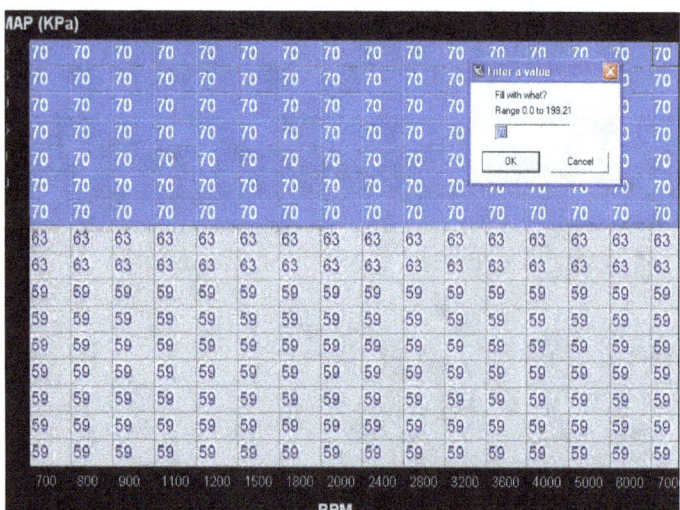

Again at a higher load value another measurement is taken showing a delivered lambda=1.11 at 90 kPa. This 11% increase over the previous value of 63 rounds to an even 70 at this load; and it's applied across all RPM breakpoints.

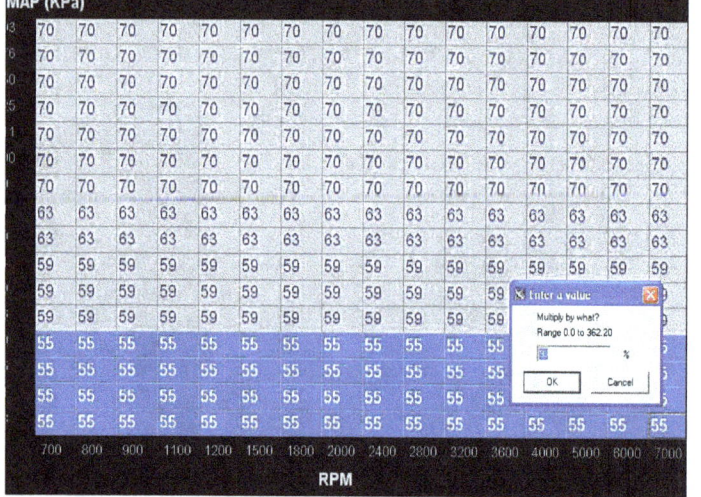

Dropping throttle position to a lower load, we see that delivered lambda went rich to an indicated lambda=0.93, so an appropriate correction is made to all low load values. We are now beginning to see the effect of throttle angle and MAP on engine pumping efficiency.

2,400 rpm. After all, if pumping efficiency improved by 8% at 2,400 rpm, it can also be expected to improve somewhat at 2,800, 3,600, and 5,000 rpm too, right? The object here is to minimize the corrections you will need to apply later when you finally get to these higher speeds. Then the engine will follow trends and this is one of them. Reducing the time spent at high speeds during calibration also reduces wear on the engine and heat buildup.

After the moderate load correction for 2,400 rpm is found and applied to everything from 2,400 rpm up, you can get more specific. Increase load again by applying throttle angle and check for error at slightly higher loads. Remember that these corrections should be applied to the "cor-

Linear MAP-MAF relationship

This first exercise is generating the fundamental relationship between MAP and airmass for a constant engine speed and temperature. If the VE and airmass (MAF) are plotted against MAP for a single engine speed, we can see an interesting relationship. Figure 10-1 shows this relationship for a sample engine. Notice that there is a straight-line relationship between VE and MAP over much of the measured MAP range. This is not an accident. At a given frequency of valve opening (engine speed), the intake port acts as a fixed pipe that simply flows more or less air in direct proportion to the pressure differential across it. One end is the cylinder at a predictable low pressure and the other is attached to the intake manifold plenum where pressure is measured by the MAP sensor. It stands to reason that the harder the intake manifold pressure is pushing upon the air column in the port, the more flow is realized to the cylinder at the other end. Certainly port tuning has an influence on this, but that is largely tied to intake runner length, volume, and excitation timing of the intake valve from the camshaft. Runner length and volume are fixed, but intake valve event timing is tied to engine speed. So for a single speed point, the relationship between manifold pressure and cylinder filling becomes much more predictable.

In engine calibration, one can use the predictable MAP-MAF relationship to help speed up the process of calibrating the VE table. Not every point along the straight line needs to be collected. We only really need to define the slope of the line and the bounds along which it exists. Points in the middle of the straight line can be interpolated fairly accurately. Below this, it is important to describe the non-linear behavior under high vacuum in order to better estimate aircharge at low loads. Some OEM speed density systems actually use the linear correlation exclusively for airmass estimation. Chances are that if the theory

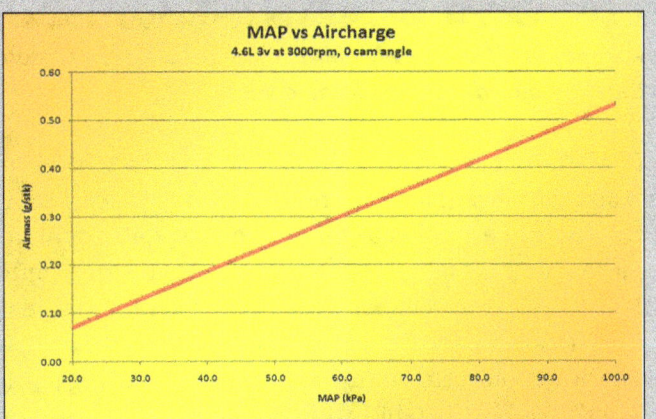

Fig. 10-1 The Ford EFI controllers use a linear MAF estimation based on a simple slope and offset from MAP equation at each RPM breakpoint for backup calculations. The result of these variables at 3,000 rpm and zero cam retard for a 4.6L 3v engine are seen here.

works well enough for these systems to pass the stringent emissions requirements today, they can be applied to the average street rod or racecar with some measure of success.

A properly tuned VE table will almost always show this linear relationship as VE values increase predictably with MAP. Common sense tells us that if the manifold pressure is increasing, the cylinder filling should also increase. Unfortunately, some less-experienced tuners miss this key concept and generate VE tables that have spots where VE is either constant or actually decreasing as MAP values increase at the same engine speed. The fundamental cause of this is usually sloppy data collection, but a common sense check should alert the tuner to the fact that this is not probable. Using the linear estimation will prevent the "roller coaster" volumetric efficiency plots that are commonly seen from less-experienced tuners.

CHAPTER 10

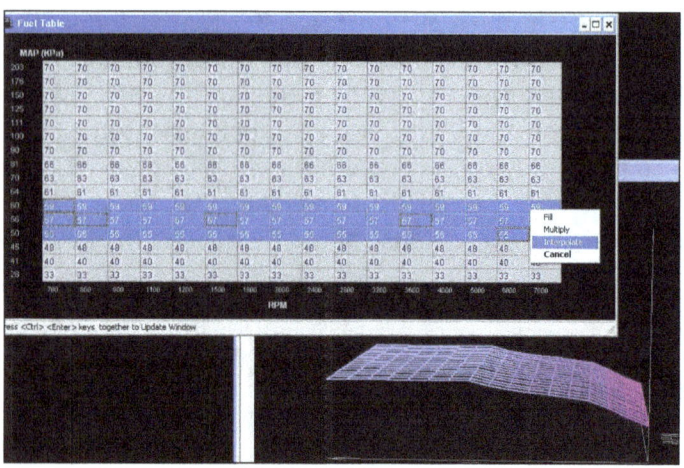

Using the software's interpolate function, it's easy to fill in the cells between the first sets of corrections. The 3D map viewed from the side now shows the charateristic quasi-linear increase in volumetric efficiency with MAP. (The flat boosted region has not yet been extrapolated or directly calibrated yet.)

ner" of the table bounded by 2,400 rpm and the current load. Increases or decreases can be applied to this entire corner of the VE table as a percent. This process is repeated for increasing load points at the same 2,400 rpm for an incrementally smaller "corner" of the VE table with each change. You will find that the earlier horizontal scaling found at 2,000 rpm has left you with less work to do here as load is increased at 2,400 rpm. The changes being applied for each smaller size "corner" of the table become smaller as you go. This is further evidence that we're getting closer to the proper VE surface shape and values as the tuning process continues. If possible, continue this process at 2,400 rpm to as high of a load as you are comfortable running near the nominal temperatures. The same holds true for decreasing loads below our starting point at 2,400 rpm. If you began measurements at 2,400 rpm at 60 kPa, you can now slowly back off the throttle to decrease load to begin mapping the bottom "corner" of the VE table. The same percent-based changes can be applied to the entire corner as you work.

Now that engine VE has been mapped at a couple different speeds in the midrange, we begin to see the general trend to the pumping efficiency of this particular hardware combination. Next up is yet another higher speed point, perhaps around 2,800 or 3,000 rpm. The same process is repeated here, starting from a moderate load point of maybe 60 to 70 kPa. Again, the entire column of load points at this speed can be quickly adjusted based on delivered lambda for this first point. Slowly work cell by cell upward in load, making corrections to the upper "corner" of the table as you go. Remember that you don't have to go all the way to 100 kPa just yet if you aren't comfortable with it. You can do that later. After the upper "corner" has been adjusted, repeat the process for the lower load "corner."

Notice that at the higher engine speeds, heat builds quickly in both engine coolant and air charge temperature. Keep a careful eye upon both of these as you work to avoid potential damage to components as well as changing air density during this reference work. It's better to back off for a minute or two and allow the radiator and dyno fans to work than to continue mapping pumping efficiency against changing air density. You want to minimize the variables during the testing process and charge temperature is a big one. The faster the engine speed, the more serious of a concern this becomes. At higher engine speeds, above 3,000 rpm or so, most automotive cooling systems will be seriously taxed by steady state chassis dyno work. Slowly collecting good data here is far more rewarding than quickly collecting questionable data.

Ideally, the high-speed VE mapping is continued all the way to redline. In practice this isn't always possible due to temperature concerns. This is why the "corner" correction

The best of both worlds, gorgeous 1960s sheetmetal surrounding a modern, powerful fuel injected powerplant. The engine in this Camaro spent some quality time on the dyno dialing-in the ECU calibration before being installed so the owner only has to worry about adding gas and driving now.

80 DESIGNING AND TUNING HIGH-PERFORMANCE FUEL INJECTION SYSTEMS

CREATING A VE TABLE FROM SCRATCH

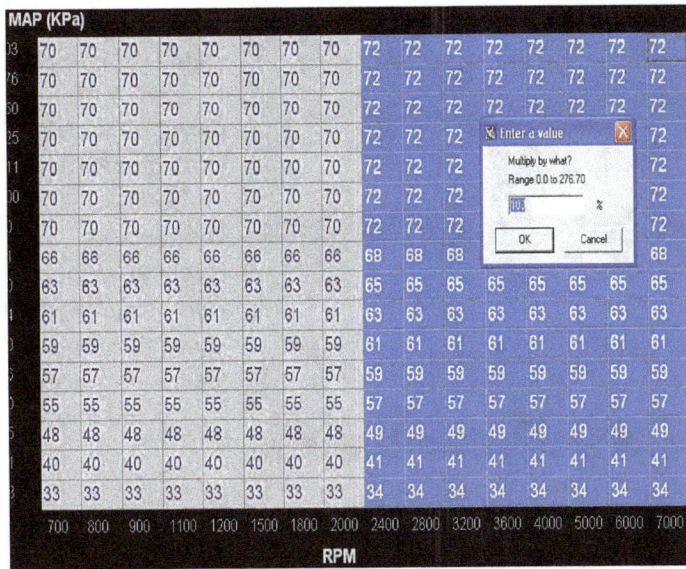

After dialing in the 2,000 rpm behavior, engine speed is allowed to increase to 2,400 rpm on the dyno and a new initial lambda measurement is taken at 60 kPa. A steady state reading of lambda=1.03 is used to correct all values ≥ 2,400 rpm in this example.

method is so effective. The corner method takes what we have learned at lower speeds and applies the trend to higher speeds. Since the engine is a mechanical pump, it can be expected that its efficiency follows some sort of predictable trend. Even if we can't collect data at every single point, we can at least extrapolate to get a good anticipation of what the data will probably look like. Generally speaking, you will find that the VE values will increase with speed all the way to the RPM where the engine makes peak torque. Beyond that speed, you will see that VE gradually rolls off with increasing speed. Keep this in mind as you work on mapping the higher speed points of the table.

Working Downward

Once the higher speeds have been mapped sufficiently, we can begin working back down toward idle. We may not be able to go all the way down to our target idle speed just yet since the lowest point we've done is only 2,000 rpm. Below this speed, we may find that volumetric efficiency drops in a nonlinear fashion with respect to speed.

Let's begin by checking a speed only slightly below our first exercise, perhaps 1,600 rpm. With the vehicle locked into gear and the dyno set to control speed, watch the delivered lambda at a moderate load once again. The delivered lambda error at this moderate load is at first applied to the entire side of the VE table bounded by 1,600 rpm. The final VE values at this lower speed will almost certainly be lower than those at 2,000 rpm because the engine's pumping efficiency generally decreases at lower speeds. After an initial adjustment based on error at moderate load, we can once again begin working on the "corners" of the VE table as load is increased at lower speeds. The dyno will be responsible for keeping the engine speed in check as load

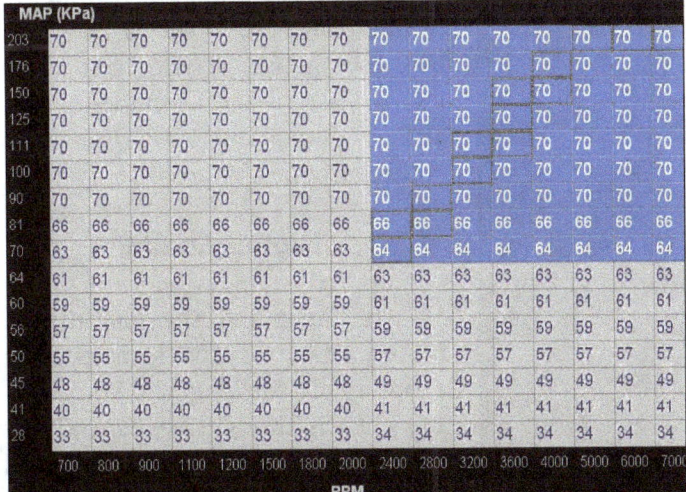

Again at the higher speed, load is increased and another steady state lambda measurement is taken. The new reading of lambda=0.98 is applied as a correction to the remaining "corner" of the VE table.

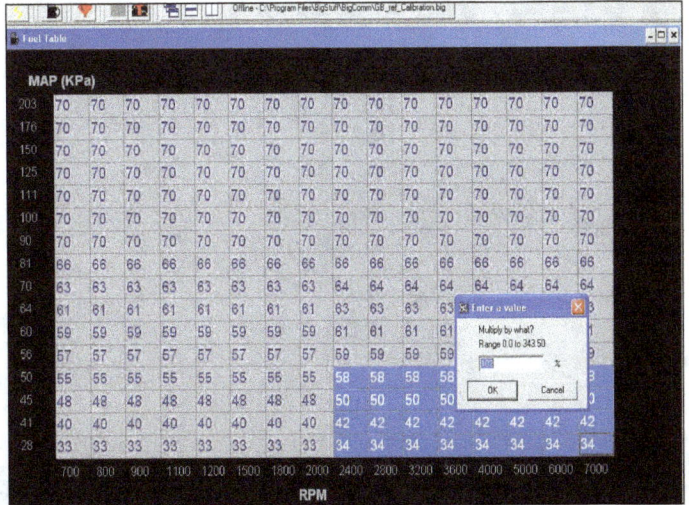

The lower "corner" of the VE table is corrected based on delivered steady state lambda at 2,400 rpm and 50 kPa. Here, a value of lambda=1.02 is used for all speeds ≥ 2,400 rpm and loads ≤ 50 kPa.

DESIGNING AND TUNING HIGH-PERFORMANCE FUEL INJECTION SYSTEMS

is increased. You will find that the general trend of increasing VE with higher MAP is similar at 1,600 rpm to what was seen at 2,000 rpm, with only slight changes percentage wise. The major difference was the speed change that was accounted for in the first measurement at 1,600 rpm. Work toward increasingly higher loads at 1,600 rpm to check each cell for accuracy being careful to listen for spark knock. It's surprisingly easy to get knock during these lugging conditions if you aren't careful. After the high load "corner" is calibrated, move down to the lower load "corner" and repeat the process.

There's a lot of repetition here, but that's the nature of calibrating a VE table. A standard 16x16 table has 256 cells in it, and you can expect to perform this process to at least half of them in many cases. Stick with it, because the more precise you are in mapping the VE table, the less work you'll have to do later when it comes

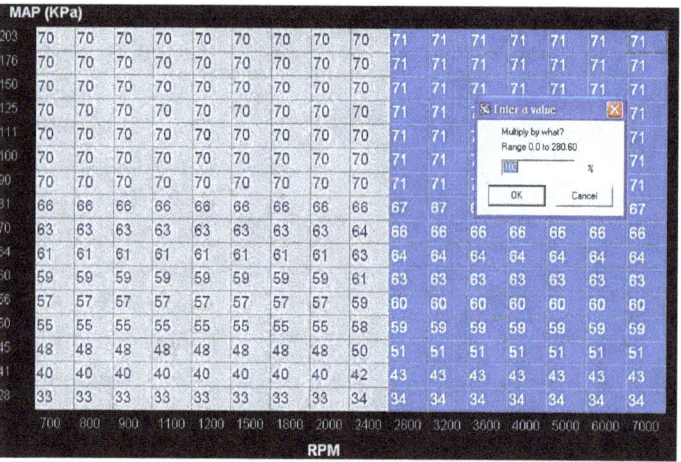

Another 2% increase is needed at 2,800 rpm based on a steady state measurement at 70 kPa. The process is repeated to increasing engine speeds as long as the cooling system is able to keep up.

time to address transient fueling and drivability.

As you complete the process of mapping the volumetric efficiency of the engine at progressively slower speeds, you will see that there is less and less error in the delivered lambda. By the time you get down to 1,000 rpm or so, you should be pretty close to the target air/fuel ratio. This means that when you actually get to idle speed, you are no longer fighting uncontrolled air/fuel ratio problems such as a lean roll or plug fouling from excessive richness. Even better, the ECU now has a pretty good estimate of actual airmass from which to pull the desired idle air control motor flow. Continue the VE mapping to as low of a stable engine speed as possible. Even if the final target idle speed is going to be 800 rpm, it helps to map the VE table about 100 to 200 rpm lower. This will allow the ECU to accurately calculate airmass whenever engine speed is pulled below idle due to clutch lugging or engagement of accessories like the air conditioning compressor or power steering pump at idle. Later on, when we work on the finer points of idle control we can at least say with confidence that airmass estimation and air/fuel ratio control are not the problem.

Higher Loads

After mapping the majority of the VE table, we have learned quite a bit about the engine's characteristics. Even though we haven't yet taken this engine to WOT, a good estimate of the expected performance can be made. By following the linear MAP-MAF trend discussed earlier, VE values at 100 kPa can be extrapolated from the part throttle values in the

At lower engine speeds, the reduced pumping efficiency is shown as a slightly rich condition before corrections. Here, a reading of lambda =0.98 drives a 2% reduction in the VE values for 1,800 rpm and below.

Working to progressively lower engine speeds and loads gets you closer to the idle region. By the time you actually reach the idle cells, the values will end up being very close and the engine is less likely to stall or load up due to fueling issues.

accompanying sidebar at each speed breakpoint. Simply follow this linear trend upward to populate the 100 kPa line and blend smoothly between there and the lower points that were more precisely measured earlier.

With a naturally aspirated engine, you are now ready to prepare for the first WOT test on the dyno. If you are testing a supercharged engine, the first test will only target 100 kPa load. This can be accomplished by either careful modulation of the throttle to avoid boost, or by removing the supercharger drive belt if possible. Turbocharged applications will likely need to stick to careful throttle modulation since some boost creep is usually present even with a fully open wastegate. Since the object is to only run the equivalent of a naturally aspirated engine's performance, a target ratio of lambda≈0.85 can be used for all applications at this load. Set the same target ratio for all engine speeds and all loads from about 90 kPa to 105 kPa. This will help ensure that you are not chasing a moving target for air/fuel ratio when recording.

Make sure that the ignition timing is set very conservatively. You don't want to experience potentially dangerous knock just because the initial VE estimation was slightly low. The purpose here is to solve for proper VE estimation based on measured lambda, not to make the big power number just yet.

Start the run from a relatively low speed, perhaps 1,500 rpm or so in third or fourth gear. Engine dynamometers can be set to a sweep rate of approximately 300 rpm/sec to match what is typically seen on the road under load. Perform the first WOT run with datalogging active to record delivered lambda, MAP, and engine speed. Continue the run as high as possible unless either knock or an excessively lean air/fuel ratio requires you to stop. Go back through the

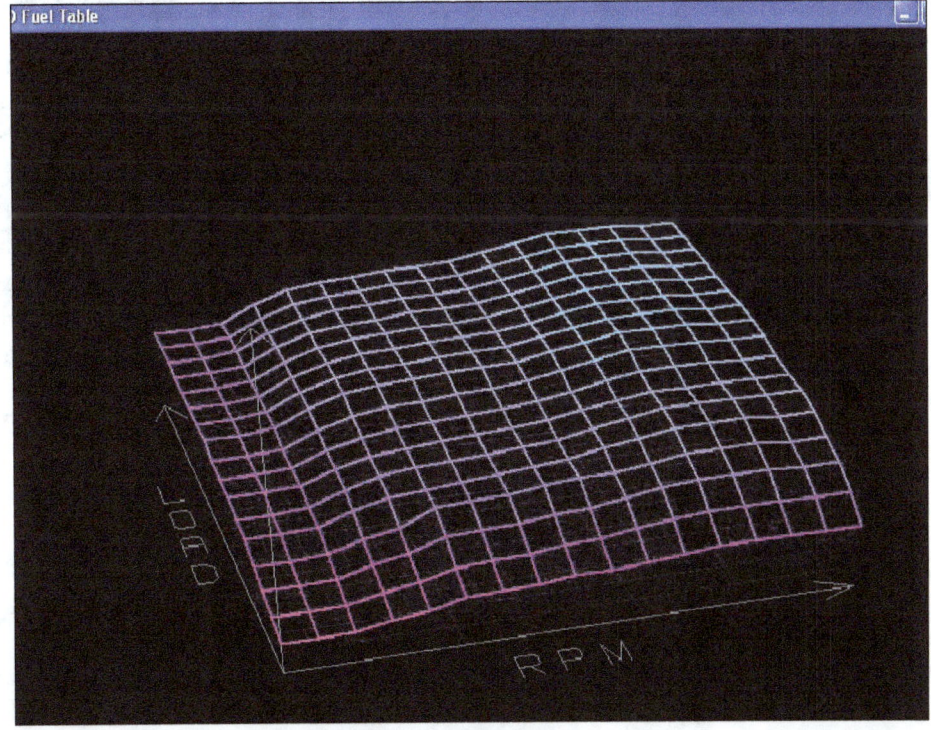

Here's the result of the VE table corrections using the "corner" method for all part-load conditions. Viewed in 3D, the table is smooth and progressive, just like the engine's actual pumping efficiency.

CHAPTER 10

100 kPa Extrapolation Demo

The concept of the linear MAF-MAP relationship is not limited to the vacuum region of engine operation. The boosted region can also be approximated by a straight-line extension of the lower load region, at least as a starting point. If starting from scratch on a supercharged or turbocharged engine calibration, using an extrapolation of the low load data to populate the boosted region's VE values can be a handy tool to reduce overall time spent on the process.

The approximation is started by examining the slope of the VE values at a single engine speed. The slope is found by finding the rise (change in VE) over the run (change in MAP) for the speed column in question. This gives us the following formula:

$$\text{Slope} = \frac{(\Delta VE)}{(\Delta kPa)} = \frac{(VE_2 - VE_1)}{(kPa_2 - kPa_1)}$$

For a pair of points of 0.735 VE at 72 kPa and 0.877 VE at 101 kPa, the slope is calculated as:

$$\text{Slope} = \frac{(0.877 - 0.735)}{(101 - 72)} = \frac{(0.142)}{(29)} \approx \frac{0.0049 \text{ VE}}{kPa}$$

This calculated slope of about 0.5% VE increase per kPa of manifold pressure can be used to solve for a new maximum boost volumetric efficiency estimate. If the engine is set up to make an additional 10 psi (69 kPa) of boost beyond atmospheric levels, then we use this slope to calculate how much higher the volumetric efficiency might go. In our example here, we calculate the increase in VE as:

VE increase = (0.0049 VE / kPa) x (69 kPa) ≈ 0.338 VE

This increase is over and above the volumetric efficiency of the engine at 101 kPa as seen earlier. If we add this theoretical increase of 0.338 to the calculated value of 0.877, we come up with an estimated 1.215 volumetric efficiency. This may not be the actual pumping efficiency seen by the engine at 10 psi of boost for our speed in question, but it gives us a good starting point before we take the engine into uncharted territory under load. Once a single point relatively high in the boosted region has been calculated, most ECUs will have an interpolate function that will fill the cells in between with a straight-line calculation, another real time saver. It may be helpful to set up a quick Excel spreadsheet to calculate the slope at each individual speed breakpoint.

It's better to overestimate the boosted region VE values at first to avoid knock or excess temperatures that may lead to engine damage. You can always lean it out later if the testing shows that this estimate was too rich, even for the safe boosted target ratio. This linear extrapolation is intended to quickly fill in an area of the VE table that can be difficult to reach and has the potential for some expensive damage if done wrong. In the end, the ideal calibration values will be found based on the usual testing where lambda errors are examined on a cell by cell basis within the VE table.

recorded data to compare the delivered lambda to the commanded reference at each table breakpoint. For example, a delivered lambda of 0.91 at one point would require a correction factor of (0.91/0.85) = 1.07 to bring fueling into line. In this case, we saw a delivered air/fuel ratio that was 7% leaner than commanded so the corresponding volumetric efficiency is increased by that same 7% locally to increase the airmass calculation. If the fuel injector characterization was right, the ECU will automatically add 7% more fuel the next time around to go along with the 7% greater airmass calculation. This process is repeated at each breakpoint until the delivered lambda matched the commanded lambda at all speeds up to redline.

Even if the spark advance isn't completely optimized, the engine should still show decent power. This will be fine tuned later.

Boosted Operation

With the engine's volumetric efficiency properly mapped up to and including atmospheric condi-

CREATING A VE TABLE FROM SCRATCH

Before running the WOT test, it's important to choose a new target air/fuel ratio. A value of lambda=0.85 (12.5:1 gasoline) should be a safe target for naturally aspirated engines or boosted engines operating at 100 kPa.

During the WOT testing at atmospheric levels, the recorded data should be analyzed on a cell-by-cell basis along the 100 kPa line (at sea level). Individual corrections can be made to a single cell at a time based on instantaneous lambda error.

tions, boosted operation is next. The lessons learned at lower loads are applied to the boosted region just as they were at 100 kPa. An extrapolation of the linear trend can be applied well into boost. In reality, this will work fairly well at moderate boost levels and most likely overestimate pumping efficiency slightly at elevated boost levels. There are diminishing returns of airmass increase with manifold pressure increases.

In an ideal environment, each boosted cell in the VE table would be mapped in steady state just as with the vacuum cells. An engine dyno can make this task exceptionally more precise as long as proper cooling capacity is available. Steady state boosted testing really isn't practical with engines installed in the vehicle,

since the cooling systems are rarely up to the task. In this case, it is advisable to slowly work upward through the MAP rows by performing WOT sweep tests at progressively higher pressures. After each sweep test, corrections are made to individual points based on delivered lambda error. Any

significant changes are also extrapolated upward to higher pressures at the same engine speed to minimize the error on each following WOT sweep. The process is continued until maximum desired boost is reached and all points are able to deliver the commanded air/fuel ratio.

After the WOT dyno run has been performed, the recorded dyno data can be reviewed in detail. This run showed a delivered lambda=0.792 at 4,500 rpm, which will be used to calculate the necessary VE correction factor based on the target lambda.

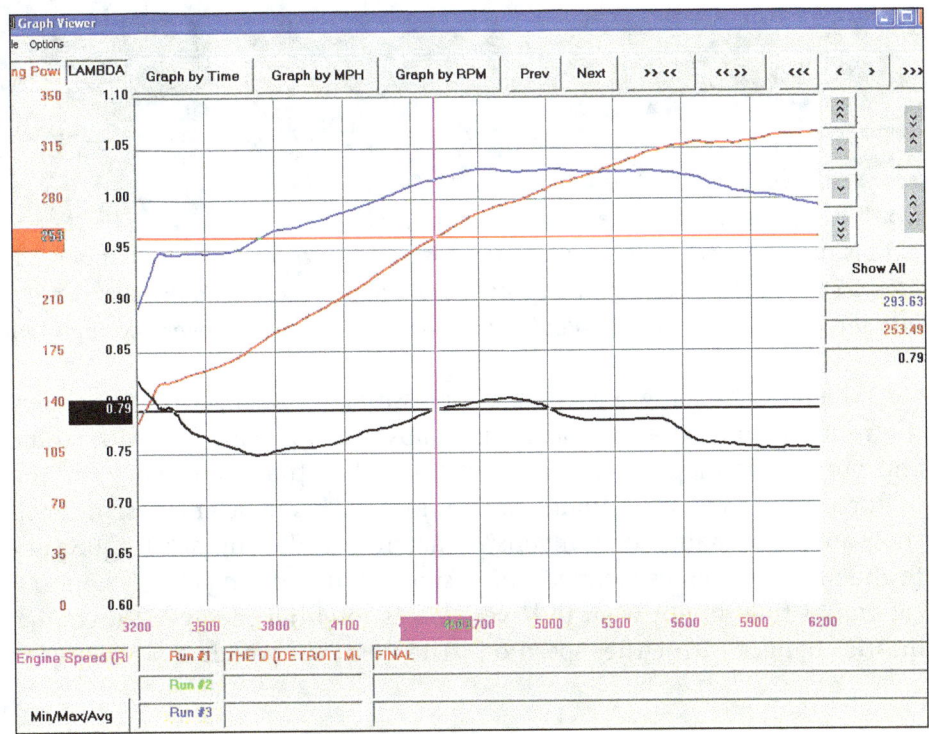

DESIGNING AND TUNING HIGH-PERFORMANCE FUEL INJECTION SYSTEMS

CHAPTER 10

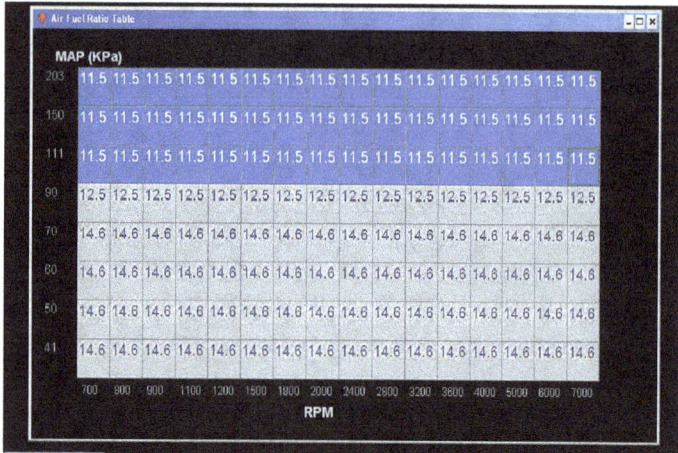

Operating in the boosted region requires some additional fueling to aid in cooling and knock control. A constant target ratio of lambda=0.78 (11.5:1 gasoline) is a good starting point just in case the initial tests are slightly leaner than the target before corrections.

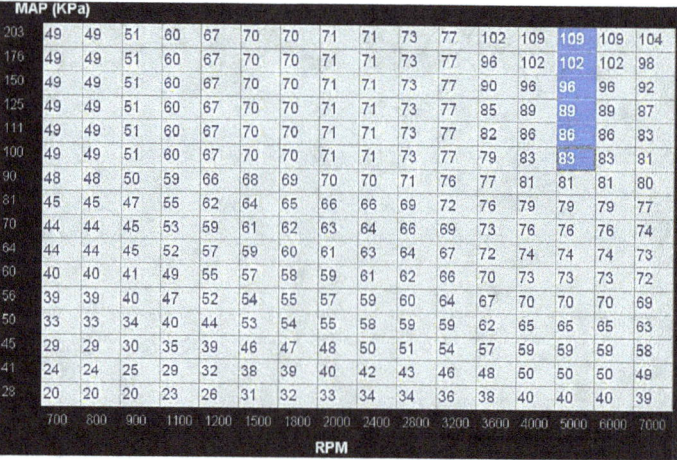

Extrapolating the slope of the VE versus MAP from the lower load region into the boosted region gives the calibration an excellent starting point. In this case, a slope of 0.25% VE per kPa is found between 60 and 100 kPa at 5,000 rpm and used to populate the table all the way up to 203 kPa.

Don't be intimidated by the huge power potential of this 8.3 L supercharged V10. Tuning this car is just like any other. Start in the midrange and slowly work your way into the boosted region to unlock the power.

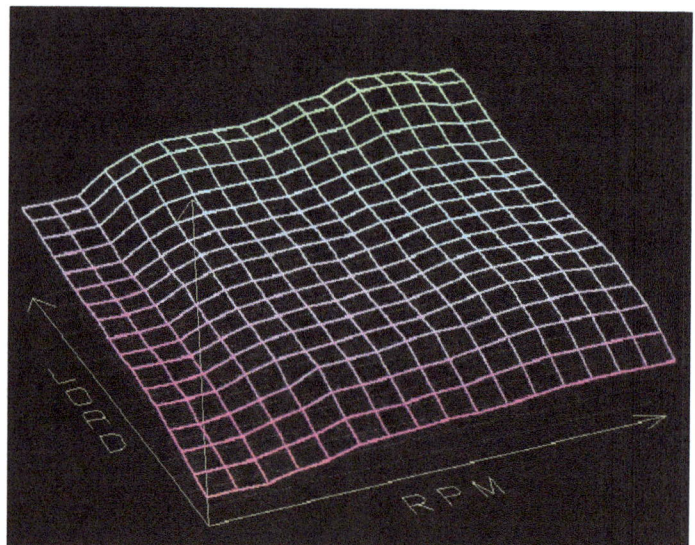

With the boosted region now updated, we get a better look at the engine's complete VE surface. Notice how even the high load region is still smooth and progressive.

When VE mapping is complete, the result should be a very smooth and progressive map. When viewed in three dimensions, it should not show any "mountains" or "canyons" in the middle. Engines are mechanical pumps that do not want to have drastic changes with either speed or pressure. As such, their efficiency maps will be smooth with some "island" of peak efficiency in the middle. This efficiency island will match with the engine's torque peak since cylinder filling closely approximates potential energy of the charge. The points at which more charge is loaded into the cylinder represent more potential cylinder pressure and torque output on the power stroke. Naturally, any point where the ram tuning of the intake, camshaft, and exhaust system enhance the engine's pumping efficiency will show up as larger local values in the VE map.

CHAPTER 11

ACCELERATION ENRICHMENT

The VE map describes the pumping efficiency of the engine during steady state conditions. This is used to estimate the airmass charge and, consequently, the fuel charge very effectively as long as conditions remain steady. Transient, or changing, conditions such as tip-in or tip-out maneuvers have special requirements of the fuel deliver calculations. If the throttle is rapidly moved in either direction, the cylinders can experience a slight change in fuel delivery. The source of this change in fuel delivery is the intake system itself. The small portion of fuel that sticks to the walls of the intake port is constantly making its own contribution to overall fueling of the cylinder. Although the ECU controls the fuel injector, there is no direct control over the film of fuel stuck to the port walls.

During an acceleration event, airflow in the port is rapidly increased. This increase in airflow tends to evaporate the wall film of fuel on the port. If this wall film reduces in magnitude, its overall contribution to the cylinder fueling is also reduced. The net result is a slightly leaner fuel mixture being delivered to the cylinder during acceleration. Left unchecked, the leaner mixture leads to a reduction in torque output until balance is restored to the wall film contribution. If the driver applies an increase in throttle, he is expecting a corresponding increase in torque output. A momentary lean condition is in direct conflict with this request, so a solution must be found. Some extra fuel must be injected into the port to offset this temporary wall film reduction and cylinder enleanment. This extra fuel shot is the EFI equivalent of a carburetor's accelerator pump.

To a lesser extent, there is also a need to offset the opposite condition during deceleration. When the throttle is closed and airflow drops dramatically, the fuel film can grow significantly on the port wall. This increased fuel film mass on the walls translates directly into an increase in fuel mass delivered to the cylinders as it evaporates. Carbureted systems simply allow the engine to run richer momentarily. Better emissions and

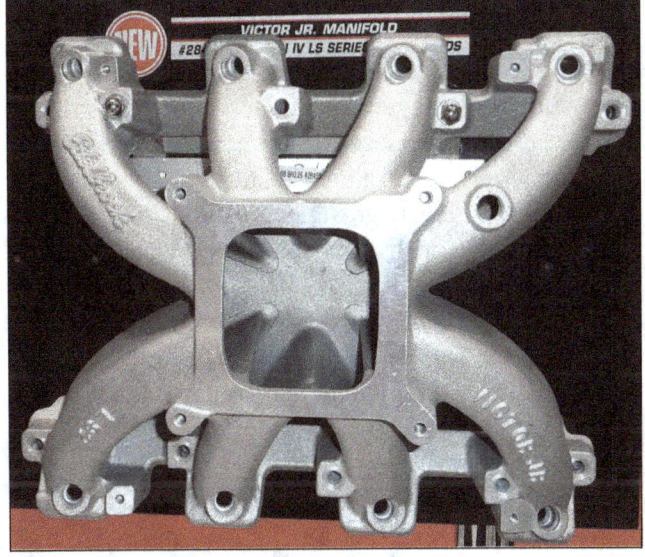

Looking down into a single-plane manifold, the difference in potential wall film area between single point fueling (CFI or carburetion) and multipoint EFI becomes evident. With single point fueling, the entire manifold has the potential to hold deposited fuel affecting transient behavior.

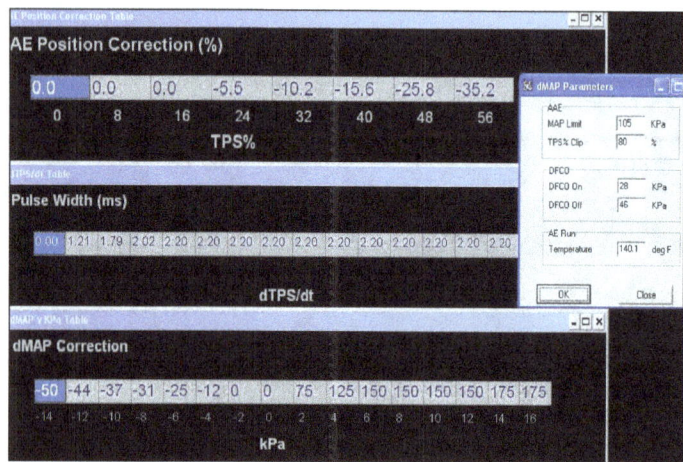

Acceleration enrichment fuel delivery is handled through its own group of tables that are adjustable with respect to throttle position, manifold pressure, and rate of change. It's important to have the steady state fuel delivery correct before attempting to adjust these tables.

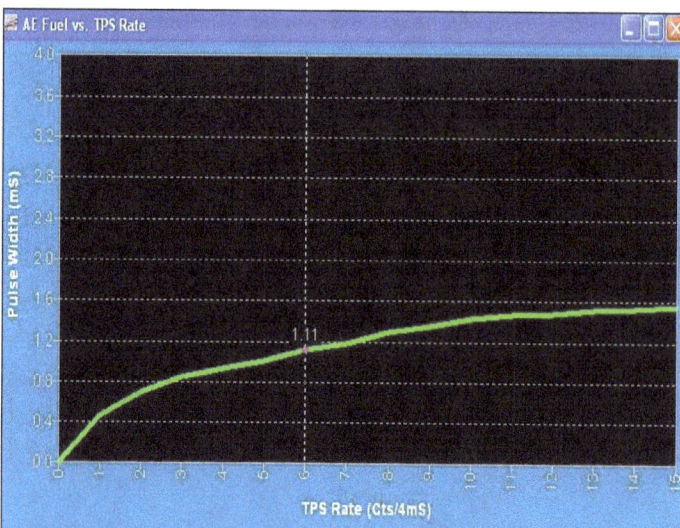

Rapid changes in throttle angle mean that an increase in air charge will soon follow. An additional fuel pulse is determined based on the rate of TPS opening.

fuel economy can be achieved by reducing this effect if the controls are present to do so.

There are several different methods that various ECUs can use to apply the necessary acceleration enrichment. The simplest method is to provide additional fuel delivery based on changes in the TPS sensor or MAP sensor output. Since it is the opening of the throttle in the first place that starts the chain reaction that results in different air and fuel delivery to the cylinder under changing conditions, the TPS sensor can be used as a good predictor of upcoming changes. If a positive change in TPS position is detected, it's a fair conclusion that some amount of additional fuel must be added to offset the change in wall film contribution. In a carburetor, this is accomplished by the mechanical linkage between the throttle arm and accelerator pump. In a simple TPS-based acceleration enrichment strategy, it is accomplished by the graph above right that shows additional fuel mass as a function of TPS rate of change.

The rate of change is usually displayed in degrees of throttle rotation per second. Larger changes in throttle angle correlate with the need for even greater additional fuel mass to offset the evaporating wall film.

Just like the throttle angle, the ECU can also monitor manifold pressure to detect highly dynamic changes in load. If the MAP sensor detects a rapid increase, it is also safe to assume that fuel mass must be increased to go along with it. A table of delta-MAP, or MAP rate of change, can also be used to estimate the necessary fuel mass increase. Some systems employ both a delta-MAP and a delta-TPS table that are summed to provide the total additional fuel mass during transient conditions.

A more elegant method of calculating the necessary fuel addition

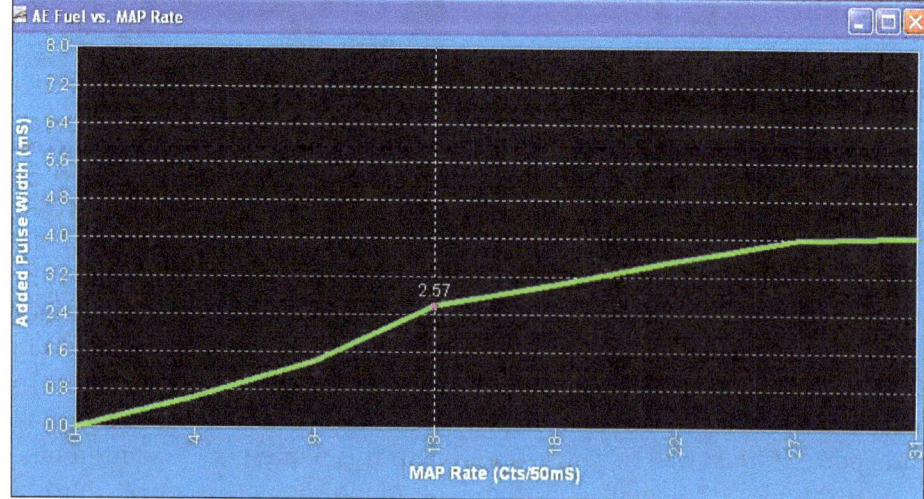

Acceleration enrichment can also be added based on changes in measured manifold pressure. This works well on turbocharged engines that may see many different boost values at the same throttle angle.

is by actually modeling the behavior of the fuel wall film. For each injection event, a percentage of the fuel injected sticks to the port wall instead of being carried directly into the cylinder. This percentage is referred to as "X" and varies significantly with temperature and load. At low temperatures, the percent of fuel effectively condensing on the cool port walls is much greater with each shot. As the engine and port walls warm up, fuel is less likely to stick and the X component decreases as seen in the top graph below. Likewise, changes in load or airflow will also affect the amount of fuel being deposited upon the port walls.

Once the fuel is deposited upon the port wall, it will evaporate over time. The rate at which it evaporates also depends upon temperature and load. Higher temperatures help evaporate the film quicker, as does lower manifold pressure. The time constant for evaporation is referred to as "τ" or the Greek letter Tau. A larger Tau value means faster evaporation. Another way to think of Tau is the portion of fuel delivered to the cylinder directly from the wall film.

Calibration of the Transient Fueling Correction

With either compensation method, the calibration procedure remains basically the same. The best method is to apply a single, positive change to the throttle position between two fixed points. Performing the test at part throttle is easiest since the engine would be going from a commanded lambda of 1.00 at the first point to a commanded lambda of 1.00 at the second point. The test is performed starting from a steady state condition and ending at another steady state condition, both of which are known to have good VE estimation and fuel delivery control. Since the beginning and ending air/fuel ratios are the same, there should be noticeable change in delivered air/fuel ratio. However, there almost certainly will be some momentary deviation if no wall film correction is applied. The objective is to add just enough wall film correction to achieve as close to zero lambda deviation as possible during the maneuver. Too little and a lean spike is shown along with soggy throttle response. Too much and a momentary rich condition is seen.

For example, one may choose to test going from 2,000 rpm and 50 kPa to 2,000 rpm and 70 kPa. This simple tip-in event is typical of a normal traffic event in the vehicle. A load-bearing chassis dyno can make this task much easier if it is set to perform a constant-speed test during the initial VE mapping. Keeping the engine speed constant helps to reduce the number of variables during the

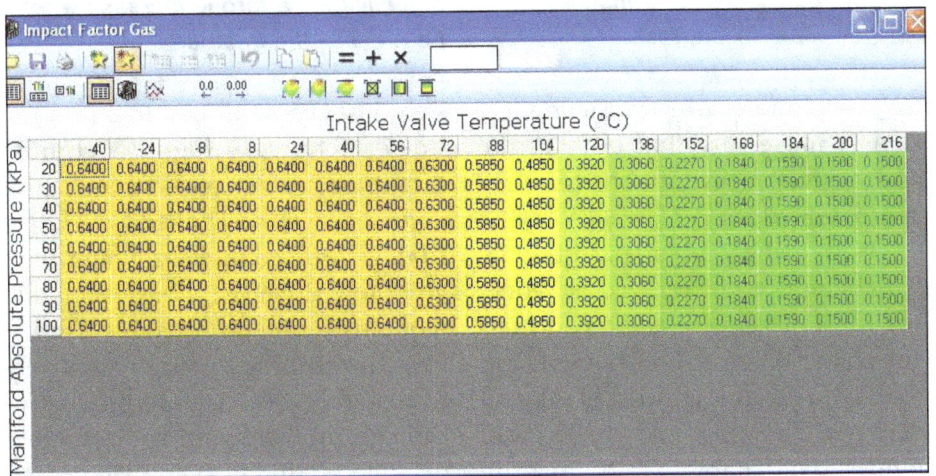

A true X-Tau system will have a table similar to this that defines the fraction of injected fuel that collects on the port wall. This amount of deposited fuel decreases significantly as engine temperature rises.

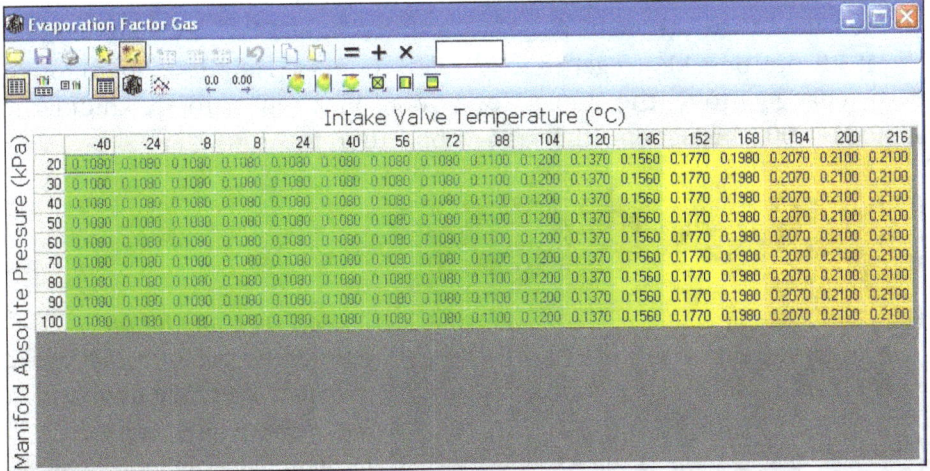

The evaporation factor (Tau) is also strongly tied to operating temperature. This is a snapshot of the OEM table in a 2009 LS3 Chevrolet Corvette as seen with HPTuners software.

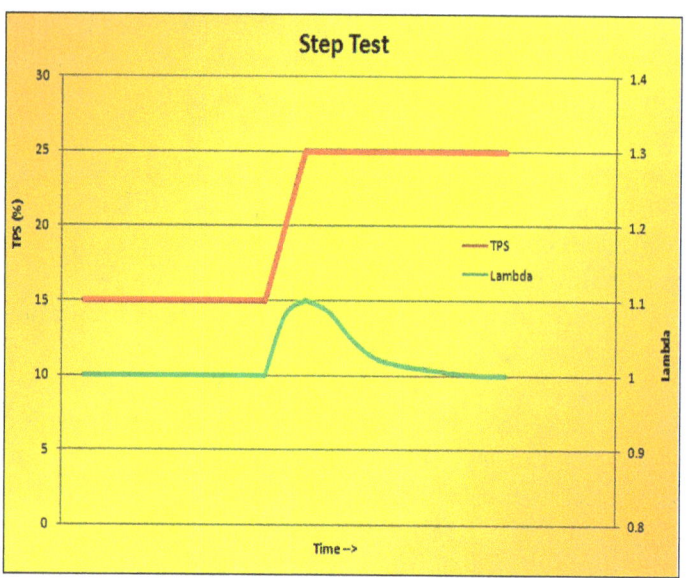

By performing a single step change in throttle postion, the calibrator can see if the transient fuel tables require adjustment. It's important to only make a single positive or negative change and allow the delivered fueling to stabilize to isolate the transient effect.

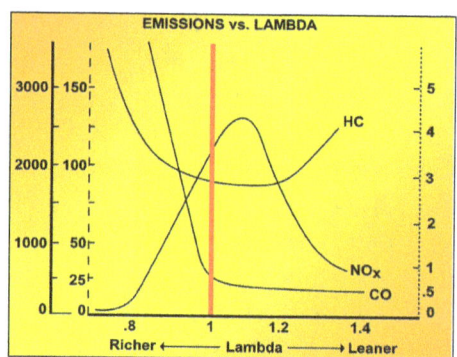

Remember this graph from earlier? During a positive transient, it's important to avoid going lean and losing torque to make sure the driver actually gets a torque increase when he presses the gas pedal.

test. Just stabilize the vehicle at 2,000 rpm and a measured load of 50 kPa with the engine at normal operating temperature. The delivered lambda should read right on the commanded 1.00 ratio and there should be minimal fluctuations in TPS, MAP, and lambda. The driver can then tip into the accelerator to increase load up to, but not exceeding, the new target of 70 kPa. It is very important to resist the temptation to release the gas pedal after hitting the higher target load. The objective is to only get a positive change, not a positive followed by a negative.

If the delivered air/fuel ratio peaks above lambda=1.00, the acceleration enrichment values must be increased and the test repeated. Increases can generally be made globally to the entire acceleration enrichment table as a percentage since the root cause of the momentary leanness is typically a function of the injector spray geometry and engine efficiency. Since the injector spray pattern remains constant, it's safe to assume that this change is almost universal for the engine in question. The test can be repeated for varying rates of throttle application to make sure that both gentle and aggressive events are properly compensated for.

If adjusting a Tau map, additional enrichment can be realized by reducing the Tau value at the second target point. When the ECU calculates that a smaller amount of fuel is being delivered from the (now smaller) wall film, it will automatically increase the fuel mass delivered from the injectors. Large negative changes in the Tau value will tell the ECU that it must provide greater compensation in the base pulsewidth delivery.

If it's not possible to get exactly zero change from the target of lambda=1.00 throughout the transient test event, it's best to err on the side of richness. A slightly rich mixture makes more torque than a stoichiometric mix. The added torque from a little richness actually feels good to a driver who has essentially requested more torque by tipping into the throttle. Going excessively rich can be counterproductive though, so avoid getting "too much of a good thing" here. There's no sense in wasting fuel with extra acceleration enrichment beyond a value of lambda≈0.92 if at all possible. An ideal case for most street driven vehicles would be only a momentary deviation to lambda≈0.96 followed by a quick return to stoichiometric operation in steady state.

There's no place for an accelerator pump on this intake manifold. All of the transient fuel delivery must happen through the eight individual injectors based on input from the TPS and MAP sensors.

CHAPTER 12

TIMING MAPS FROM SCRATCH

Quite frankly, the best way to create a timing map is not to create it from scratch. If there exists a factory timing map for your application, that's almost always the best place to start. Factory timing maps have already done a lot of the difficult work and can be easily adjusted in specific areas to better match the specific engine at hand. Even if a factory map is not available for the exact engine being tuned, starting with a similar engine's timing map is still much more time efficient than starting from nothing.

In general, a completed timing map will look very similar to the VE map. There should not be any surprises in the form of drastic jumps upward or downward in the values shown. Everything should be smooth and progressive. There are a handful of simple rules that will help when tuning spark advance.

Rule #1: Don't Knock!

Regardless of what else is going on, knock should be avoided at all costs. Spark knock is one of the two biggest killers of engines, excessive

Using an existing spark advance table from a similar engine to start from can be a real time saver. The table will almost certainly require adjustments, but the major trends of timing versus speed and load are already there, along with some starting values.

engine speed is the other. Ideally, we'd like to run the engine at its most mechanically efficient point for spark advance. Known as MBT, or maximum brake torque, it is the spark advance value at which torque output is optimized at a single speed, load, lambda, and temperature point. Although we'd like to optimize for torque almost all the time, it's just

DESIGNING AND TUNING HIGH-PERFORMANCE FUEL INJECTION SYSTEMS

CHAPTER 12

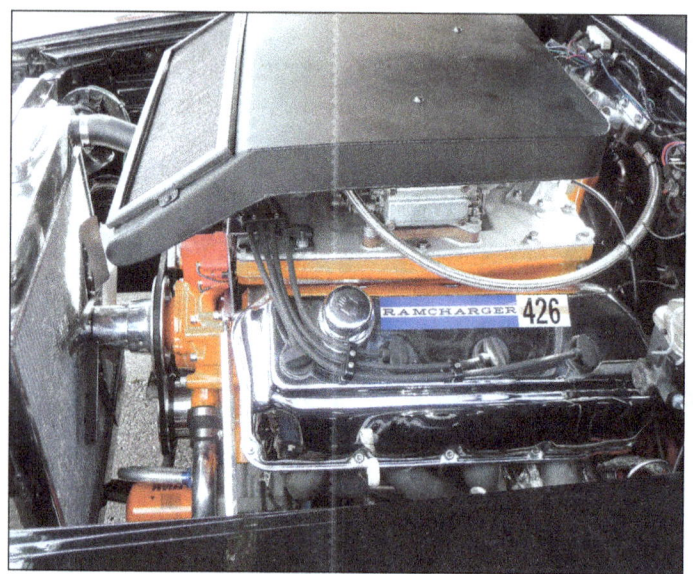

When it comes to tuning the ignition timing, the engine doesn't really care how the fuel got into the cylinder. The same rules apply for both carbureted and fuel injected engines, the EFI system just gives much more precise control across a wider range of conditions.

Modern DOHC engines are both expensive and time consuming to repair. Avoiding spark knock goes a long way toward preventing premature destruction.

not possible with higher loads or temperatures.

Spark knock is the result of uncontrolled combustion that is exhibited by colliding pressure waves within the cylinder, usually at the most inopportune time. These colliding waves can combine to deliver pressures well above the normal combustion loads on the heads, gaskets, pistons, rings, rods, and bearings. Left unchecked, the excess pressure tries to find the easiest way out of the cylinder, often resulting in broken parts. In the best of cases, knock pressures are contained without mechanical failure but the increased pressures are present mostly during the compression stroke. The excess pressure upon the piston during compression literally tries to turn the crankshaft backward and significantly reduces engine torque as measured at the flywheel.

If the engine is exhibiting spark knock, the only real option is to retard the ignition timing until it's gone. The need to protect the engine hardware trumps all other spark advance tuning strategies.

Rule #2: Advance Timing with Increasing Engine Speed

The whole point of advancing ignition timing is to provide peak cylinder pressure at the most effective point in the cycle. This is typically about 12 to 15 degrees ATDC for piston engines, due to the nature of the connecting rod geometry and expansion ratios. Since the air/fuel mixture takes some amount of time to burn, the process must be started ahead of this target in order to peak the cylinder pressure at the right time. With a relatively consistent rate of burn for the mixture, total burn time remains predictable as well. If we want to be about halfway through this burn time by a specific engine angle, it must be timed to the engine's rate of angle change. Fortunately, we have just such a measurement available from the typical engine speed measurement of revolutions per minute. Each revolution is 360 degrees, so we are effectively measuring degrees per minute, or angular velocity, anyway. As this angular velocity increases, the time window for starting the burn moves forward. Degrees of rotation effectively become flexible units of time that change their magnitude with RPM. Higher engine speeds mean more degrees per second, yet the burn time in seconds remains relatively consistent. In order to time the peak pressures that occur just after 50% burn time with a point 12 to 15 degrees ATDC at higher speeds, the burn must be initiated earlier. "Earlier" in this sense means more degrees before TDC. Failure to compensate for speed would result in a burn that

The choice you make here will usually affect how much timing the engine will be able to tolerate during high-load operation. Before tuning an engine's timing tables, it's imperative to verify the fuel specification and make sure that same fuel is always used.

Turbocharged or supercharged engines like this highly modified Subaru Sti are more likely to experience spark knock at WOT than their naturally aspirated counterparts. Luckily, this engine is also equipped with an efficient front-mounted intercooler that allows the engine to safely run higher timing under boost.

With its short intake runners and high-duration camshafts, this Ferrari Testarossa engine is tuned to operate at high engine speeds. These higher engine speeds also require a relatively high spark-advance value to keep the combustion pressure from happening too late in the cycle.

is less complete as the optimal crank angle approaches and the piston has less pressure acting upon it when it would be most useful. Essentially, the gas expansion from combustion isn't harnessed effectively because the piston on the expansion stroke is already running away from it.

Just like hitting a fastball versus a changeup, a faster moving target (higher RPM) requires more lead (spark advance) to make contact (produce peak pressure) at the right time. The faster the speed, the more lead required.

Looking at a finished OEM timing map, it's easy to see this in action. The spark advance values trend higher and higher with engine speed almost without exception. Even older mechanical advance distributors delivered a similar response as the weights were pulled outward against the spring as speed rose. The EFI tables have the advantage of being able to tailor these increases with a wider range of speed breakpoints and even allow for non-linear increases.

Rule #3: Reduce Timing with Increasing Cylinder Load

Any time more potential energy is placed in the cylinder in the form of additional air and fuel mixture, the rate at which it reacts is slightly increased. The reacting molecules are literally tighter packed, such that the "relay race" of flame propagation is handled quicker between them. Additionally, the larger quantity of reacting molecules means greater total heat release and rate of pressure rise. Heat and pressure are catalysts for the reaction, so more of both means that things literally happen quicker. Once again, "quicker" means over the course of fewer crank degrees of rotation.

Since the reaction does not take as many crank degrees to build and complete, less lead in terms of crank degrees is required to get peak pressure once again near the optimal point in the cycle.

Load, in this sense, really refers to total cylinder airmass. We often measure load for spark tables with the same units as the VE table, kilopascals of pressure. This is not necessarily wrong since increases in manifold pressure correlate to increases in cylinder airmass. Anytime manifold pressure is increased at the same engine RPM, it is safe to assume that cylinder airmass has also increased and timing can be retarded to compensate.

However, there is a trap to avoid when using MAP as the load indicator for spark advance. When looking across engine speeds for a single MAP row of the spark table, it doesn't necessarily mean that cylinder load is staying constant. Remember that volumetric efficiency (and consequently airmass) varies with engine speed at the same manifold pressure.

Near-peak-torque engine speeds, the engine exhibits more efficient pumping and cylinder filling, so actual load may be higher here than at the same MAP reading for other engine speeds. It's not surprising to see a dip in the base spark map values across all MAP rows for the peak torque RPM columns. This is simply a case where the engine load is increasing faster than engine speed, so the net result is a drop in ignition timing.

Rule #4: Don't Run MBT at Idle

Most of the time an engine is running, we want it to be as efficient as possible. A key step to obtaining optimum engine efficiency is operating at MBT timing in order to make the most of the cylinder pressure being generated. Retarding the timing from MBT at any point means that there is some untapped potential torque left in reserve. It's possible to intentionally build up a torque reserve simply by retarding the timing from the mechanically ideal MBT point.

When an engine is idling, the ECU is constantly trying to find a way to balance all of the torques in the system. Friction, pumping losses, accessories, and the transmission all provide negative torques to the crankshaft that are constantly trying to slow the speed to a stop. To offset this, the combustion of air and fuel in the cylinder is used to generate just enough positive torque to maintain a constant idle speed. If the losses outweigh the positive torque being generated by the combustion, engine speed drops below the target idle setpoint. Anytime the losses are reduced while the combustion torque remains constant, the engine speed flares upward until a new equi-

Adding a supercharger is a great way to add more cylinder loading at WOT. This higher cylinder filling requires a reduction in ignition lead to offset the faster burn rate to avoid knock.

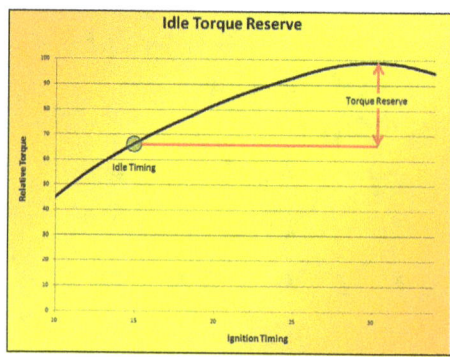

Ignition timing at idle is intentionally decreased from MBT. This allows the ECU to add or subtract torque very quickly when trying to control engine speed.

librium point is reached.

The driver often changes the torque losses by pulling the vehicle into gear, turning on the air conditioning compressor, or applying a load to the power steering pump. During all of these operations, there is an expectation that the engine will not stall or otherwise surprise the driver. Since the ECU cannot always predict when these losses will come and go, it must have some mechanism of dealing with their sudden appearance and disappearance. What the ECU needs is a bank of additional torque to draw from if there is any sudden increase in the system losses at idle. This is accomplished by normally running the engine at less-than-MBT timing at idle. Running at a lower ignition advance angle means that at any moment, the ECU has the option to increase torque output to the crankshaft to overcome any sudden increase in losses. This torque reserve is critical to maintaining good idle control.

When setting up the ignition timing map on an ECU, it's best to check for MBT timing at speeds just above

	Scaled Engine Speed RPM														
	200	800	1000	1200	1800	2200	2600	3000	3400	3800	4200	4600	5000	5400	5800	6200
13.44	17.00	17.00	20.00	27.00	38.75	39.75	42.75	42.75	42.75	41.75	40.75	40.75	43.75	44.75	45.75	46.75
19.29	17.00	17.00	20.00	26.00	37.75	39.50	41.75	41.75	41.75	40.75	39.75	39.75	42.75	43.75	44.75	45.75
25.14	17.00	17.00	20.00	26.00	34.50	36.60	39.25	39.25	39.25	38.25	37.25	37.25	40.25	41.25	42.25	43.25
31.00	17.00	17.00	20.00	25.50	34.50	35.00	38.00	36.00	36.00	35.00	34.00	34.00	37.00	38.00	39.00	40.00
36.85	17.00	17.00	20.00	24.00	34.00	34.00	37.00	35.00	35.00	34.00	33.00	33.00	36.00	37.00	38.00	39.00
42.70	17.00	17.00	20.00	24.00	32.00	32.00	35.00	35.00	35.00	34.00	33.00	33.00	36.00	37.00	38.00	39.00
48.55	17.00	17.00	20.00	24.00	31.00	32.00	35.00	35.00	35.00	34.00	33.00	33.00	36.00	37.00	38.00	39.00
54.40	17.00	17.00	20.00	24.00	31.00	32.00	35.00	35.00	35.00	34.00	33.00	33.00	36.00	37.00	38.00	39.00
60.26	17.00	17.00	20.00	24.00	31.00	32.00	35.00	35.00	35.00	34.00	33.00	33.00	36.00	37.00	38.00	39.00
66.11	17.00	17.00	20.00	24.00	31.00	32.00	34.00	34.00	34.00	33.00	32.00	32.00	35.00	36.00	37.00	38.00
71.96	17.00	17.00	20.00	24.00	31.00	32.00	34.00	34.00	34.00	33.00	32.00	32.00	35.00	36.00	37.00	38.00
77.81	17.00	17.00	20.00	24.00	31.00	32.00	34.00	34.00	34.00	33.00	32.00	32.00	35.00	36.00	37.00	38.00
83.66	17.00	17.00	20.00	24.00	31.00	31.00	33.00	33.00	33.00	32.00	31.00	31.00	34.00	35.00	36.00	37.00
89.52	17.00	17.00	20.00	22.00	29.00	29.00	31.00	31.00	31.00	30.00	29.00	29.00	32.00	33.00	34.00	35.00
95.37	17.00	17.00	20.00	20.00	26.00	28.00	30.00	30.00	30.00	29.00	28.00	28.00	31.00	32.00	33.00	34.00
101.22	17.00	17.00	20.00	20.00	26.00	28.00	30.00	30.00	30.00	29.00	28.00	28.00	31.00	32.00	33.00	34.00

Even though engine speed is slightly higher in the highlighted region, there is still a dip in commanded timing near peak torque. This is a case where cylinder filling from ram tuning is picked up faster than the mechanical delay of increasing speed.

TIMING MAPS FROM SCRATCH

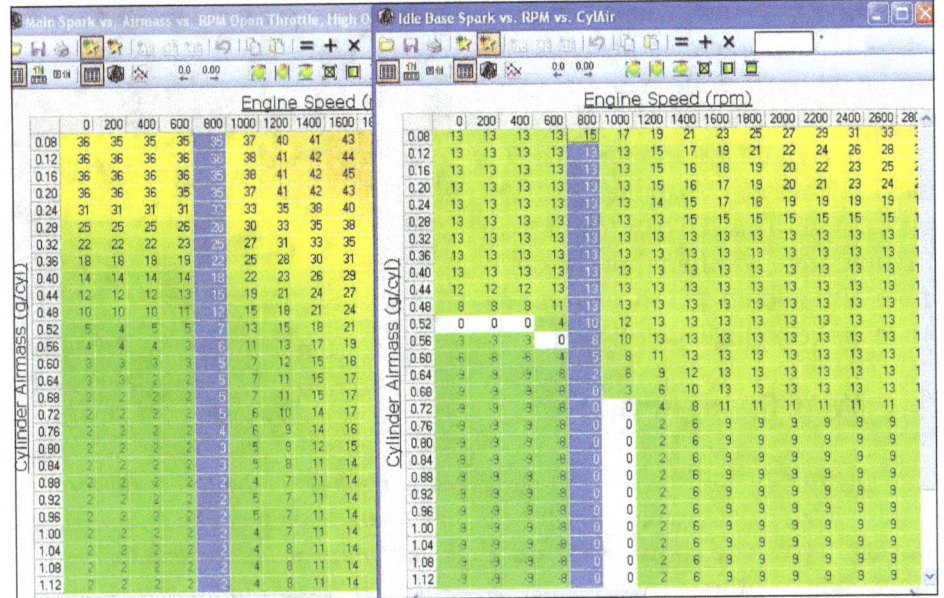

Modern ECUs often have separate tables for closed-throttle (idle) and part-throttle ignition timing. Notice how the idle table (right) has much lower values than the reference table at low speeds.

idle. Chances are that the engine will have a similar value for MBT at idle, and this will give the calibrator a good idea of just how far back they are from MBT when idling. It's not unusual to operate an engine with 10 degrees or more of spark retard from MBT at idle to provide the necessary cushion of available torque. Keeping this torque reserve available at idle goes a long way toward being able to maintain a stable idle speed under a wide variety of conditions.

Finding MBT on the Dyno

With the right equipment, it's not very difficult to find MBT timing for an engine at most points. The objective is to find the ignition angle that delivers the most torque at the crankshaft for a given engine speed, load, charge temperature, and lambda. Timing below this point results in reduced torque, effectively creating a torque reserve as discussed earlier. Advancing the timing too far loses power as the early combustion fights the piston's upward movement too much during the compression stroke. Going even further can lead to spark knock and potential engine damage, which should definitely be avoided.

So how do you find MBT timing at a single point? The test is performed on a load-bearing dyno. This is necessary since we must take an instantaneous torque reading. It can be done on either an engine or chassis dynamometer checking either crankshaft or wheel torque respectively. Much like during the steady state VE testing, the engine is held at a single speed by the dynamometer's controls and the driver uses throttle control to hold the engine to a specific load point in the spark advance map. Intake air temperatures should be checked to ensure that they are close to the same nominal temperatures seen during VE mapping, and delivered lambda should be 1.00 for this part-throttle test.

After the engine has stabilized into a single operation point, a torque reading is recorded along

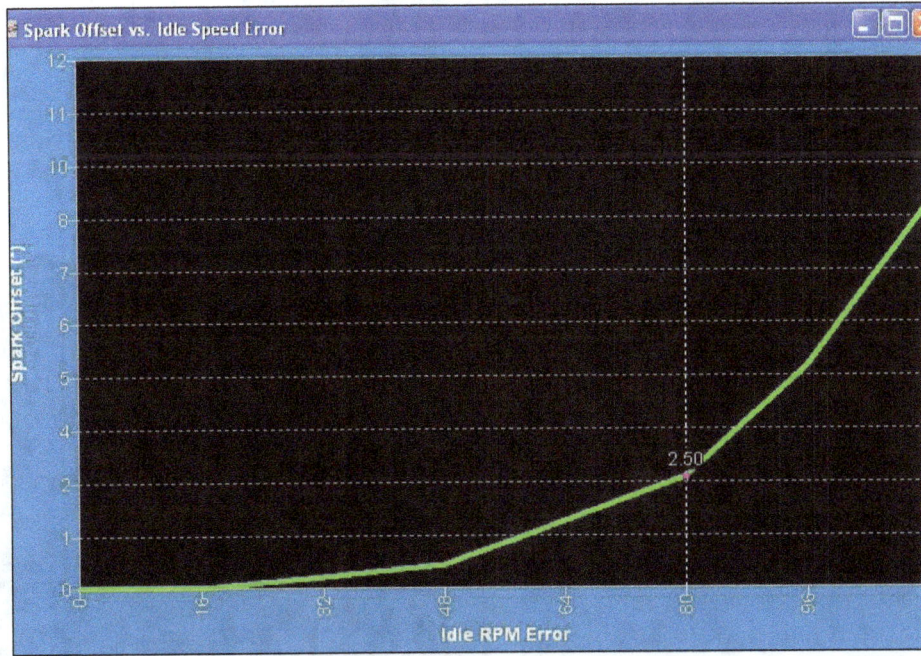

Timing is an effective method of controlling idle speed. The further away from the target idle speed, the greater ignition angle adjustment is applied to correct the error.

DESIGNING AND TUNING HIGH-PERFORMANCE FUEL INJECTION SYSTEMS

with the current spark advance value. Timing is then advanced by about 2 degrees and a new torque reading is taken. If the advance in ignition timing results in an increase of output torque, we are getting somewhere. The timing is once again advanced a few more degrees and another steady state torque reading is taken. This process is repeated until the torque no longer increases with ignition angle. If the second testing point did not show any increase in torque from the baseline measurement, timing should be reduced by a few degrees and another torque reading taken. The objective is to be able to plot the output torque against ignition angle. Once this data is plotted, it is easy to see what precise timing value results in the maximum amount of output torque, MBT. The resulting plot will have some sort of hook or curve to it with a plateau of sorts near the maximum. This is what gives the procedure the name "spark hook test." If several values of ignition angle all result in statistically similar output torques (within about 2% of each other), it's usually best to pick the lower spark angle necessary to make the torque. This will allow for a larger margin of error in the event of the occasional bad tank of gas or extreme operating conditions.

As long as the calibrator can accurately hold the engine to individual speed, load, temperature, and lambda conditions, the spark hook test is easy to run. The test can be repeated for a wide array of speed-load points within the spark advance map. Ideally, every single point would be checked as they are in an OEM application. However, running a few spot checks spaced out across the map can be a much quicker indicator of what changes are necessary.

If both 2,000 rpm and 3,000 rpm at 60 kPa are found to benefit from an additional 4 degrees of spark advance over the starting table, it is a relatively safe assumption that the same change can be applied at 2,500 rpm as well. This can be a major time saving strategy when hourly dyno time costs add up quickly with trying to map every single point.

WOT Spark Advance

For wide-open-throttle testing at higher loads, many engines will not be able to operate continuously at a single point without protest. Just as with the volumetric efficiency mapping of the 100 kPa line, a sweep test is the best alternative. By this point, the VE map should already be established and the calibrator can simply dial-in whatever air/fuel ratio he wants and have a reasonable expectation of getting it. Timing is the tool that will be used to unlock the engine's maximum power and torque potential.

Since there is typically only a marginal change in power output for a naturally aspirated engine once in the vicinity of peak flame speed

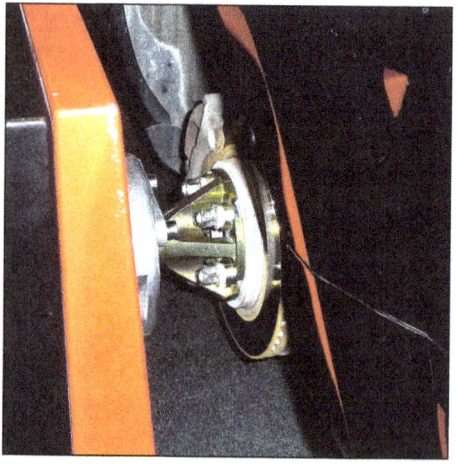

Load control is required to perform the spark hook test and find MBT. This Dynapack unit bolts a load absorber directly to the wheel hub that can hold the vehicle at a constant wheel speed and eliminate tire slippage.

lambdas from ≈0.85 to ≈0.92 or so, a safe starting point is chosen that should err a little on the rich side. Lambda≈0.86 is a good starting point for naturally aspirated engines. Super or turbocharged engines can run this same air/fuel ratio at 100 kPa MAP, but should run richer (lambda≈0.79 to start) once into boost.

The sweep test is conducted first with a very conservative timing curve

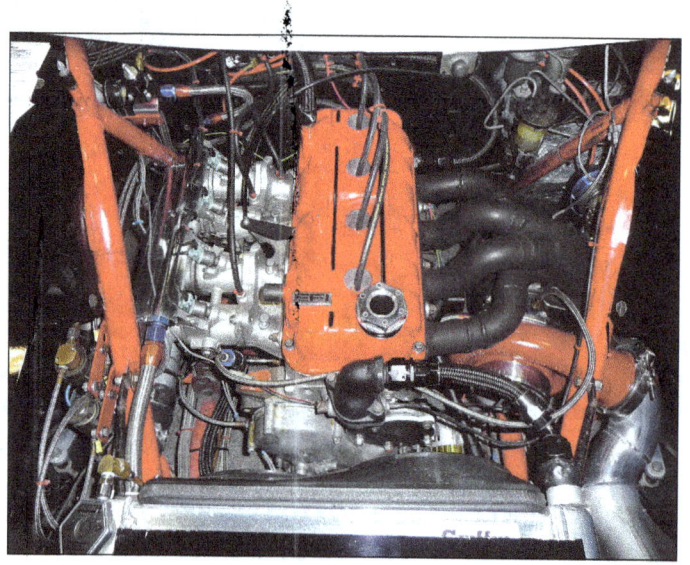

WOT ignition timing calibration should be performed on a fully warmed up or heat soaked engine to check the worst case conditions. Turbocharged engines, in particular, are very sensitive to temperature for their knock resistance.

across all engine speeds. If there are any deviations in delivered air/fuel ratio from the target setpoint, it's time to revisit the VE table before continuing. Provided the air/fuel ratio looks good, we can take a look at the engine's torque curve. Remember that the torque curve is an indication of cylinder filling as well as cylinder pressure. A second run can be made with a global increase of about 2 degrees to the WOT timing. Overlay the delivered torque curves and compare them to see if the added timing resulted in an increase of torque at each point. If torque increased at a point, it means that the engine stepped a little closer to MBT without hitting the knock limit and the timing is helping to increase engine output. If torque either stays the same or decreases as a result of increased ignition advance, you are done with that particular point. Return the timing to the previous run so that the engine continues to run only as much spark advance as necessary to achieve maximum output. Once again, you're trying to keep some safety margin here. If at any time knock is detected, timing should be reduced to avoid it. Additional power sweep tests with increased local timing can be run until all points deliver the maximum torque without knock. This will result in a completely optimized torque curve for the engine, and the corresponding maximum power output.

If an engine prematurely exhibits spark knock during this testing with what appears to be low spark values, there are still a few options. First, check for mechanical issues or oil ingestion. Very small amounts of oil can quickly reduce the effective octane of the air/fuel mixture. Depending on the blend, oils can have effective octane ratings of about 48. It doesn't take very much 48 octane mixed with 93 octane premium fuel to bring down the average very quickly. Don't look for a calibration solution to a mechanical problem here.

The other option, assuming there is no mechanical issue, is to run with a richer air/fuel ratio. The added fuel will slightly reduce the burn rate of the mixture, allowing for an earlier ignition point before combustion pressures become favorable for knock. This is the same strategy used with supercharged engines, just to a lesser extent on a naturally aspirated engine. It may be found that more power is consistently available from the engine with a slightly richer mixture along with increased timing. Either way, set the air/fuel ratio first and then use spark advance to creep up on torque output.

After the optimal 100 kPa line has been determined for spark advance values, some blending can be done to make a smooth transition between the part-throttle and WOT regions of the map. If a handful of part-throttle points have been clearly defined for MBT timing, it becomes easier to draw smooth connections between them and the newly derived WOT spark curve. Just like the VE table, the final spark map should be smooth and progressive.

Boosted Spark Advance

For a boosted engine, the 100 kPa line should still be carefully tuned for spark advance. This line gives the calibrator a valuable series of reference points from which to smooth the

By adding a couple degrees of timing across the entire WOT range for the second run (dotted line), we can see which areas benefitted from the added lead. This test showed increases in torque across the entire WOT range, with an increase of over 16 ft-lbs to the wheels on average that the driver will really enjoy.

whole table in both load directions. The calibrator will still need to test to find the optimum spark advance for various levels of boost across the RPM range. Power sweeps with careful application of the throttle angle can once again be used to test at progressively higher boost levels up to the intended maximum. Just like at 100 kPa, the timing that results in the highest torque output without knock at each point is the goal. Compare torque curves between runs to verify that timing changes are having the desired effect and keep the lowest value necessary to make clean torque without knocking.

Just as with the 100 kPa tuning, additional fuel can be used to control spark knock or burn rate. The higher the boost pressure or inlet temperatures, the more useful this may become. Non-intercooled systems in particular will usually benefit from running richer since the extra fuel's evaporation has a noticeable cooling effect within the cylinder that will usually allow for more ignition advance without knock. The same holds true for older, less efficient, positive displacement superchargers such as roots blowers. These tend to heat soak very quickly due to their lower compression efficiency and adding a bit of extra fuel goes a long way toward helping these engines run smoother at high load.

When performing WOT testing, it's always a good idea to verify engine speed against wheel speed to check for clutch slip. The stock clutch is often no match for the torque modern engines are capable of generating with modifications, so a stronger unit like this twin disc may be required.

The final spark table for a boosted vehicle should just look like an extension of the naturally aspirated equivalent. It still follows Rule #3 above, just much further up the scale. As the increased boost adds to the actual cylinder airmass loading, spark advance is still progressively pulled. Even in boosted operation, Rule #2 still applies. Don't be surprised to see that spark advance can be increased significantly at speeds above peak engine torque, even well into boost.

Most importantly, don't forget Rule #1 when tuning a boosted engine. When operating in boost, knock can appear very quickly and cause significant damage. Listen very carefully for the telltale "marbles in a can" noise and lift immediately if the engine knocks. It may be helpful to employ an outboard knock sensor or set of "chassis ears" to catch the knock even earlier. If you can hear the knock, the engine is already several degrees past the threshold. Check the air/fuel ratio for accuracy and either add fuel or retard the timing to reduce the knock to zero.

Remember that just because an engine doesn't knock on a single dynamometer test doesn't mean you're permanently safe. It's always a good idea to maintain some safety margin for that occasion tank of bad gas, especially on street driven vehicles.

Dedicated race engines can be tuned to run much closer to the knock limit than street cars. When the fuel is always purchased from a high-quality supplier in sealed containers, there is less chance for contamination and a smaller safety margin can be used when tuning.

CHAPTER 13

STARTUP MAPS

By this point, the engine should run really well once warmed up. There should be no concerns of steady state air/fuel ratio errors, tip-in stumbles, idle control, or knock. In short, it should be right as long as it's up to operating temperature. If there are any issues with operation at normal temperatures, go back and fix them right now before getting into this part of the calibration procedure. All of the startup calibrations work upon the assumption that everything is working correctly at nominal temperatures, and their only reason for existence is to fix the physical changes to the engine's operation due to low coolant temperature and lack of wall film.

In most cases, standalone controllers already have some values in the startup or cold-start tables. Chances are that if the majority of the engine mapping was done properly at normal temperatures, there really won't be too much work to do here. If you must start from a completely empty set of tables for these values, it's a good idea to copy the values from another file just to have something with which to start. Most engines have similar trends during cold start and therefore require similar calibration values for these tables. With any luck, you will only be making moderate changes to whatever values are already populated in the tables. Remember that you are typically making adjustments that are in addition to the normal, warmed up operation of the engine. The biggest differences between engines are typically their fundamental pumping efficiencies, which should have already been corrected by now in the VE and transient fuel control tables. It's almost always better to start with something rather than nothing for cold-start calibration. Don't be afraid to copy here, it can be a real time saver.

After being parked for a while, the engine is soaked to the ambient temperature where fuel does not evaporate as readily as it does at full operating temperature. When the engine is first started, a little extra fuel will be added to establish an initial wall film.

The startup tables are there primarily to address two key issues: temperature and wall film establishment. When an engine is cold, it has more friction. Sliding parts have tighter tolerances when cold and the oil has higher viscosity, making it more difficult to not only pump through the galleys, but also to squeeze past each bearing. Just turning the engine over requires more effort when cold. This means that the combustion that provides the power to rotate the engine must be greater just to maintain the same operation speeds as a warm engine.

Unfortunately, a cold engine is less consistent at delivering small

CHAPTER 13

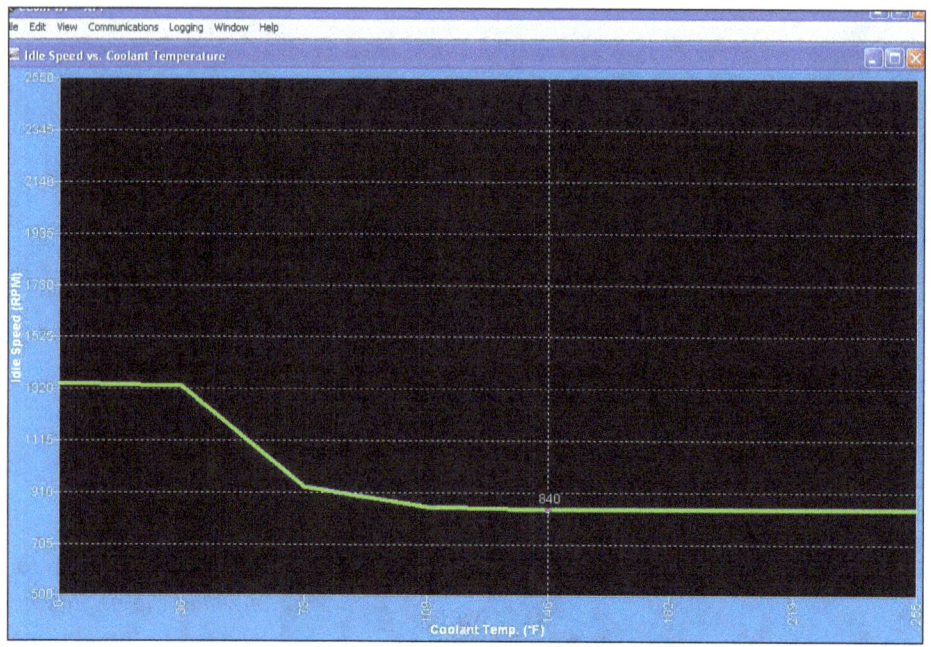

The idle speed setpoint is usually determined by a table that varies with temperature. A higher setpoint is used at cold temperatures to offset the added friction and aid warmup.

amounts of power, so a higher target is usually chosen. With a higher stabilized engine power, the balanced idle speed ends up also being higher. Most ECUs provide the ability to set a target engine idle speed based on engine coolant temperature. Low temperatures are usually calibrated to request significantly higher target idle speeds. It's common to see an increase of 400 rpm or so above the nominal idle target when coolant temperatures are close to 0 degrees C (32 degrees F). On the bright side, this higher engine speed for a cold engine leads to faster heat addition to the block and coolant, reducing the time until a normal operating temperature is reached. Even better, the vehicle's passenger heater and defroster are also able to more quickly benefit from the engine heat when idle speeds are set faster. As coolant temperatures approach the normal operating range, the idle speed target is smoothly reduced to normal.

This table should be populated prior to attempting any cold-start work. It's not critical to be very precise at first, just pick a noticeably faster idle speed target for cold temperatures to avoid stalling. Later on, this table can be fine tuned after the fuel delivery is under control during startup. A faster idle target speed can be used on purpose to reduce overall warmup time at the expense of fuel consumption and noise. Most OEM applications try to get just enough speed to avoid stalling and make adequate heater performance while minimizing fuel consumption and NVH to the driver.

Fuel Delivery

Gasoline engines burn fuel, but not liquid fuel. The liquid gasoline is injected into the intake manifold and it must evaporate into a gaseous state before it can be ignited in the cylinder. In a fully warmed up engine, the liquid fuel is partially atomized as it leaves the injector

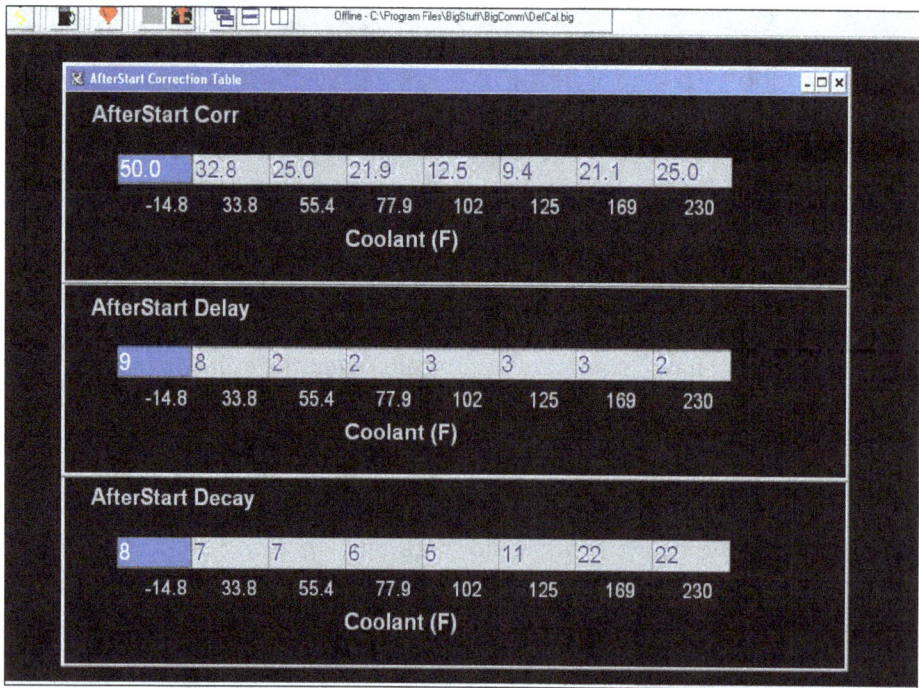

The amount of additional fuel delivered after starting is calibrated in these tables. Notice how the extra enrichment tapers off (and the decay rate increases) as temperature approaches the normal operating range.

and then almost completely evaporates as it hits the back of a very warm intake valve. When the valve is not as hot, the amount of evaporated fuel is greatly reduced. A cold engine may only evaporate a small portion of the injected fuel before the ignition event. At –40 degrees C (–40 degrees F), most blends of gasoline do not want to evaporate at all under atmospheric conditions, and only do so slightly due to the heat of the compression stroke. Whenever the fuel does not completely evaporate, more fuel than normal must be added to the engine in order to get the necessary amount of evaporated fuel for combustion. In very cold weather, there may be large amounts of unburned fuel pumped through an engine as only the evaporated portion is able to burn. The colder the engine is, the more total fuel delivery is required

The intake air temperature sensor helps compensate fueling for extremely cold air temperatures for warm engines, but vehicles must also start in frigid conditions where the block and heads are also cold. The trick is to add just enough extra fuel to compensate for the unevaporated amount at startup without adding so much that it won't start or fouls spark plugs.

just to get the desired fuel mass for combustion. Startup fuel tables will typically have one axis of engine temperature to allow the calibrator to adjust for this behavior. The amount of additional fuel injected tapers to zero as the engine reaches a fully warmed up state.

It is common to have to add a significant amount of extra fuel at cold temperatures. This table is calibrated by monitoring wideband output immediately after startup. Make sure that the wideband sensor is fully powered and warmed up before turning the key to start the engine. If the resulting lambda measurement is lean, chances are that more fuel must be added even though you may already be at the right actual fuel mass for the measured airmass. Remember that not all of the fuel being injected here is actually burning, and the UEGO only reports how much unburned oxygen is being measured. If anything, it's better to err on the side of moderately rich during startup. A cold engine start reading of anywhere between lambda=0.80 and 0.95 is fine, depending on the temperature. This should taper to a measured lambda=1.00 relatively quickly though. Achieving a measured lambda=1.00 at cold start may require as much as 30% extra fuel beyond the normal calculation.

When we previously looked at fuel injector operation, it was established that some portion of the injected fuel would not directly enter the combustion chamber. A portion of the fuel would become stuck to the port wall to establish a film that evaporates with time and airflow. At startup, this film does not yet exist if the engine has not run in a while. When the first injection events are happening, some of the fuel being sprayed into the engine will be "lost"

 Hot Restart

During a hot restart, much of the existing wall film may have evaporated due to the temperature of the port. It's often necessary to increase the after-start fuel delivery slightly at high temperatures in order to reestablish the wall film on a hot engine. If this is done, just make sure to also increase the decay rate to quickly remove the extra fuel adder so that the engine does not run too rich after the wall film has been quickly established.

as it forms the initial application of the wall film layer. If the port walls are cold, as in startup, the fuel is more likely to condense upon them to form a larger boundary layer. The colder the engine is, the more fuel mass that is lost to the formation of the wall film. At cooler temperatures, this film is also less likely to evaporate on its own, delivering even less actual evaporated gaseous fuel to the cylinders. This has the double penalty of not only requiring more fuel just to hit the desired air/fuel ratio at cold temperatures, but also making transient fuel delivery more difficult when cold.

As the engine slowly warms up, the amount of fuel contained in the wall film gradually reduces. Many ECUs will model this with a decay rate table that slowly reduces the extra fuel delivery in cold conditions as the engine approaches normal operating temperatures. The trick when tuning this table is to remove the extra fuel at a smooth rate so that the measured lambda in the exhaust remains constant and on target as the engine warms up.

CHAPTER 14

AUXILIARY OUTPUTS

Most basic engine combinations will be done with the tuning process by this point. The typical fixed-camshaft-angle engine that is either naturally aspirated or controlled to a known boost curve doesn't need much more than fuel and spark control to operate gracefully for years of reliable operation. The EFI system can be used as a more precise carburetor and distributor replacement, or some systems can begin to integrate a great deal of additional functions. Once the ECU already has a handful of critical engine function inputs such as RPM, spark angle, MAP, throttle position, or temperatures, these can be used as triggers for more complex controls.

Modern standalone systems recognize this potential flexibility and almost all of them offer some degree of additional output control support. These additional functions of the ECU can range from simple switches to infinitely variable controls, depending on the configuration. The controls can be used as either base engine functions such as camshaft positioning, throttle controls, and fueling source or they can be used to control external devices such as a transmission, nitrous oxide system, or wastegate actuator.

Cooling fans are one of the simplest auxilliary ECU outputs to control. Most controls are just a simple on/off switch based on the engine coolant temperature sensor reading.

Cooling Fans

The simplest of auxiliary ECU output controls is for cooling fans. The ECU typically has a low current output that is either switched to 12-volt power or ground that is used to trigger a relay that switches the high current power circuit for the fan motor(s). When using a standalone controller, make sure to check the setup instructions or user's manual for that particular system to make sure the correct wiring polarity is chosen. Also be sure to use a properly sized fuse for the actual power lead to the fan motor. Many electric fans can draw 30 amps or more during startup.

Setting the actual trigger temperature is simple. Most ECUs will have a single turn-on point based on measured engine coolant temperature from the ECT sensor. The turn-off point can be defined either as its own discreet temperature or as a hysteresis band, a fixed number of degrees below the trigger point to exit the "ON" condition. These two

AUXILIARY OUTPUTS

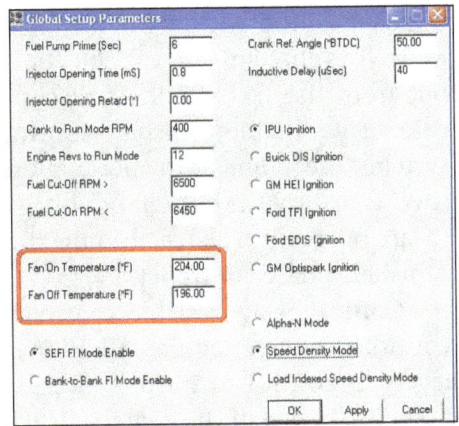

The fan trigger temperatures (red box) are adjusted in this controller along with other basic setup parameters. The setpoint should be higher than the thermostat opening point.

temperatures should have a noticeable separation to avoid constant toggling of the fan output.

The turn-on point for the electric fan should be set above the thermostat's control temperature as well. This will allow the thermostat and radiator to do their job without consuming extra electrical power in cases where it is not required. The fan should not be on as long as the radiator has sufficient capacity to cool the engine. Turning the fans on if the coolant temperature gets above the thermostatic control point will increase the effectiveness of the radiator at slow vehicle speeds where there is not very much natural airflow from the outside. Cooling fans do not have much effect at speeds above 30 mph on most vehicles, and some ECUs turn them off above a calibrated speed threshold to save energy.

Camshaft Actuation

One of the first applications of the standalone controllers' external control capabilities was for binary camshaft controls. Systems like Honda's VTEC or early BMW VANOS hardware are controlled by a single switched output from the ECU. These binary systems have only two states, "Off" and "On." The switch between the two states is usually an engine speed trigger coupled with either throttle position or MAP. The typical strategy is to recognize high load through either RPM, TPS, or MAP thresholds and turn the system "On" at a certain engine speed to switch to a more aggressive camshaft position that promotes better top-end power production. When dipping back below the thresholds, the camshaft control returns to the "Off" position where a more docile position promotes better idle characteristics and drivability.

Choosing the best engine speed to switch between two camshaft set points is fairly simple. Generally, the idea is to find the best compromise for engine torque output across the entire operation range. To make the most of the entire speed range for the engine, the ideal situation is to have the high speed tuning point ("On") pick up right where the low speed tuning point ("Off") left off. Two torque sweep tests should be run across a wide range of overlapping engine speeds. The first test is run with the camshaft control locked into the "Off" position and the second locked into the "On" position. The resulting torque curves can be overlaid in the common engine speeds using the same scale for torque output. Wherever the two torque curves cross will indicate the best switch point to make the most of the engine's entire speed range and deliver the flattest torque curve possible.

If the ECU does not have any additional volumetric efficiency

This Mitsubishi EVO engine is equipped with continuously variable valve timing on both camshafts. The volumetric efficiency and EGR percentage can be adjusted with changes in valve overlap and timing relative to TDC.

CHAPTER 14

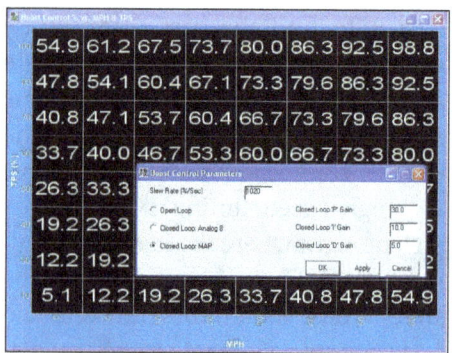

This ECU allows the desired boost level to be controlled with a closed loop correction against the MAP sensor. The table in the background is configured to adjust boost controller duty cycle based on both TPS and vehicle speed to apply more boost as traction increases with speed.

Variable cam timing systems work best with a multi-tooth target wheel installed on the camshaft. This allows the ECU to have an accurate measurement of exact camshaft position relative to the crankshaft at all times.

compensation to accompany the camshaft control activation, some careful thought is required when using these systems. The camshaft position switch point should be used as one of the breakpoints on the VE table. Even better, have two closely spaced breakpoints immediately on either side of the intended camshaft switching point. When the system is actuated, it is very probable that there will be some noticeable increase in pumping efficiency, causing a knee in the torque and VE curves. To get the best modeling of this switching's effect upon airflow, the knee point should correlate with the VE table breakpoints so that the ECU is not left trying to interpolate across the table during a very non-linear physical response. Having the switch point chosen as a pair of very close breakpoints means that any interpolation on either side of the switching point will always be referenced to known values in both directions. This will go a long way toward preventing a momentary rich or lean condition every time the camshaft actuation circuit is triggered. Any time a variable camshaft system is used, it is important to spend some quality time mapping the volumetric efficiency on both sides of the intended switch point.

Variable intake manifold systems that switch between two different sets or lengths of intake runners can be treated just like binary camshaft control for the purposes of volumetric efficiency tuning and torque output. Fundamentally, the cylinders don't really care if the increase in charge loading is a result of camshaft or intake manifold tuning. What matters here is that whatever change is mechanically executed has a corresponding ECU calibration change to describe the mechanical adjustment. As long as the ECU "knows" that a change in volumetric efficiency has occurred, a lot of other things should just fall into place without much trouble.

As engines have become more complicated, it is becoming increasingly common to see continuously variable camshaft phasing systems. These systems allow for the selection of any position within the operable range by changing a variable output from the ECU itself. Most continuously variable camshaft control systems use pulsewidth modulation (PWM) to vary the current or voltage to an oil control valve feeding the camshaft phase controller.

Continuously variable camshaft control systems require additional layers of control to operate at their best. This is one of the characteristics that separates the more affordable budget controllers from the more serious and expensive hardware. Since they have the potential to operate at a wide variety of camshaft positions for a given speed and manifold pressure, there must be some third dimension of description available to properly model the changing pumping efficiency. Additional layers of controls cost real money to develop both the software and ECU hardware to support, so there is a significant leap in capability associated with these controls.

The additional dimension of control necessary to run a continuously variable camshaft may be done several different ways. Most continuously variable systems have a base VE table that describes the pumping efficiency of the engine with the camshaft locked into its default position, usually fully advanced. This provides a failsafe mode in the event of actuator failure so that the engine control system can still properly meter fuel delivery and spark advance. It also serves as the reference point from which additional pumping efficiencies can be added or subtracted in proportion to camshaft phasing. Before any variable camshaft work is done, the base VE table must be calibrated in the same manner as any other non-variable camshaft engine.

DESIGNING AND TUNING HIGH-PERFORMANCE FUEL INJECTION SYSTEMS

AUXILIARY OUTPUTS

A turbocharger's compressor is driven by a shaft linked directly to a turbine located in the exhaust gas flow. The amount of energy being added to the compressor through the shaft can be regulated by controlling the flow of exhaust either to or around the turbine.

Once the reference table is properly calibrated, it is possible to progress on to the variable controls and volumetric efficiency compensation. Most continuously variable camshaft controls work by having a second VE table or modifier. The second VE table usually represents the engine's pumping efficiency at a different camshaft position, usually the opposite extreme from the reference position. The final volumetric efficiency is then calculated as a linear interpolation between the two tables' results, based upon what percent phasing is currently delivered between the two extremes. (See Sidebar "Working Example for Variable Cams" on page 106.) Alternatively, an adder to the reference VE can be calculated based on degrees of camshaft phasing. This requires a map of VE modifiers per degree at various speed and load points. The final VE is calculated by using the modifier table to determine a VE adder based upon current position and adding this to the reference value.

Boost Control

Many turbocharged vehicles can benefit from having a variable control of the boost level. This option allows the user to dial-in the desired power level by adjusting the maximum allowed intake manifold pressure, using more boost to make more total power. Lower boost levels are often desirable at low vehicle speed where available traction is limited. In higher gears, applying more engine power to the tires may be

The turbochargers in this V-8 kit use a single-port wastegate. Boost is controlled by a vacuum line connected from the top of the wastegates to the intake manifold plenum.

The boost control solenoid can be seen on this engine, to the left of the tubular manifold. This racer has opted to use threaded fittings and -AN lines to prevent separation of the boost connections under high pressure.

possible, so the desired boost level may be raised with speed. It may also be useful to save different boost settings for various fuel octane levels. Some users prefer to have one setting for pump gas and another for race fuel, which becomes surprisingly easy with ECU controls.

The actual adjustment to engine boost level is made by controlling the turbocharger's wastegate. The wastegate is the "brains" of the turbocharger that diverts just enough exhaust gas flow around the outside of the turbine to deliver only enough total energy to the turbine and shaft to make the desired pressure at the compressor's outlet. Diverting a larger percent of the total exhaust flow around the turbine reduces the available energy to the turbine and results in lower boost levels. The opposite is also true where the act of forcing more of the engine's hot, high velocity exhaust gases through the turbine generates more shaft power that is used by the compressor wheel to generate more pressure being fed to the intake manifold. Regulating this diversion to maintain a delicate bal-

Dual-port wastegates can have pressure applied to both sides of the diaphragm. Controlling the pressure differential with an outboard control solenoid can more than double the boost compared to the static spring pressure.

ance right at the expected pressure level is the job of the wastegate.

The wastegate works by applying pressure to a diaphragm that is directly attached to the diverter valve controlling the direction of exhaust gas flow. A closed valve forces 100% of the exhaust flow through the turbine and increases the energy supplied to the compressor. Opening the valve more progressively decreases the energy delivered to the compressor through the turbocharger shaft. The force placed on the diaphragm from gas pressure fed by the boost reference line is the product of the pressure (1 kPa = $0.1 N/cm^2$, or 0.145 lbs/in^2) times the working area (cm^2, or in^2) of the diaphragm itself. A higher pressure on the same area equals more total force on the diaphragm trying to open the valve. A spring of known compliance (mm/N or in/lb) is placed behind the diaphragm of the wastegate so that the valve begins to open at a specific pressure level.

If the balance between pressure applied to the diaphragm and spring pressure is changed, a new equilibrium pressure is reached at the intake manifold. The mechanics of the wastegate do not allow for this equilibrium to be below the constant spring pressure, but it can be moved higher by one of two methods. The first is by regulating the actual pressure delivered to the wastegate. The second is by applying pressure to the opposite side of the same diaphragm to deliver a pressure differential that equals the spring pressure.

In the first method, some sort of controlled leak is created to reduce the available pressure at the feed to the wastegate diaphragm. By delivering a lower pressure to the wastegate actuator than what is actually in the intake manifold, the wastegate reacts and performs its normal regulation routine around this lower, regulated pressure. The simplest version of this is the "fish tank valve" used by racers over the years that is just a simple regulated bleed orifice controlled by a knob. A more elegant solution is to use a solenoid that is open to atmosphere on one side. If the solenoid opens, pressure from the reference line escapes to the atmosphere and the downstream pressure on the line is reduced in direct relation to how much the solenoid is opened.

Now we're getting somewhere in terms of ECU control. The ECU

Working Example for Variable Cams

Let's look at an engine with a variable camshaft position range of 0 to 60 degrees of movement. At a reference speed and load, it has a volumetric efficiency of 72% with zero camshaft phasing. At maximum camshaft retard, the volumetric efficiency is increased to 88% for the same speed and load point. If the camshaft is run at 28 degrees of retard from the reference position, the engine is calculated as operating at a factor of 28/60, or 0.467 between the two tables. This factor is then used to determine the final weighting of the two tables, with 46.7% weighting on the upper table and (100% to 46.7%) upon the reference table:

Final VE = (0.467) x (72%) + (.533) x (88%) = 33.624 + 42.64 ≈ 76.3%

The same engine can be mapped using a variable adder based on cam position. If the speed load point in question has a VE compensation of 0.266% per degree of camshaft retard, the adder is found by multiplying this by the current position. Using the same position of 28 degrees of retard, we find the corrective VE adder to be (0.266 x 28) or about 7.5%. Adding this to the same reference value of 72%, we get:

Final VE = 72% + (0.266 x 28) = 72% + 7.5% ≈ 79.5%

Note that the final VE value differs using the two methods. The numerical difference is a function of different methods of interpolation, but both get relatively close to the desired outcome. In this case, the difference is about 3%, which is as close as many engine calibrations ever get once tolerances and stackups are added to the long list of possible variables. The moral here is that if you really want to be precise with continuously variable camshaft control, make sure to read and understand the ECU's manual where they will typically list the exact formula used to derive the final position.

AUXILIARY OUTPUTS

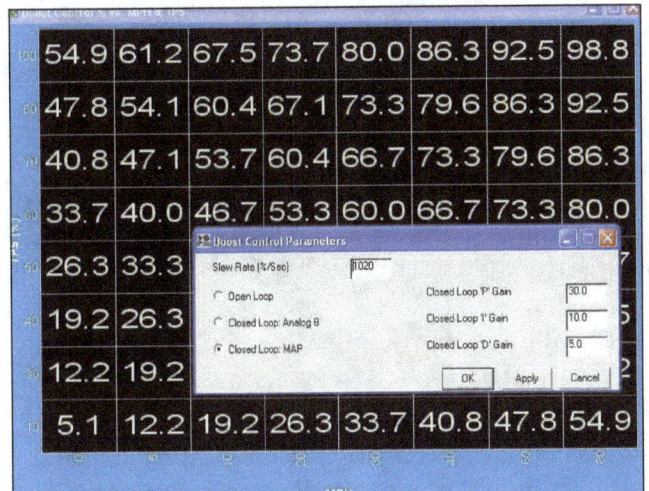

This ECU allows the desired boost level to be controlled with a closed loop correction against the MAP sensor. The table in the background is configured to adjust boost controller duty cycle based on both TPS and vehicle speed to apply more boost as traction increases with speed.

TECH TIP: Boost Control

Whenever ECU boost control is active, it is important to properly tune as many cells of the base fuel maps in the boosted region as possible. This helps to ensure that even if an incorrect boost control setting is selected, at least the fuel and spark control will be appropriate to help avoid engine damage.

can control a solenoid with its pulse width modulation (PWM) output drivers to be either open, closed, or constantly toggling at some known duty cycle. The greater the duty cycle, the more opportunity for flow there is across the solenoid. The ECU can then effectively regulate the control pressure to the wastegate through this PWM solenoid driver control, which in turn is actually regulating the compressor output and manifold pressure. Even better, the ECU can compare the measured MAP value to a preset target and adjust the boost control solenoid duty cycle up or down as necessary in closed loop control to hold the desired manifold pressure. This approach works well on most single-port wastegates, but ultimate precision is still a function of ECU processor speed and control loop refinement.

If a dual-port wastegate is used, a slightly better control system can be applied. Dual-port wastegates have two pressure fittings. The standard fitting opposite the spring remains, but it is accompanied by another fitting that feeds a chamber on the same side as the spring. If the second spring side chamber is left open to the atmosphere, the dual-port wastegate behaves just like its conventional single-port counterpart. The benefit of the dual-port wastegate is that regulated pressure can be applied to both sides, resulting in a pressure differential across the diaphragm. The wastegate does not begin to open until this pressure differential equalizes with the spring force. By splitting the boost reference line from the intake manifold or compressor outlet and applying a regulator to on-line feeding the spring side of the diaphragm the pressure differential can be adjusted while working at pressures well above the nominal equilibrium point of the spring and manifold pressure.

Once again, the ECU is put in charge of a solenoid to act as a regulator for this arrangement. The PWM output controls are connected to the boost control solenoid and pressure is measured by the MAP sensor. Instead of bleeding reference pressure to the atmosphere, regulated pressure is directed to the spring side chamber where it works against what is now a higher primary pressure. Since the resulting pressure differential across the solenoid is not as large as the bleed type mentioned earlier (where the differential is full boost pressure minus atmospheric pressure), smaller increments of adjustment are possible. This gives the ECU finer control over adjustments to the control loop as it tries to achieve the target manifold pressure setting.

Traction Control

Some ECUs offer the ability to adjust engine power based on vehicle speed. By limiting the power at low speeds, tire spin can be reduced to aid in overall acceleration. With some slightly more involved control logic, tire slip itself can be detected by looking at the rate of acceleration versus speed. Whenever the acceleration rate is too great for a given speed, the ECU assumes that the tires must be spinning and it can enter a power reduction mode. In order to work properly, the ECU must have some form of vehicle speed input from either a wheel speed sensor, driveshaft RPM sensor, or transmission output shaft speed sensor. Before attempting to tune the traction control system, it's always a good idea to verify that the ECU is registering the correct speed. A chassis dyno will make verifying vehicle speed a snap. The actual power reduction

DESIGNING AND TUNING HIGH-PERFORMANCE FUEL INJECTION SYSTEMS

With more than 2,000 hp on tap, this vehicle has no chance of making it down the quarter-mile cleanly at full throttle. Using speed based traction control to reduce power off the line results in much better acceleration than just spinning the tires from too much torque.

for traction control strategies can come from one of three basic sources: airflow, spark advance, or fuel cut.

Reducing airflow is usually reserved for applications where the ECU is also actively controlling the boost via a wastegate solenoid output. In the event of tire slip with boost control, the target boost level is simply reduced and the ECU performs all normal fuel and spark functions based on this lower resulting manifold pressure. Most ECUs that employ traction control via boost level have these controls integrated with the other boost control variables. The user typically just enters a maximum MAP allowed for each wheel speed. On electronic-throttle-control-equipped vehicles, the ECU would also have the option to reduce the blade angle to restrict airflow whether the engine is supercharged or naturally aspirated. Either of the airflow control methods will give a relatively "slow" path to engine torque control and, as a result, traction control. It takes time for the actual engine torque to be reduced as the manifold pressure drops, and it will also take time to rebuild manifold pressure once traction has been established and more power is desired.

A more immediate control method is retarding the spark advance. Reductions in delivered ignition angle can happen almost instantaneously, so they make for very good "fast" control paths for engine torque. If wheel slip is detected, some amount of ignition angle is removed until the slip goes to zero. Once full torque is desired again, spark advance is returned to the optimum setting of MBT or the knock limit as was previously done during normal calibration.

A final method of traction control is elimination of fuel delivery. This method is not usually desirable because it's often an "all or nothing" approach to torque delivery. While this can be very effective for rev limits where great intervention is preferred to avoid possible engine damage due to high speed, it usually does not result in smooth control even if done on a cylinder-by-cylinder basis. Additionally, the wall film effect dictates that 100% of the fuel does not get shut off to the cylinder on the first couple cycles. Shutting off the injector leaves the cylinder with a small amount of fuel evaporating from the port wall. Combining this with forced induction or nitrous oxide can be a recipe for disaster. Likewise, when the fuel is turned back on after a cutoff event, there is a delay before the total fuel delivered to the cylinder matches the target ratio as the wall film is being established again. It's usually best to just avoid using fuel cuts as a method of traction control at full power if possible.

More advanced control systems use electronic throttle controls instead of a cable. These systems can override the driver request for open throttle to satisfy a traction-control algorithm request.

Nitrous Oxide

Many modern standalone ECUs now have the ability to seamlessly integrate controls for a nitrous oxide injection system with the rest of the normal engine operation. Triggering the system is still done by some external switch, but the wires are run directly to the ECU for processing. Closing this circuit switches the ECU over to a new set of control parameters designed to optimize performance with the nitrous oxide flowing.

The wide-open-throttle switch is no longer necessary since the ECU already has a reliable signal from the throttle position sensor. Triggering the system at WOT is now as simple as setting the appropriate voltage that correlates with a wide-open blade position. This means there's one less physical component in the system to fail under the hood, a very good thing considering the marginal quality of many WOT switches and their precarious mounting positions. Even better, the outboard window switch is also replaced by software. The ECU will typically have adjustable minimum and maximum engine speed set points for activation to prevent overdosing of the cylinders at low speeds and runaway conditions near redline. Setting the shutoff point for the nitrous oxide system below the ECU's normal rev limit also greatly reduces the risk of damage due to leanout if the rev limiter shuts off the injectors while the nitrous system continues to inject just enough fuel to break things at high speed.

One important note regarding nitrous oxide injection is that the injected gas is rapidly expanding and displaces air in the ports. The result is actually a slight drop in engine volumetric efficiency. This can be confirmed with a MAF sensor (provided the Nitrous injection point is downstream of the sensor) where the activation of a nitrous system will show a lower measured total airflow across the RPM range at WOT compared to a naturally aspirated run on the same engine. Luckily, no real power is lost since the gas being injected to the port contains a higher oxygen concentration than the air it is displacing. The net result is an increase in total oxygen delivery to the cylinders, at a cooler temperature as well. The total fuel mass delivery must also be increased if the engine is to maintain the same combustion balance of hydrocarbons to oxygen within the cylinder. The added oxygen load to the cylinder also typically requires a reduction in ignition lead to avoid knock at the higher cylinder pressures being generated.

The black spacer between the throttle body and intake manifold here is a single-stage nitrous oxide injection plate. Since this engine uses an intake that is a derivative of an older carbureted design, a wet-flow nitrous oxide system works well here. (Photo courtesy of Motor City Steel)

Newer dry flow intake manifolds may cause puddling with larger amounts of nitrous when injected upstream of the plenum. A direct-port nitrous injection system like this one will allow for very large amounts of nitrous oxide to be safely injected along with the additional fuel through the individual nozzles closer to each intake valve.

With a wet-flow nitrous oxide injection system, all of the additional fuel is injected at the nozzle (or nozzles) completely separate from the conventional fuel injectors. In this case, no adjustment to the ECU's fuel delivery should be necessary. Any fuel trimming should be done by changing the fuel jet size in the nozzle to achieve the desired target lambda. The ECU still has the ability to employ a secondary ignition timing table or adder value

CHAPTER 14

Always check the bottle pressure before starting to tune a nitrous oxide system. Testing should always be done with a full bottle at high pressure to see the leanest possible condition. A bottle heater may be needed for repeated tests in order to maintain full pressure. (Photo courtesy of Motor City Steel)

whenever the nitrous oxide system is active. These ignition modifiers or alternative tables should be tuned only when the nitrous oxide is flowing, preferably at the highest bottle pressure that is intended to be run.

Tuning at a high bottle pressure means that the highest possible cylinder load is used to find a safe spark advance value and fuel delivery through the jets. As bottle pressure drops, the actual cylinder load will drop as well. The result is a slightly richer mixture with a greater safety margin for knock on the spark advance, often as the car is farther down the track fighting a higher aerodynamic resistance and slowing the engine's sweep rate as temperatures climb in the cylinder. Tuning for the worst case scenario is definitely a good idea.

Since most modern EFI intake manifolds were not designed for wet fuel flow and even distribution of a suspended fuel mixture between cylinders, it is preferable to use a dry flow nitrous oxide injection system on these engines. The nitrous is still injected as normal to the port or plenum, but all additional fuel is injected through the existing fuel injectors. This solves the concern of uneven cylinder distribution of the nitrous oxide and fuel as long as the nitrous itself is being evenly mixed with the incoming air charge.

Getting more fuel flow through the existing injectors can be done either with increase pressure or increased pulsewidth. Older nitrous oxide systems often applied pressure to the vacuum reference of the fuel pressure regulator in order to raise the fuel rail pressure. This rail pressure increase effectively raises the static flow rate of the fuel injectors as demonstrated by *Equation 5.7* (page 44). Remember that most ECUs do not have any way of knowing that this pressure and effective flow rate change has occurred. Therefore, it's preferable to just make a larger fuel request, provided the existing injectors can handle it. In this case, injector selection should be done based on the total fuel requirements of both the naturally aspirated engine and the nitrous oxide system's maximum delivery rate.

As long as the injectors have sufficient duty-cycle headroom, the larger fuel mass request that accompanies the nitrous injection is just calculated as some increase to the delivered injector pulsewidth. The calibrator is able to use the ECU's fuel adder functions to adjust actual fuel delivery to hit the desired target lambda during testing with the highest intended bottle pressure. Again, the testing is done at high bottle pressures to monitor the leanest and hottest possible condition, insuring that later operation on the track will always be safe.

Whether running a wet or dry nitrous system in multiple stages, the same tuning guidelines should still be followed. Many standalone ECUs allow the nitrous injection to be controlled by two or three stages. Often, a smaller initial stage is used to allow for a more gentle application of power early-on with a larger second stage that can really crank up the output when traction is not so difficult

 Injector Size

Traditional injector size calculators can still be employed as long as the inputs are total horsepower (including driveline and accessory losses), estimated Brake Specific Fuel Consumption, and number of injectors. The change in chemistry will shift the actual air/fuel ratio in relation to how much nitrous oxide is being used versus atmospheric air to make the total delivered power, but BFSC units are lb/hp-hr (which already takes this into account). Start out with a safe estimate of about 0.6 lb/hp-hr and work from there for most street systems.

Even if the actual air/fuel ratio changes due to the chemistry of nitrous oxide, the measured lambda should still read similar to what would be expected for a supercharged engine. The added fuel for cooling and knock control for increased loads should still register lambda≈0.80 for moderate doses, going richer with increased cylinder load and shot size. The UEGO sensor does not care whether the oxygen it is measuring came from the air or another injected gas. It just displays the total chemical balance, which is what's important for clean combustion.

---

110   DESIGNING AND TUNING HIGH-PERFORMANCE FUEL INJECTION SYSTEMS

AUXILIARY OUTPUTS

Bottle Heater

It's a good idea to have a bottle heater available during these tuning sessions in order to keep nitrous pressure near the optimum setting. If the vehicle is not equipped with one, there are several good 110v alternatives on the market that can be plugged into a wall outlet near the chassis dyno. Never attempt to heat a pressurized cylinder with an open flame.

A two-step ignition control can result in better launches at the drag strip. Engine speed is controlled to a point just below the limit of tire adhesion on launch by using a spark cut above the RPM limit. (Photo courtesy of Motor City Steel)

to find farther down the track. Each stage should still have its own fuel and spark modifiers that are tuned to offset only that stage's nitrous injection. Be sure to completely dial in the first stage before attempting to tune a second or third stage of nitrous. This will make the overall tuning process easier and more consistent.

Two-Step Control

A two-step controller is used to aid in drag racing launches. The two-step functionality sets a second engine speed limiter at a lower point when some other input switch is engaged. The input for the two-step activation is tied to a momentary external switch that is either directly held by the driver or some other mechanical linkage such as a clutch switch or line lock. When the switch is closed, the ECU cuts spark delivery to hold the optional (lower) speed limit. Running against the limiter, the engine can be consistently held at the desired launch RPM for an aggressive drag racing start with a specific amount of available torque to the wheels upon release. Releasing the switch disengages the lower speed limit, applying normal spark delivery to the engine at what is much greater than normal idle speed. The result is an almost-instant application of tremendous power to the transmission input and a stronger vehicle launch.

Turbocharged vehicles can also use the two-step function to build boost when stopped. Since the turbine is driven by exhaust gas heat and flow, it's difficult to fully power it by merely "free-revving" the engine without any load. When the spark is cut to a few cylinders by the lower rev limiter in the two-step, some amount of unburned fuel and air is passed to the exhaust system. This unburned mixture reacts almost instantly once it is subjected to the hot environment of the exhaust manifold and burned gases from the other cylinders. When this reaction occurs in the manifold and turbine housing, it rapidly expands and creates pressure. Instead of pushing down on a piston, this pressure now drives the turbine very effectively, creating shaft work for the compressor and consequently, boost in the intake tract. This external combustion can be very loud, but it's effective enough to help spool even the largest of turbochargers at the starting line.

Setting the two-step control point is pretty simple in most ECUs with this functionality. The trick is to make sure that before it is used the point at which the engine will be operating is already properly tuned for steady state operation. For an intended setpoint of 4,000 rpm on the two-step, this means taking the time to check delivered air/fuel ratio and optimal timing at 4,000 rpm and all boost points on the dyno without the limiter active. This will make sure that the air/fuel ratio being delivered to the cylinders that are actually seeing spark is appropriate and will not cause knock or other potential piston and head gasket damage.

When the two-step is activated on a turbocharged engine, boost will progressively build, so all manifold pressure points between atmospheric and maximum boost along the engine speed line may be hit as the driver holds the switch waiting for launch. This is not the time to realize that one of these points is a bit low on the volumetric efficiency table. Taking the time earlier to properly map every point in the table really begins to pay off here. If the earlier work was done correctly, there is surprisingly little work to be done after selecting the desired speed limit.

Transmission Control

If the ECU has an input for vehicle speed, chances are that it also has the ability to actuate a lockup solenoid for the torque converter on an automatic transmission. Locking the torque converter eliminates the slip between engine speed and transmission input shaft speed, reducing losses in the system at the expense of losing the torque multiplication of the torque converter. At low speeds (and in low gear), it is usually desirable to have more torque available to help accelerate a relatively heavy vehicle from a stop. Once up to speed, torque can be traded for power and we want to avoid wasting energy wherever possible. When cruising down the freeway, excessive slip in the torque converter not only wastes energy (read: lowers fuel economy), but also generates a significant amount of heat. This added heat can shorten the life of the transmission if the cooler is not sufficient, be sure

Lambda Lies

If the measured air/fuel ratio is checked while the limiter is active, it will undoubtedly read lean as the unburned oxygen passes the sensor. The wideband is just an oxygen sensor and doesn't know the difference between burned and unburned gases. The raw fuel being passed out the cylinders may smell rich to you, but the oxygen sensor can't detect it. Don't believe the lambda reading while a two-step is operating.

your vehicle has an adequate transmission oil cooler. Locking the torque converter reduces the slip within the torque converter that heats the fluid so much, so it not only can improve life expectancy of the powertrain, but also give better fuel economy.

If the clutches in the torque converter are strong enough, they can also be held closed during WOT at high speeds. Locking the converter in high gear can often added a couple MPH to the trap speed in the quarter-mile just by making more of the engine's power actually enter the transmission's gear sets instead of pumping the fluid in a loose converter housing. Only experimentation on each particular engine and vehicle combination will show the best time to make the switch between optimizing for input torque with an unlocked converter and optimizing for input power with a locked converter. Just make sure that no matter what engine speed and load result from the transmission settings, the engine fuel and spark maps are properly tuned for the worst-case-scenario loading.

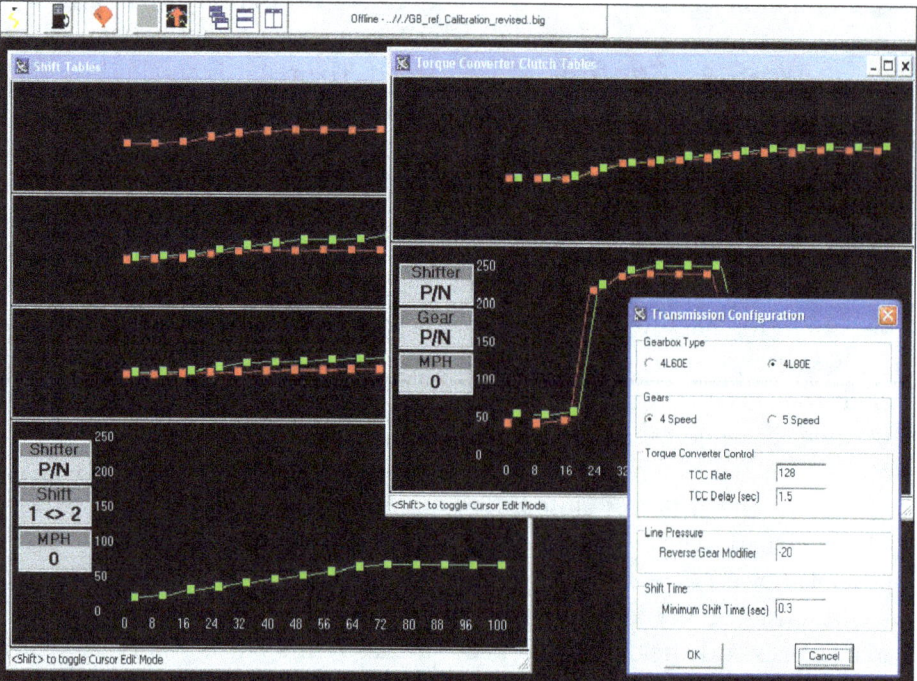

Transmission controls can be integrated with the ECU to activate either a converter lockup solenoid or the entire shift strategy if properly configured. This BigStuff3 ECU is able to control the popular GM four-speed automatics without any external devices.

CHAPTER 15

ALCOHOL AND ETHANOL

For years, a significant number of racers have been running alternative fuels. Historically, the most popular has been "alcohol," which in the automotive context typically refers to methanol. Methanol has been used by USAC, IRL, Champ Car, and NHRA Top Alcohol class racers through the years. It burns with a clear flame with minimal soot production and is very corrosive in its liquid form. Methanol is available from several sources such as Sunoco Racing Fuels, VP Racing Fuels, and Torco.

Methanol is a relatively simple molecule that starts out looking like methane (CH_4), but replaces one of the hydrogen legs with an –OH group that now qualifies it as an actual alcohol to chemists. Because the fuel carries some amount of oxygen within it, the stoichiometric balance for clean combustion in air is shifted. If methanol were to be burned at the same mass ratio of 14.64:1 as most gasoline blends, there would just be too many oxygen molecules available for each hydrogen and carbon in the mix. The result would be a lean burn with less-than-optimal power. To fix this, more fuel is added per unit of air in order to achieve a balance of all the hydrogens, carbons, and oxygens (which may come from either the air or the fuel itself) during combustion. With methanol, this balance is a ratio of 6:1 in Earth's atmosphere.

The IRL circuit currently runs on ethanol fuel, with the car making about 700 hp from naturally aspirated engines. The exhaust port is seen here just above the halfshaft on the side of the closeout panel ahead of the tranmission case.

Methanol contains slightly less energy per unit, but because the stoichiometric ratio is so rich (relatively speaking, of course!), more total fuel is burned on each cycle with the same amount of airflow. Once the correct ratio of fuel is delivered, the loss of specific energy per unit volume becomes irrelevant, as more total energy can be released with methanol than with gasoline for the same airmass. The limiting factor on how much power most engines can deliver is usually their maximum airflow limit. A limit on maximum airflow with a given target air/fuel ratio means a limit on total fuel delivery without going excessively rich and hurting power. If there is a limited amount of chemical energy to be released from the fuel, this also limits the potential mechanical energy out of the engine. With alcohol fuels that run at much richer mixtures in order to achieve the same chemical balance between the hydrogens, carbons, and oxygens, more total fuel can be burned with the same amount of outside air being pumped through the engine. As long as the fuel system is able to keep up with the higher flow rate demands of an alcohol-based system, more total power can be delivered even though the specific energy of the fuel may be slightly lower. Alcohol fuels also tend to burn at a noticeably lower temperature than gasoline. This can greatly reduce loads on the cooling system thermal concerns within the exhaust system at high power. Making large amounts of power from an engine with a fixed pumping capability gets easier when the fuel itself is helping to deliver oxygen to the cylinders.

A six-to-one ratio of air and fuel looks pretty rich at first glance. Keep in mind that this is actually the balance point. If burned at that ratio, the chemistry does not see it as "richer" than gasoline that is being burned at 14.64:1. Rather, it's just a smaller molecule that happens to be contributing to the oxygen source of the air during the reaction. A ratio of 9:1 may be extremely rich with gasoline, but with methanol it's exceptionally lean.

To make things more clear, let's go back to using units of lambda. Lambda is just the excess air ratio for combustion. It does not care what type of fuel is being burned because it is really a reference of where things are at the moment compared to whatever the chemical balance point is. *Equation 3.1* gave us the definition of lambda:

$$\lambda = \frac{\text{(Current AFR)}}{\text{(Stoichiometric AFR)}}$$

Equation 3.1

In the case of alcohol blends as fuels, the stoichiometric air/fuel ratio is just different than what we're used to seeing for gasoline. Using methanol's stoichiometric balance point of 6:1, lambda can be calculated in much the same manner as with gasoline. If the actual ratio of 9:1 from our earlier example is to be observed in units of lambda, we find that the current excess air ratio is actually:

$$\lambda = \frac{(9.00)}{(6.00)} = 1.50$$

The resulting lambda of 1.50 is so lean that combustion may not occur at all due to being near the lean ignition limit of the fuel, depending upon conditions. To get a clean burn, much more fuel is required. In this case, 50% more fuel would be necessary just to get back to the chemically ideal balance that is desirable at idle and cruise in most engines.

Oxygen Sensors and Alcohol

Lambda sensors, both wideband or narrowband, do not know what

Using a wideband oxygen sensor with alcohol blends when tuning is a must. Just stick with units of lambda to avoid confusion with numeric air/fuel ratios when the stoichiometric point is unfamiliar.

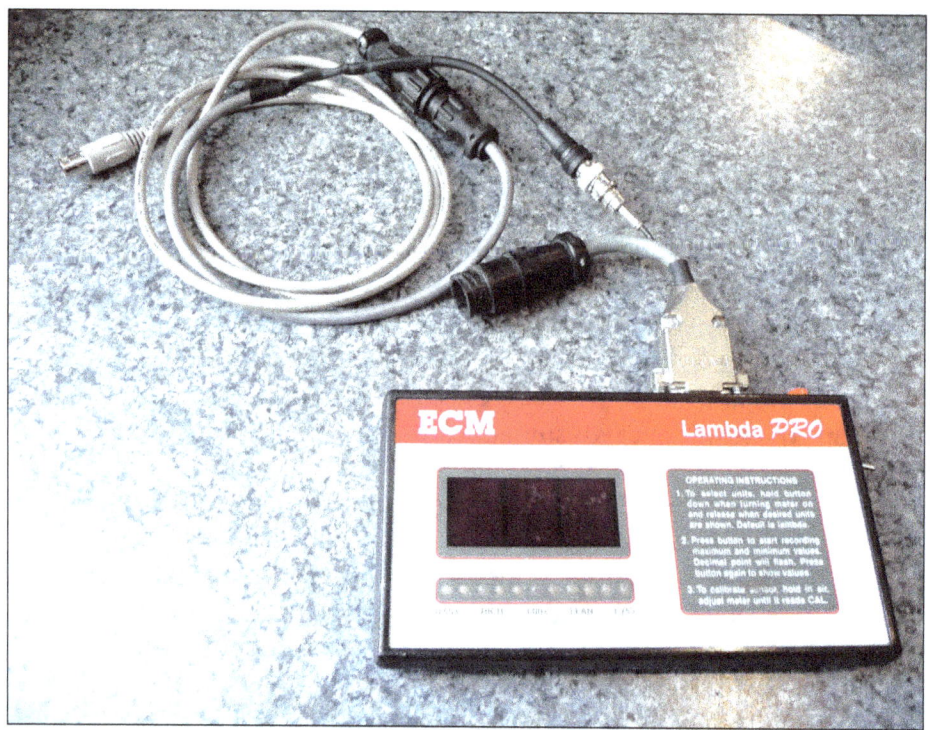

type of fuel is being burned in the cylinders. Frankly, they don't care and neither should you. What they tell you is which side of the chemical balance the engine is on at any given point. With a wideband, you just have the added benefit of knowing how far on either side of the balance the engine is. Although this may sound like a bit of a handicap at first, it's really a blessing in disguise.

Remember that the oxygen sensor is really only measuring oxygen content and not fuel content in the exhaust gases. The display that is returned for "air/fuel ratio" on many cheaper units is really just lambda multiplied by about 14.64 to give the less-educated user something he is used to seeing. If methanol is being burned at a ratio of 6.00:1 in an engine, the wideband sensor will detect a ratio of lambda=1.00. The cheaper units will display this as (1.00) x (14.64) for an indicated ratio of 14.64:1. Obviously, there is a mismatch here. The problem arises from the assumption that the engine is burning gasoline when, in fact, it's really burning methanol. The wideband sensor is actually doing its job perfectly, it's just that the display configuration is misleading. The best course of action is to configure the display to only show lambda. That way, the calibrator is not confused by the conversion factor. Most experienced calibrators are used to working in units of lambda anyway, so there is no problem with stopping here. If you really want to see an actual air/fuel ratio with methanol, the wideband output configuration must be modified to show lambda multiplied by the stoichiometric balance point of 6.00:1. Once you can get used to looking at units of lambda rather than air/fuel ratio, it becomes far easier to tune almost any alternative fuel blend.

Calibration Setup for Alcohol

So how does one set an EFI system up to properly control a methanol fueled engine? The answer is surprisingly simple. All that's really needed is to open the target air/fuel ratio table and input new targets based upon the chemistry of the fuel being used. With methanol, most of Zones 1, 2, 3, 4, 5, and 7 are set to lambda=1.00, which is a ratio of 6.00:1 in this case. When tuning the VE table, just look at the wideband output in units of lambda, not air/fuel ratio. Lambda will show the exact error if the target is stoichiometric operation, so corrections to the VE surface can be made based upon lambda alone. Make corrections to the VE table in the same exact manner as with gasoline by using the delivered lambda as a correction factor.

When the time comes for WOT tuning with alcohol fuels, just keep working in units of lambda. The same lambda setpoints can be used with alcohol fuels as with gasoline. A naturally aspirated engine can be run at lambda≈0.87. With alcohol just like gasoline, the only difference will be the actual commanded air/fuel ratio. If the base fuel map does not support units of lambda, simply calculate the desired ratio using a variant of *Equation 3.1* as before:

Target AFR = λ x (Stoichiometric AFR)

In this case, the target ratio is lambda=0.86, so the actual desired air/fuel ratio with methanol for our naturally aspirated engine is calculated as:

Target AFR = (0.86) x (6.00) = 5.16:1

Stay On Target

Whenever tuning with an alcohol-based fuel, just set the target air/fuel ratio in the base map according to the proper stoichiometric shift and continue working as normal using lambda exclusively. Before long, you'll forget how hard alcohols are to tune as you just work toward the usual target of lambda=1.00 for most of the map.

The target air/fuel ratio within Zone 6 can be populated with a ratio of 5.16:1 for use with methanol. This provides a safe starting point from which the WOT volumetric efficiencies can be calculated. Because alcohol fuels burn cooler, it may be found that this much extra enrichment is not necessary. Running slightly leaner, closer to LBT, around lambda≈0.92 may be possible without damage on alcohol-fueled engines. Only actual testing of the engine in question with a loaded dyno or at the track will tell if this approach is acceptable.

Alcohol-based fuels also have inherently high octane ratings. This high octane rating means that the fuel is not very likely to experience knock under higher loads and temperatures. Many alcohol engines will be able to run ignition angles all the way up to MBT timing at WOT without knock. Keep this in mind as testing is performed. Air/fuel ratios should still be corrected before optimizing ignition angle. Once the delivered air/fuel ratio matches the target, timing sweeps can be done to find the best power and torque for the engine. Don't wait for spark

CHAPTER 15

It's becoming increasingly easier to find E85 fuel as it gains popularity with both environmental types and performance enthusiasts. Remember that the actual alcohol content may change with seasonal blends when bought at a gas station's pump.

knock to tell you when too much timing has been delivered, as this may be well past MBT with alcohol. Just watch the torque output as timing is added. If delivered torque drops with added timing, chances are that MBT timing has been passed. Backing off the timing may actually deliver more torque output. Even in boost, timing may still be able to reach MBT with alcohol without knock. Don't be afraid of what looks like large timing numbers compared to gasoline, but be careful not to go too far and lose power. Always try to run the minimum amount of ignition lead necessary to deliver maximum torque without knock or abnormal combustion.

Ethanol

One of the unintended benefits of the environmental movement has been the availability of cheap race fuel. E85 is billed as a "greener" alternative to gasoline because its combustion results in lower CO_2 production. Carbon dioxide is a greenhouse gas that contributes to the warming of the Earth, so many efforts have been made to reduce the overall generation of it. By blending conventional gasoline with a percentage of ethanol, the carbon content of the fuel is reduced, which in turn reduces production of CO_2 by the vehicles burning this fuel.

Much like methanol, ethanol starts out as a simple hydrocarbon molecule. In this case, the base molecule would be ethane (C_2H_6), which is a two-carbon chain. To make ethane into its alcohol equivalent, ethanol, an –OH group again replaces one of the hydrogen atoms on the molecule. The result is another oxygen-bearing fuel that has a different stoichiometric combustion balance point that is somewhere between that of gasoline and methanol. The stoichiometric balance for clean

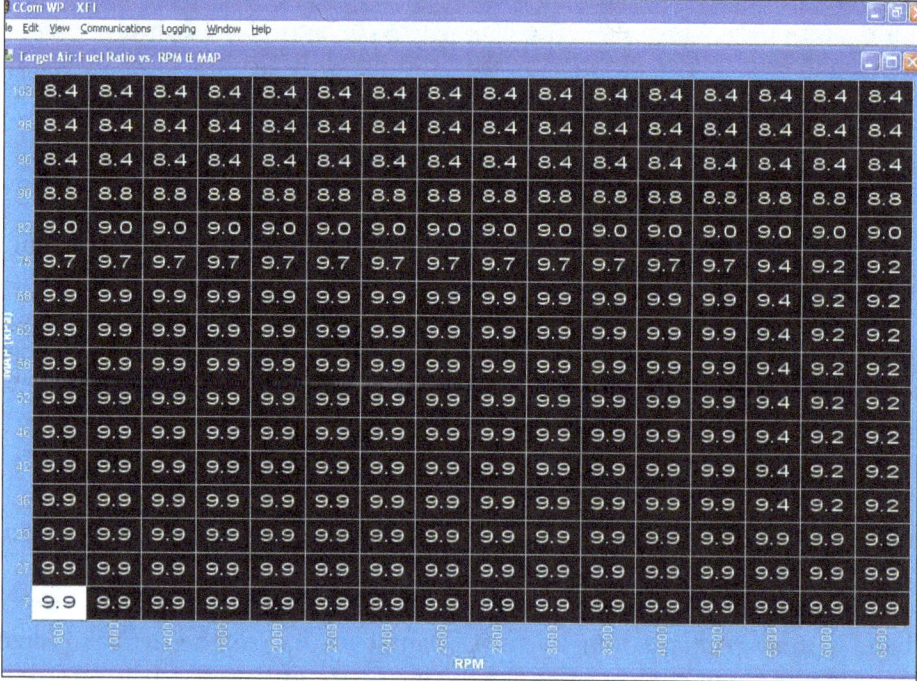

One of the first steps when performing a calibration for alcohol fuels is to determine the proper target air/fuel ratio based on the new chemistry. This table is set up for E85 and will result in lambda=1.00 for the idle and cruise ranges along with lambda=0.85 at WOT.

116 DESIGNING AND TUNING HIGH-PERFORMANCE FUEL INJECTION SYSTEMS

combustion of pure ethanol is a mass ratio of 9.00:1. Ethanol itself has an inherently high octane rating due to the compact shape of the molecule. The octane rating of pure ethanol is approximately 129 RON (Research Octane Number, the higher of the two [MON, Motoring Octane Number is the other]). So in a rare coincidence, the environmental movement has lead to widespread availability of cheap, high octane fuel.

Many different blends of ethanol are available today. Pure ethanol is actually rare, and usually only available as a research fuel with correspondingly high pricing. However, E85 has become far more common at gas stations today. E85 is typically a blend of 85% ethanol and 15% gasoline. Adding the 15% gasoline to the mixture greatly helps cold temperature evaporation rates and makes storage less of a concern for water absorption. The blend between ethanol and gasoline in E85 results in a stoichiometric balance point of a 9.85:1 mass ratio. When tuning an E85 application, simply use 9.85 instead of the 14.64 used for gasoline or 6.00 used for methanol for zones 1, 2, 3, 4, 5, and 7. For a naturally aspirated engine looking to run at lambda≈0.86 at WOT, the actual target ratio is found as before by:

Target AFR = (0.86) x (9.85) = 8.47:1

Remember that even though this looks like an extremely rich ratio at first glance, it's going to behave similar to a gasoline engine operating at about 12.6:1. Also remember that a cheaper wideband may actually display "12.6" at this ratio when it really is measuring lambda=0.86 and converting it to a gasoline-based display number. Just stick with the lambda reading to avoid confusion during testing. E85 has an octane rating of approximately 105 (R+M)/2, depending on the blend. This high octane rating is what makes this "green" fuel attractive for many racing applications.

In winter months, the fuel sold as "E85" is usually actually closer to E70, a 70% blend of ethanol that contains more gasoline. This is done to aid in cold starting of the engine since the alcohol fuels have lower vapor pressures than their gasoline equivalent and have trouble evaporating completely at low temperatures. During the transition months, the fuel in the tanks at gas stations selling E85 may vary anywhere between these two blends, so it's important to know what you're burning before getting too far into the calibration exercises.

Most OEM vehicles that are designated as "flex fuel" vehicles have the ability to detect the difference between the seasonal blends of ethanol-based fuels and normal gasoline. This is done either by a specific sensor or by a more complex logic within the ECU. The logic-based systems employ a "virtual sensor" that solves for alcohol content by examining fuel trims and knock sensor feedback immediately after startup if the fuel level has changed. The logic used here is pretty involved and closely guarded by the manufacturers who have invented it, so it should not be expected to show up in the garden-variety standalone controller any time soon. The fuel composition sensor is typically installed either in the fuel tank or on the fuel feed line leading to the engine and is active anytime the ECU is running. One such example is GM's flex fuel sensor used in some truck applications. This sensor returns a PWM signal to the ECU that indicates both alcohol concentration percentage and fuel temperature. If the ECU has the software to adjust fueling based on this input, it can make tuning with various blends of alcohol fuels a breeze.

Two primary hardware concerns must be addressed when running alcohol fuels: capacity and corrosion. Because these fuels require larger volumes of flow to reach their stoichiometric and power enrichment ratios, the fuel system must be sized to support these higher flow rates. It takes about 50% more fuel volume to support the same air/fuel ratio with E85 as it would gasoline. This means that the fuel pump, lines, filters, rails, and injectors all need to be sized accordingly. Before simply buying larger capacity components, it's also important to consider the materials used. Alcohol fuels can be corrosive to the parts in many older fuel systems. Rubber and EPDM seals can literally be dissolved by alcohols, and the deposits may clog filters and injectors. Viton, Teflon, or another equivalent material should be used instead. Aluminum will oxidize in the presence of alcohols too, so stainless steel fittings, rails, and hard lines should be used whenever possible with alcohol fuels.

> **Single Tune**
>
> The latest F.A.S.T. XFI standalone controllers have the ability to monitor the GM fuel composition sensor (P/N 12570260) when connected to the auxiliary discrete input. This means a single tune file can be used with premium pump gas as well as summer blend E85.

CHAPTER 15

Teflon

I have seen expensive rubber core stainless braided fuel lines ruined by alcohol erosion in just a matter of days after installation. Use Teflon-based flexible lines or stainless hard lines with alcohol fuel systems to avoid this expensive lesson.

Pump Gas

Even those of you running standard pump gasoline are probably getting a mild alcohol blend. By law, most gas stations today are now allowed to sell blends of as much as 10% ethanol as "gasoline." The ethanol is being used to displace the MTBE (methyl tert-butyl ether), which has its own environmental and health concerns. It used to be that stations were required to post a sticker on the pump declaring the alcohol content, but that's no longer happening. Some regions were quicker to adopt the maximum allowable ethanol content in the pump gasoline. In my travels and discussions with shop owners and calibrators across the country, I've found that almost every station can be assumed to be selling some alcohol blend unless stated otherwise. In most cases, this means assuming a blend of 10% ethanol.

Any addition of alcohol blends to the gasoline will shift the stoichiometric balance point. The more oxygen carried by the fuel, the richer the stoichiometric point will be. Where

Pump Gas

When tuning with pump gas, just treat it as an E10 blend and set the stoichiometric regions to a target value of 14.2:1. Use lambda instead of air/fuel ratio and make corrections based on the oxygen balance.

E85 has a stoichiometric ratio of 9.85:1, E10 (most pump gas blends) will balance at about 14.2:1. This means that tuning to an assumed pure gasoline composition with a stoichiometric point of 14.64:1 may include a 3% error before the engine is ever started. The wideband oxygen sensor will still typically display "14.64:1" at lambda=1.00, even though this is really an actual ratio of 14.2:1 with a 10% ethanol blend. Three percent may not sound like much, and it really isn't, but the idea behind engine calibration is to get all variables as close to optimal as possible. Leaving a 3% error in the fuel's stoichiometric point just makes tuning the volumetric efficiency table, startup fuel, and transient fueling that much less accurate. It's a good idea to just adjust at the beginning before baking that error into every other calculation later on.

The only trick with E10 gasoline blends is that they must be treated like normal gasoline for the purposes of spark tuning. The alcohol in the fuel is part of the cocktail of additives used to get the desired octane rating. In this case, 91 octane really is just 91 octane, so the same care must be taken to avoid knock at high loads with E10 blends as is typically done with conventional gasoline.

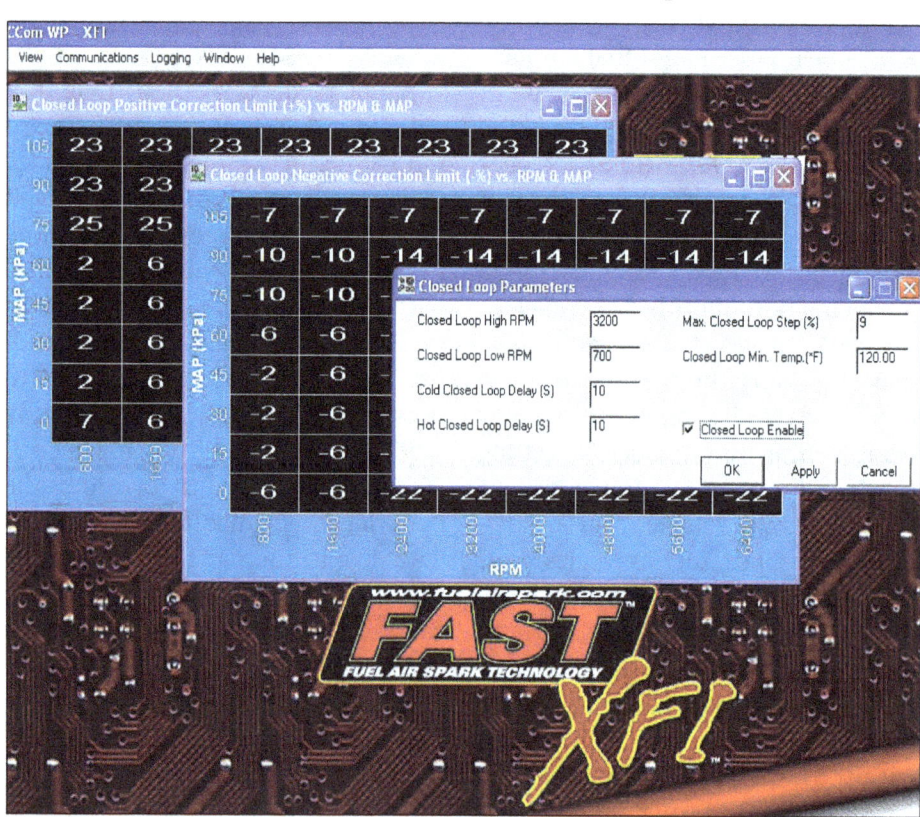

Closed loop fuel correction can be a big help when using E85. The variable alcohol content from the seasonal blends can be tolerated if these tables are set up with enough flexibility.

118   DESIGNING AND TUNING HIGH-PERFORMANCE FUEL INJECTION SYSTEMS

APPENDIX

Tuning Example

Let's take a look at putting everything discussed earlier in this book to work in a real application. This demonstration discusses the start-to-finish tuning process as performed on a typical enthusiast application. The vehicle used here is a 1969 Chevrolet Corvette with a big-block 427-ci engine. The factory intake and fuel systems have been replaced with an Edelbrock dual-plane aluminum manifold that is fitted with injector bungs on each intake port, aimed at the valve. A four-hole throttle body replaces the carburetor and includes an integral TPS sensor along with the IAC valve. A high-pressure electric fuel pump is installed on the frame rail feeding a pair of aluminum rails and a single adjustable fuel-pressure regulator set to 42.5 psi (3 bar) without any vacuum signal. The 30 lb/hr "Red Top" fuel injectors were sourced from the Ford Motorsport catalog.

The owner opted for a Megasquirt ECU as a low-cost solution to converting his carbureted classic into a more civilized fuel injected machine. The Megasquirt is a do-it-yourself-oriented kit that includes instructions for adapting the controller to a wide variety of engines, ignition systems, and vehicle applications. It uses a fairly straight forward MAP-based speed density control algorithm with a couple unique twists that will be discussed as we go. Tuning this system, it becomes apparent that the controller was designed more by software and code specialists than combustion experts, but that's not a show stopper as long as we keep the real goals in mind during the tuning process.

The first steps in our tuning adventure are to enter as many known parameters as possible before starting the engine. In this case, the easiest to find would be the fuel injector characteristics. Many fuel injector sales websites and retail outlets freely publish the static flow rate of the injectors but, as we learned in Chapter 5, there's more to it than just pounds per hour. A quick internet search leads us to the Ford Racing Performance Parts website where the entire injector "Calibration Summary" datasheet has been published in the units used by Ford OEM controllers. These values can be adapted for use with the Megasquirt ECU if we make a couple adjustments to correct for our actual fuel pressure.

Rated Pressure	39.15	psid
"Hi Slope"	0.008398	lb/sec
	30.23	lb/hr

Offset Curve	Volts	Offset
	6	3.253
	8	1.669
	10	1.057
	11	0.872
	12	0.730
	13	0.627
	14	0.519
	15	0.441

Since the Ford datasheet shows flow rates at a differential pressure of 39.15 psi (2.7 bar), the Bernoulli equation is used to find a new linear flow rate:

$$\text{New Flow Rate} = 30.23 \text{ lb/hr} \times \sqrt{(42.5/39.15)}$$
$$= 30.23 \times 1.042$$
$$= 31.496 \text{ lb/hr at } 42.5 \text{ psid}$$

DESIGNING AND TUNING HIGH-PERFORMANCE FUEL INJECTION SYSTEMS

APPENDIX

This corrected flow rate is entered into the injector settings screen in the software along with a nominal value for offset time at normal operating voltage. In this case, the Ford spec sheet showed us that increasing the rail pressure slightly increases the injector offset, so the 12 volt offset of 0.73 ms was increased to a more realistic 0.75 ms and entered into the ECU data. The Megasquirt ECU uses a straight-line compensation for opening delay versus operating voltage instead of the real curve that injectors experience. This is one of those cases where the code guys have simplified the actual physics at the expense of a little accuracy. In order to satisfy their straight-line estimation, the slope was taken from the difference between the 11-volt and 15-volt offsets provided by Ford Racing:

$$\text{ms/v} = \frac{(0.871 - 0.441)}{(15-11)} = 0.1075$$

Since these are high impedance injectors, the ECU is configured to operate with saturation driving of the injector output transistors. This is accomplished in the Megasquirt by setting the PWM current to 100% across the board. This is a key area where taking the time to carefully read the users' manual is required to understand how the entered calibration values will affect ECU performance. This is not optional!

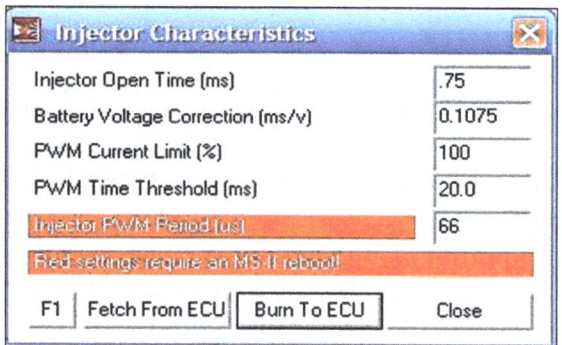

Moving forward, the rest of the ECU's fundamentals must be configured as well. In order to satisfy the speed density equations, engine displacement must be entered along with the number of cylinders and injection pattern. This ECU is configured for batch fire operation across two banks and a MAP based calculation. The reference air/fuel ratio is set to 14.6:1 to account for a small amount of alcohol content in the pump gas instead of an ideal 14.68:1 with pure gasoline. This ECU also takes the engine size, number of cylinders, and a few other

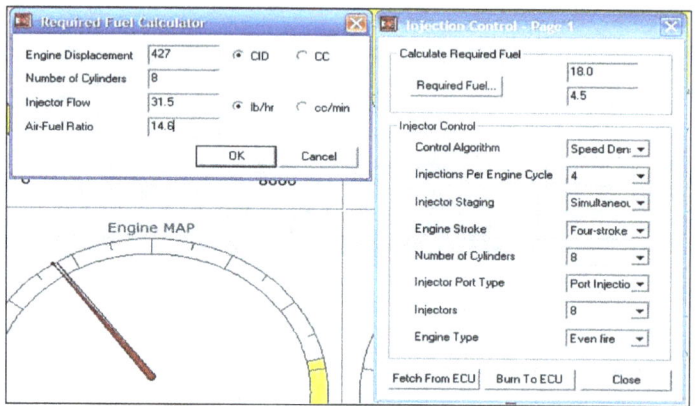

assumptions to auto-generate a starting VE table. Don't expect this to be correct right out of the box, but it's a decent starting point to work from.

The top number in the "Required Fuel" box represents the injector pulsewidth at maximum output for the target air/fuel ratio. Since we know the target air/fuel ratio at WOT will be richer than this, we'll need to make corrections somewhere else later on to get the ratio we really want. In this specific ECU case, it means that the VE values will only really equal the engine's actual VE when the target ratio is 14.6:1. If we want the engine to run richer anywhere, this enrichment ratio (phi) must be "baked into" the VE table values, forcing a richer actual fuel delivery under those conditions.

Before running the engine too much, we must also verify that the ignition system is properly configured. This is the point where we double-check our settings for coil output (this vehicle uses a Ford EDIS module), and reading the users' manual is once again critical to getting all the correct settings on this screen for the vehicle's hardware. The crank trigger angle is verified by checking ignition with a timing light. Any error in crank trigger angle will show up in the delivered timing, so grab a timing light and check things the old fashioned way. This vehicle required a 5 degree offset in order to align the ECU with the engine.

Once the ignition settings are correct, we begin to prepare for open loop fuel calibration on the dyno. The

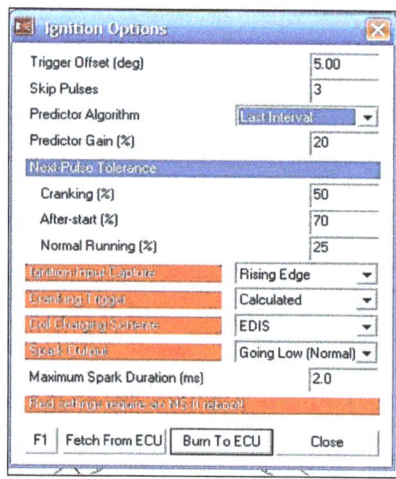

TUNING EXAMPLE

key here is to make sure we're not aiming at a moving target. Closed loop corrections are disabled by either setting the allowable correction to 0% or setting a master disable switch.

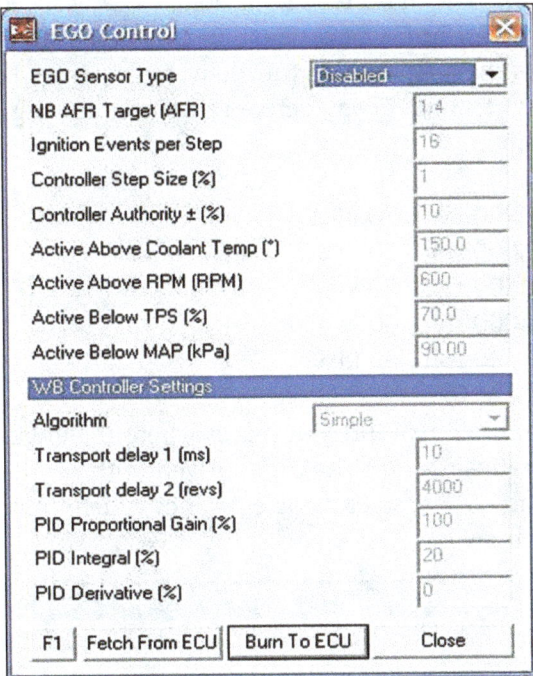

The target air/fuel ratios are also entered into the appropriate table. The Megasquirt ECU only references this table when closed loop correction is active with an integral wideband. This table displays a good final target ratio setup, but we'll be using an external ECM LambdaPro wideband during the calibration of the VE table to make sure we can really trust the data.

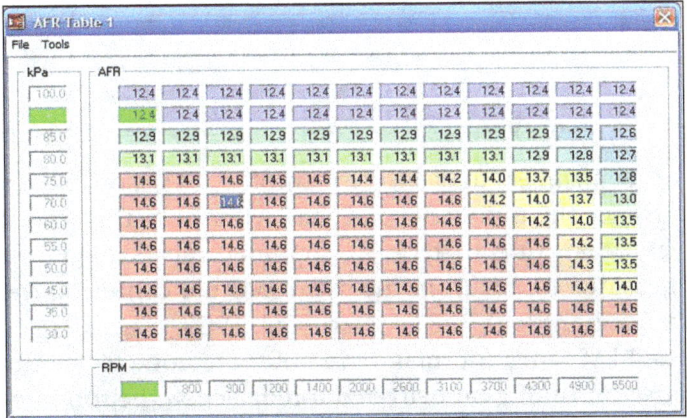

With the targets clearly defined, it's time to fire up the engine and use the dyno as a real calibration tool. To avoid headaches initially, we skip right past the idle tuning temporarily and hold the engine at a more forgiving speed and load point where it is less likely to stall or give us inconsistent data. In this case, we'll start at 2,000 rpm and 60 kPa with a target of lambda=1.00 to begin roughing in the VE table corrections.

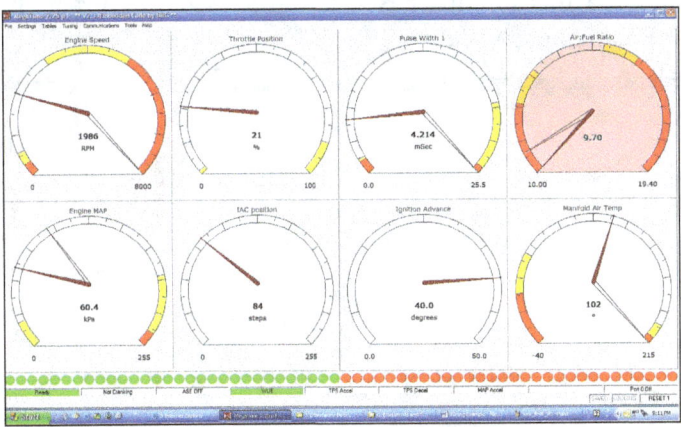

The engine is held in steady state long enough to get a consistent reading on the wideband. Notice that the "Air Fuel Ratio" gauge indicates extremely rich because the on-board wideband is not in use. Instead, we simply look at the professional UEGO display in units of lambda and use that value as our correction factor, as discussed in Chapter 10. It's important to take steady state data here to make our work on the transients later that much easier and more accurate. You'll also notice that the engine speed is not precisely 2,000 rpm. The key is to be as close to the VE table breakpoints as possible while avoiding oscillations. If you stabilize within 100 rpm or so, there should be negligible difference in actual volumetric efficiency. Temperatures are also key to watch. This ECU will automatically adjust for inlet temperature changes, but these should be held as consistent as possible throughout the mapping of the VE table.

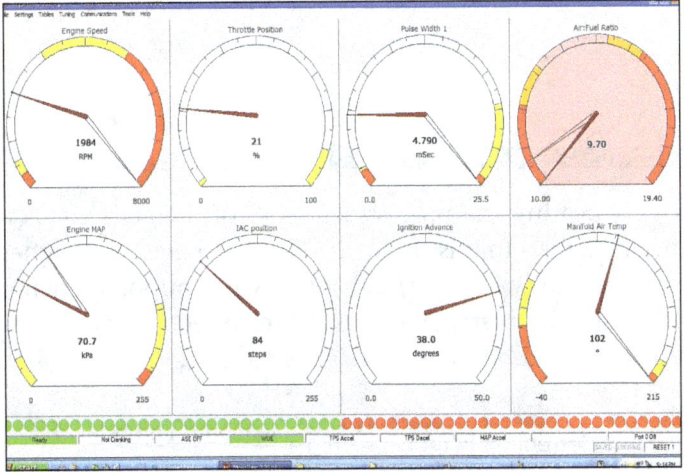

APPENDIX

With the 60 kPa cell properly adjusted, we use the dyno's speed controls to hold the engine at 2,000 rpm while load is increased to deliver 70 kPa to the intake manifold. After a brief stabilization period, another lambda measurement is taken and used to correct the VE table appropriately.

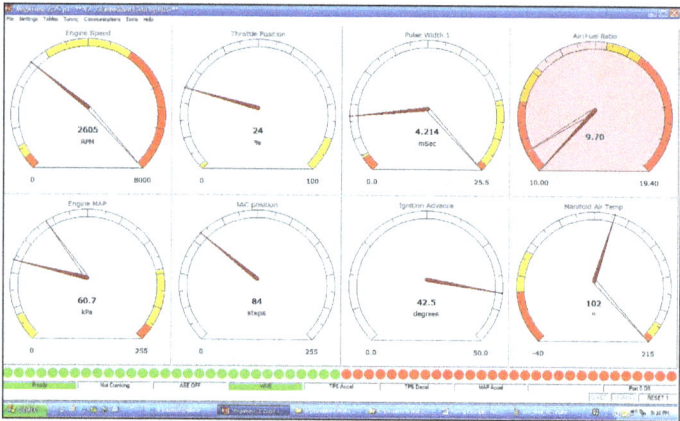

After going through most of the load points at 2,000 rpm, engine speed can be changed to the next breakpoint in the VE table. We start again at about 60 kPa to see the RPM influence and then progress to various loads at this new speed. Along the way, we use measured lambda to make corrections to the table at each cell or "corner" of the table.

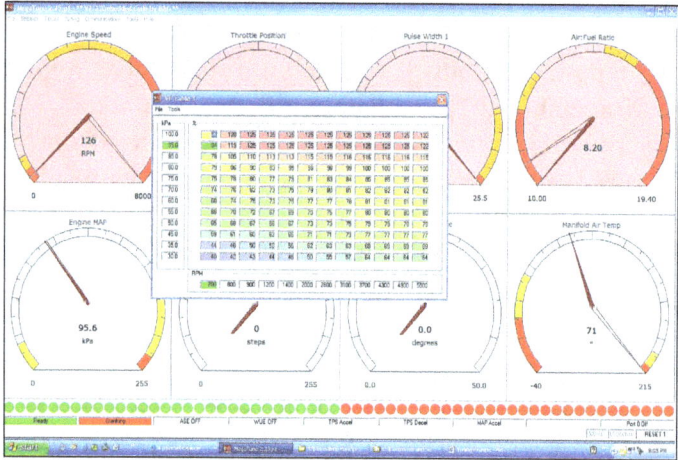

Repeating the process across all of the cells yields a final VE map that is smooth and progressive. The higher load points where air/fuel ratio is intentionally richer than stoichiometry meant that the correction factor was calculated based on error relative to the target:

$$\text{Correction Factor} = \frac{\text{(Actual Measured Lambda)}}{\text{(Target Lambda)}}$$

With the delivered air/fuel ratio closely matching the target values in steady state, we can then progress to spark calibration. The objective is to pick a handful of critical points and find MBT by performing the spark hook test. The dyno is used to hold a steady speed again as the driver holds throttle (load) constant while adjusting timing and noting the delivered torque. For this exercise, the MBT was derived at the following speed-load points:

- 1,900 rpm, 70 kPa
- 2,000 rpm, 50 kPa
- 2,500 rpm, 50 kPa
- 3,000 rpm, 60 kPa
- 3,500 rpm, 60 kPa

These points represent places where the engine may see significant duty. The car is driven both on the street and road course, so cruising efficiency is definitely a plus for the owner.

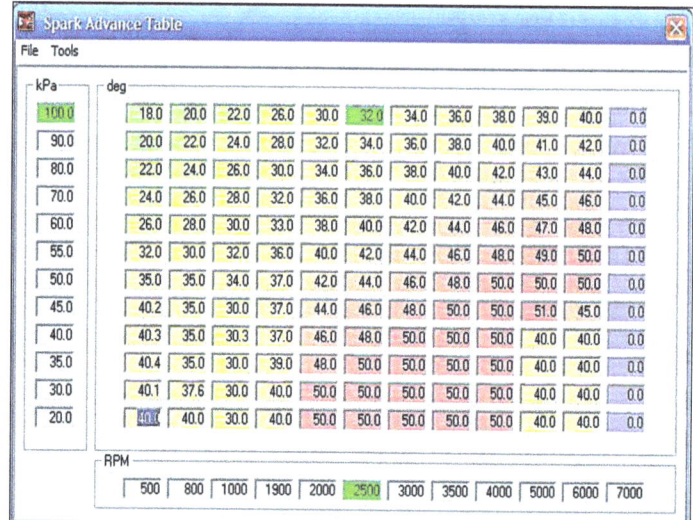

Remember that at part throttle, it's possible to advance the timing beyond MBT without hitting knock yet. Make sure to base the optimum spark angle on measured torque from the dyno to avoid confusing the knock limit with MBT at part load. WOT sweeps across the RPM range (normal dyno pulls) are done to see the effect of timing on delivered torque across the top lines of the base spark advance table. Simply add two degrees to the top lines and perform a second WOT sweep test. Anywhere the resulting torque is higher without knock, you will keep the increased spark advance in the table. If torque is lost or you hear knock as a result of the increased timing, go back to the previous value and consider this part of the spark advance calibration done. Again, the timing value that delivers the best torque without knock is the winner. Just make sure to avoid crowding the knock limit if it only gains a couple foot-pounds of torque. The safety margin is worth more than the statistically insignificant power increase in most applications.

With the spark advance table dialed-in at both part- and full-throttle conditions, we can return to fueling. This time, we'll check the transient behavior by performing a step test. The step test is done by holding the engine speed constant with the dynamometer while the driver makes a discrete step input to the gas pedal. It's important to only make a single, positive change in throttle position while checking the transient fuel settings. When done correctly, we see the effect of wall film evaporation on the total cylinder fueling and can make adjustments to the transient fuel tables to offset this. Our test ECU has an "acceleration wizard" screen that contains the transient fuel calibration values that will be adjusted until the step test shows only a minimal change in air/fuel ratio throughout the test. Several different engine speeds are checked to make sure that an adequate amount of acceleration enrichment is provided without over-fueling in other areas.

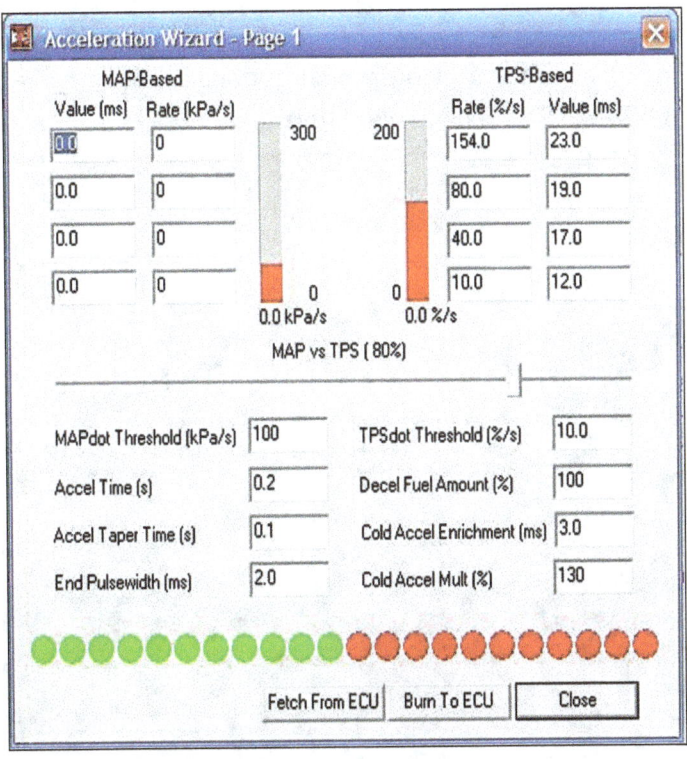

With the acceleration enrichment values dialed in, the vehicle's behavior is really beginning to shine. Driver inputs are met with crisp throttle response and clean combustion. Any time the driver increases throttle position, engine torque is consistently increased without wasting fuel or generating excessive emissions. The result is what most calibrators and vehicle owners will agree to be good drivability in traffic and on the track. Now it's time to refine the idle performance.

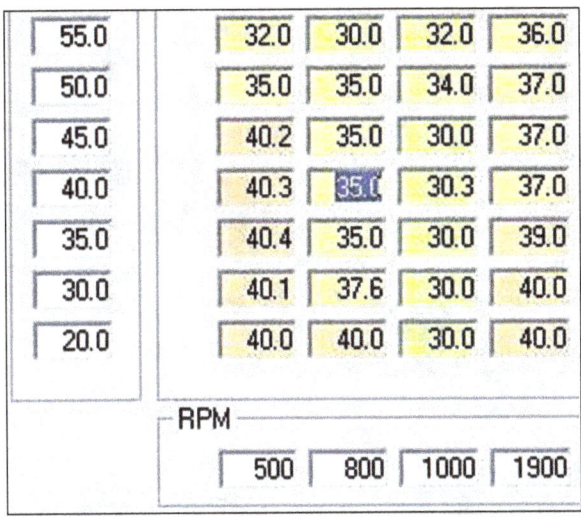

Since there is no dedicated idle spark advance table, it is baked into the base ignition table on this Megasquirt ECU. While many ECUs will have their own dedicated idle timing tables, this is a case where we must work within the limitations of this budget-minded system. Not to worry, though, since a skilled calibrator can still make this table work properly. The target idle point is highlighted in the table above. The value in this cell does not represent MBT, but rather a significant reduction from there in order to create a torque reserve on the hook test curve.

Notice how the timing at speeds below the idle target is increased. This will effectively use up some of the torque reserve to prevent stalling if the engine speed is pulled down by releasing the clutch or pulling an automatic transmission into gear. Above the target idle speed, timing is reduced even further, but only in low vacuum conditions. This will effectively reduce engine torque if the engine speed surges above our idle target and help reduce speed back to our target. The next column showing an even higher engine speed returns to MBT timing to preserve efficiency above idle.

With normal temperature idle speed effectively controlled by the timing trims above and below the target speed, we can now look at improving the behavior during cold starts and warm up. Timing is added at low temperatures to offset the increased friction of closer tolerances. This timing will be added to whatever is in the base ignition table.

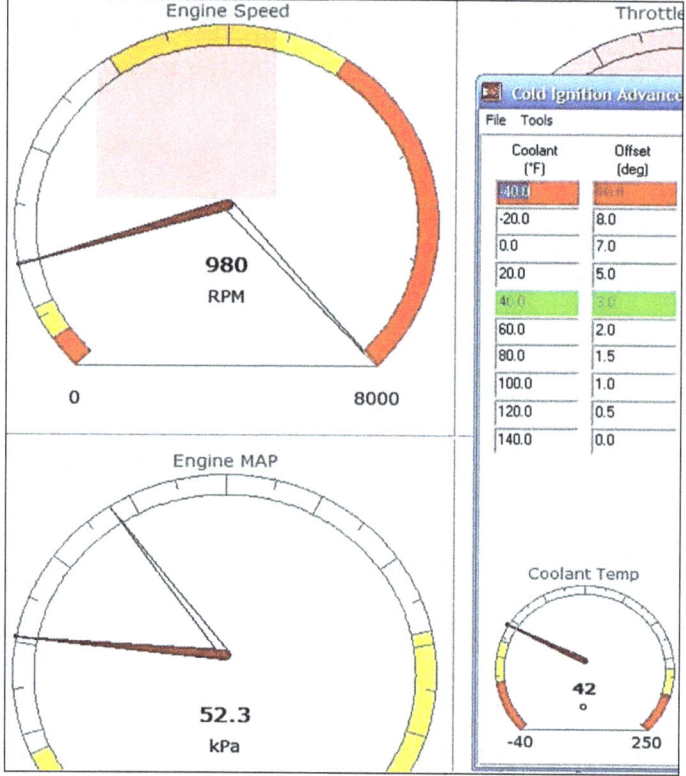

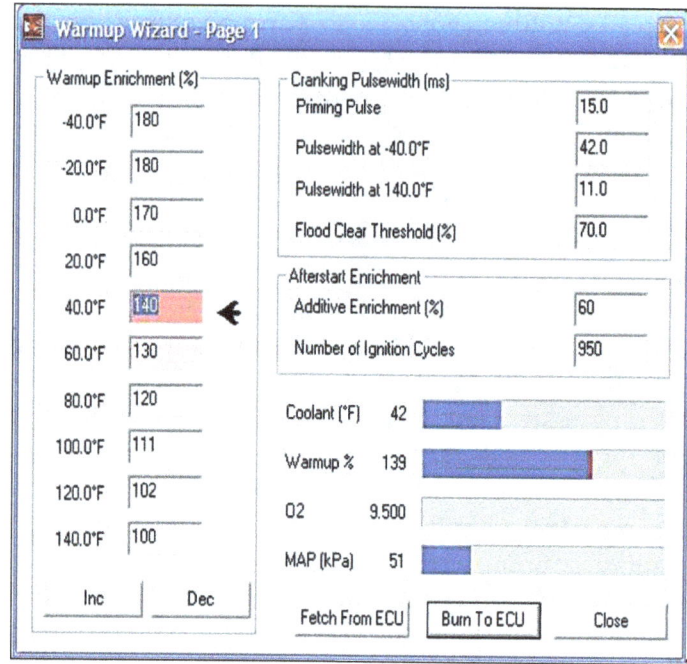

Along with added ignition timing in cold conditions, some extra fuel must also be used to offset the lower evaporation rates that accompany a cold engine. The amount of extra fuel is tuned by checking the wideband air/fuel ratio throughout a cold start. If we know that the fundamental VE table is correct, we can safely assume that any apparent leanness during startup is due to poor mixture preparation and fuel evaporation. Some extra fuel is added until the measured lambda shows 1.00 or slightly less. Remember that a slightly rich mixture will make more torque and can be helpful in offsetting the cold friction as well as making for more stable combustion. Going slightly rich at cold engine temperatures is preferable to be lean, so don't be afraid to overshoot by a little here.

One can also see that the priming pulse is defined in this screen and is significantly larger at cold temperatures. There is also an after-start enrichment of 60% that decays to zero over a period of 950 cycles, a little under a minute for this engine.

At this point, we should have a vehicle that starts right up with the key and settles into a stable idle. Upon driving off, both timing and fuel are handled seamlessly so that the driver merely controls torque with his right foot without really thinking about it. WOT is also optimized for power, and deceleration is controlled and smooth. The only thing left is to take the vehicle off the dyno and drive it in the real world. The test drive should be merely a confirmation of what we already know to be true. If all of the previous work was done correctly, there's nothing left to do here but enjoy.

APPENDIX

Conversion Charts

Length			Mass			Volume		
Inches	Meters	mm	Pounds	Grams	kg	Liters	cc	Inches^3
1	0.0254	25.40	1	453.59	0.454	1	1000	61.02
Meters	mm	Inches	kg	Grams	Pounds	Inches^3	cc	Liters
1	1000	39.37	1	1000	2.205	1	16.39	0.01639

Power			Torque			Velocity		
HP	ft-lb/s	kW	ft-lb	in-lb	Nm	MPH	KPH	m/s
1	550	0.746	1	12.0	1.356	1	1.609	0.447
kW	HP	ft-lb/s	Nm	ft-lb	in-lb	KPH	m/s	MPH
1	1.34	737.3	1	0.738	8.85	1	0.277	0.621

Pressure					Airflow			
bar	in Hg	in H20	kPa	PSI	g/s	kg/hr	lb/min	CFM
1	29.53	401.5	100.0	14.504	1	3.6	0.132	0.0101
PSI	bar	in Hg	in H20	kPa	kg/hr	g/s	lb/min	CFM
1	0.0689	2.04	27.7	6.895	1	0.2778	0.037	0.0028
kPa	PSI	bar	in Hg	in H20	lb/min	CFM	kg/hr	g/s
1	0.145	0.010	0.295	4.015	1	0.0763	27.22	7.560
in Hg	in H20	kPa	PSI	bar	CFM	lb/min	kg/hr	g/s
1	13.6	3.386	0.491	0.034	1	0.0763	2.08	0.576

Temperature			
Celsius	Kelvin	°F	Rankine
-273.15	0	-459.67	0
-40	233.15	-40	419.67
-10	263.15	14	473.67
0	273.15	32	491.67
10	283.15	50	509.67
20	293.15	68	527.67
30	303.15	86	545.67
40	313.15	104	563.67
50	323.15	122	581.67
70	343.15	158	617.67
80	353.15	176	635.67
90	363.15	194	653.67
100	373.15	212	671.67
120	393.15	248	707.67

Kelvin = Celsius + 273.15

Kelvin = (°F + 459.67) x (5/9)

Celsius = (°F - 32) x (5/9)

Rankine = Kelvin x (9/5)

Rankine = °F + 459.67

°F = [Celsius x (9/5)] + 32

GLOSSARY

ACT – Air Charge Temperature (also known as IAT, Intake Air Temperature) Sensor used to determine the temperature of air entering the engine, usually variable resistance thermistor.

AE – Acceleration Enrichment. Additional fuel added to the normal delivery to account for the rapid onset of airflow and evaporation of the wall film during tip-in maneuvers.

AFR – Air to Fuel Ratio. Comparison in units of mass between airflow and fuel flow. Since pounds are divided by pounds, AFR is a ratio without units.

Aircharge – Also known as Airmass. The amount of air present inside the cylinder on a single intake event, measured in units of mass.

Alpha-N – Type of speed density control logic based upon two primary inputs, throttle angle (alpha) and engine speed (N). This control logic is especially well suited to applications without a stable MAP signal, such as "stack" injection systems.

CO – Carbon Monoxide. An emissions component that is the result of combustion with a rich condition.

Coefficient – Multiplier, as used to modify another table or value for an additional condition.

Correction Factor – 1) Multiplier applied to dynamometer data (horsepower and torque) to simulate actual output at reference conditions. 2) Multiplier applied to calibration data to bring calculated values in line with actual physical values.

Cycle Time – Duration between intake valve opening events. In a four-stroke engine, cycle time represents two complete engine revolutions or 720 degrees of rotation.

DE – Deceleration Enleanment. Removal of fuel mass in the normal delivery to account for the rapid decrease of airflow and buildup of the wall film during tip-out maneuvers.

Deadtime – Delay between initial energization of the injector coil and the time at which it reaches an open position. Opening delay.

DFCO – Deceleration Fuel Cut Off. Complete removal of fuel injection events during closed throttle at elevated engine speeds resulting in a negative net engine torque (engine braking).

DTC – Diagnostic Test Code. Numeric or alpha-numeric code used to indicate a specific fault condition. These often vary by manufacturer.

Dwell – Duration of time that power is applied to an ignition coil. Increases in dwell increase available spark energy as well as heat applied to the coil. A spark event occurs at the end of dwell when primary voltage is removed.

ECM – Engine Control Module. Common acronym for an electronic engine control box or system.

ECT – Engine Coolant Temperature. Sensor used to determine the temperature of the water or other cooling fluid of an engine, usually variable resistor thermistor.

ECU – Engine Control Unit. Common acronym for an electronic engine control box or system.

EEC – Electronic Engine Controller. Common acronym for an electronic engine control box or system.

GLOSSARY

EGR – Exhaust Gas Recirculation. 1-n) Amount of previously combusted gases either retained in the cylinder or reintroduced to the intake charge. 2-v) The motion by which spent gases are retained or reintroduced into the cylinder. Increases in EGR reduce bulk burn temperature and slow combustion speed.

EMS – Engine Management System. Common acronym for an electronic engine control box or system.

ETC – Electronic Throttle Control. A motor assembly attached to the throttle blade shaft that is able to replace the traditional cable connection. This system requires the addition of a pedal position sensor and ECU control logic that provides the necessary output to move the motor on the throttle shaft.

HC – Hydrocarbons. An emissions component that usually represents unburned fuel, typically the result of combustion with either an excessively rich or lean condition.

Horsepower (hp) – Unit of measure for engine output representing available torque per unit of time. 1 hp is equal to 550 ft-lb/sec, 33,000 ft-lb/min, or 0.7457 kW.

IAC – Idle Air Control. A variable output control that diverts a small amount of airflow around the throttle blade to precisely control airflow into the engine during closed throttle and idle conditions. The IAC acts as a "slow path" control for idle speed.

IAT – Intake Air Temperature, see ACT.

Injector Offset – Additional time added to a target pulsewidth to compensate for both opening and closing delays.

Joule (J) – Metric unit of energy equal to 1 Pascal times 1 cubic meter. $1J = 1\ Pa\text{-}m^3$.

Kelvin (K) – Unit of temperature measure with identical increments to Celsius, but where 0K is equal to absolute zero. 0 degrees C (32 degrees F) is equal to 273.15K.

Lambda (λ) – Excess air ratio (percent enleanment), an engineering unit of measure used to describe air to fuel ratio divided by the stoichiometric mixture. A value of lambda=1.00 is equal to 14.68:1 for gasoline.

LBT – Lean Best Torque. Air/fuel ratio that correlates to the minimum fuel enrichment required to achieve near maximum engine torque output.

Load – Numeric representation of cylinder mass charge filling usually expressed as a percent. It represents the current mass of intake charge divided by the theoretical maximum airmass that would occupy the cylinder volume at standard temperature and pressure conditions.

MAF – Mass Air Flow. 1) Total amount of air entering an engine per unit time, measured in weight (mass). 2) Sensor that measures number of molecules of air entering the engine and returns either a voltage or frequency output proportional to the flow rate.

MAP – Manifold Absolute Pressure. 1) Pressure as measured between the throttle body and intake valve. Absolute pressure indicates that the reference is absolute zero (0 bar), such that atmospheric pressure is shown as 1 bar (14.5 psi). 2) Sensor that measures intake pressure relative to zero. A 2 bar MAP sensor has the ability to measure up to 1 bar (14.5psi) gauge pressure or "boost."

MBT – Maximum Brake Torque. Ignition angle that provides the greatest engine torque output for a given speed, load, and ambient conditions.

Newton (N) – Metric unit of force equal to the amount necessary to give one kilogram an acceleration of one meter per second squared. $1N = 1\ kg\text{-}m/s^2$.

NO$_x$ – Oxides of Nitrogen. An emissions component that forms under high combustion temperatures when the nitrogen in air is broken down and allowed to mix with oxygen ions.

OEM – Original Equipment Manufacturer. A company whose prime business is the design, testing, and production of automobiles such as GM, Ford, Chrysler, BMW, Honda, and Toyota.

Opening Delay – Length of time between energization of a solenoid (e.g., fuel injector) and movement of the pintle. This is primarily a function of the inductance of the coil and resistive force applied to the pintle.

Pascal (Pa) – Metric unit of pressure equal to one Newton of force per square meter or one Joule per cubic meter. $1Pa = 1N/m^2 = 1J/m^3$. Most EFI systems display intake pressure in kilopascals (kPa) where 1 kPa = 1000 Pa. Standard atmospheric pressure is 101.3 kPa.

PCM – Powertrain Control Module. Engine controller that also includes transmission control capability.

Phi (φ) – Enrichment Ratio (percent enrichment). An engineering unit of measure used to describe the stoichiometric ratio divided by the current air to fuel ratio. A value of lambda=1.00 is equal to 14.68:1 for gasoline.

GLOSSARY

Pulsewidth – Time that a fuel injector is energized and the driver circuit (transistor) is subject to current flow. It is not possible for injector pulsewidth to exceed available cycle time.

PWM – Pulse Width Modulation. A method of electronic output control that switches a device on and off at known frequency. Percent of "on" time is varied, resulting in a change of average output value. This allows for variable control of an otherwise binary device or system.

R – Universal Gas Constant. For air, this is equal to 287.05 J/Kg-K or 8.3145 J/mol-K.

RBT – Rich Best Torque. Air/fuel ratio that correlates to the maximum amount of fuel enrichment that still provides near peak engine torque output.

SAE – Society of Automotive Engineers. 1) Organization responsible for developing standards for testing and measurement of a wide range of automotive components, including engines. 2) Reference used to define "normal" environmental conditions for engine testing, 25 degrees C (77 degrees F), 99 kPa (29.23" Hg), 0% humidity, and 85% mechanical efficiency.

Speed Density – Control logic for an engine that estimates the current aircharge based on engine speed and pressure present within the intake manifold.

Steady State – A condition in which all characteristics of engine function are not changing significantly. Most importantly, speed, manifold pressure, throttle angle, airflow, air/fuel ratio, ignition angle, air and coolant temperature.

Standalone – A control unit that does not require interaction with any other vehicle modules.

Stoichiometry (Stoich) – A condition in which the chemical components of a reaction are balanced, often stated as a ratio. If a complete reaction occurs, this condition will result in no leftover components. For combustion of gasoline in air, this is a ratio of approximately 14.68 parts air to 1 part fuel.

STP – Standard Temperature and Pressure. Reference defining "normal" environmental conditions. 15.5 degrees C (60 degrees F) and 101.3 kPa (29.92" Hg) STP conditions typically result in horsepower numbers about 4% higher than SAE conditions.

Tau (τ) – Time constant for evaporation of the fuel wall film.

TDC – Top Dead Center. The point at which a piston has reached its maximum vertical movement and minimum clearance volume to the cylinder head as the connecting rod reaches full extension on the crankshaft's movement.

Thermistor – A resistor whose impedance changes with respect to temperature; often used for ECT and ACT sensor applications.

Tip-in – Positive change in throttle angle resulting from an increase in driver demand at the gas pedal.

Torque – Twisting force measured in units of mass per unit length. Most engines are measured in units of foot-pounds (ft-lbs) or Newton-meters (Nm). At a given torque value, the available force (pounds) increases as the acting radius (feet) decreases.

TPS – Throttle Position Sensor. A rotary resistor installed on the throttle shaft that changes impedance with respect to angle.

Transient Fueling – Additional fuel used to offset the wall film effect during acceleration. Also refers to fuel removed during deceleration to avoid excess enrichment.

UEGO – Universal Exhaust Gas Oxygen (sensor). A wideband sensor that has an extended accurate range of air/fuel ratios. Output from the sensor itself is milliamps of pump cell current, which must be converted to a useful display or analog voltage by an external controller.

Volumetric Efficiency (VE) – Numeric representation of cylinder volume charge filling, usually expressed as a percent. It represents the equivalent volume that the intake charge would occupy if it were at STP conditions divided by the actual cylinder volume.

Wall Film – Volume of fuel that clings to the inside of an intake port or runner. Its size and location are the result of the injector spray pattern and targeting. Fuel that evaporates from the wall film joins fuel from the injector spray to form the complete fuel charge entering the cylinder. Increases in port temperature or airflow will tend to decrease its size.

Wideband – Generic term for a wide-range UEGO sensor. This is often used to describe both the sensor itself and the external controller or display unit. Most wideband oxygen sensors have an approximate accurate range of lambda=0.7-1.1 (10:1 up to 16:1 air/fuel ratio with gasoline)

WOT – Wide Open Throttle. Condition where the throttle blade is completely open, allowing the engine to move as much air through it as possible.

www.ingramcontent.com/pod-product-compliance
Lightning Source LLC
Chambersburg PA
CBHW081459070526
44586CB00019B/2420